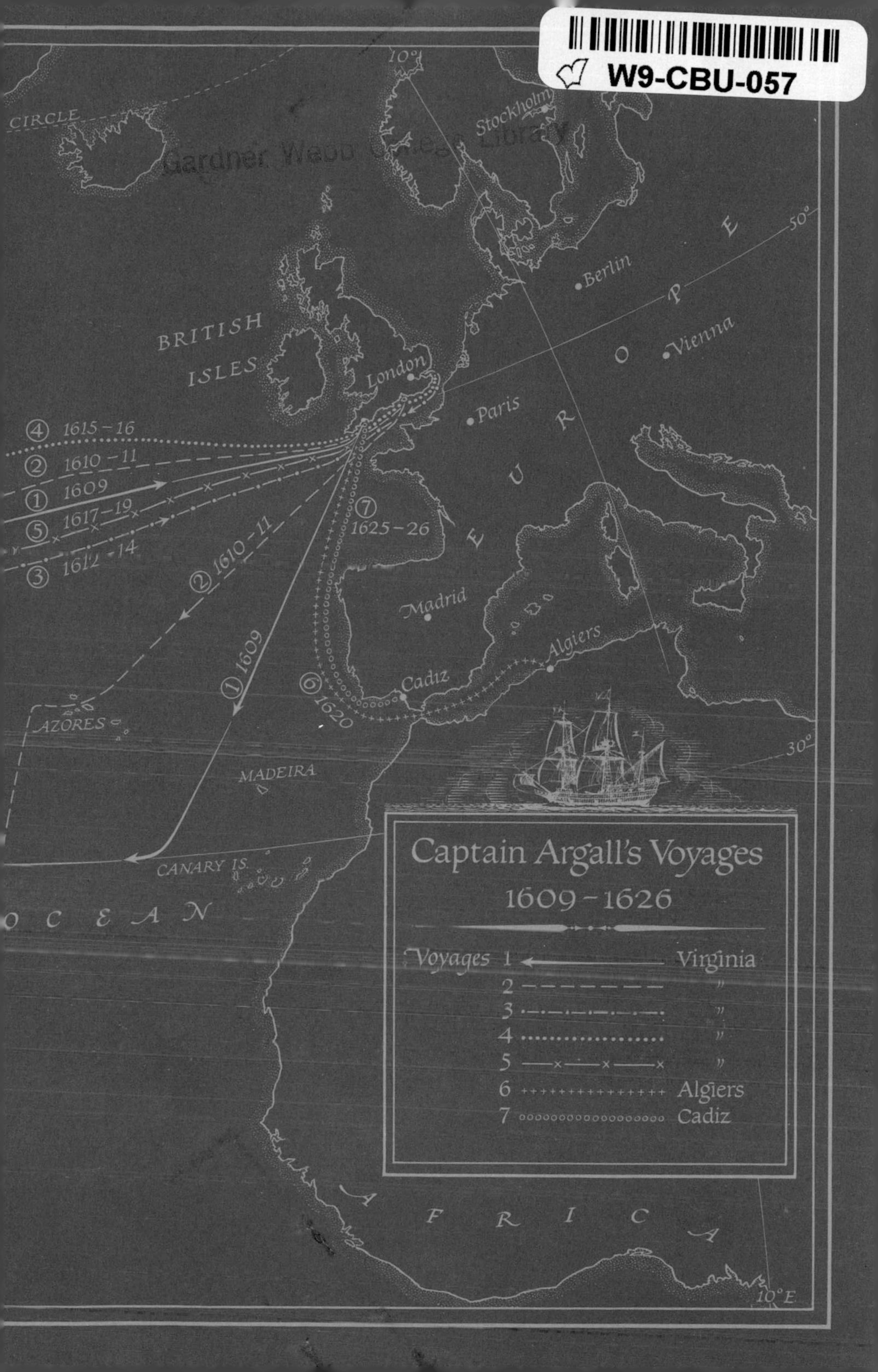

W9-CBU-057
Gardner Webb College Library
CIRCLE
10°
Stockholm
BRITISH
ISLES
London
Berlin
E
P
O
R
U
E
50°
Vienna
Paris
④ 1615–16
② 1610–11
① 1609
⑤ 1617–19
③ 1612–14
② 1610–11
⑦ 1625–26
① 1609
⑥ 1620
Madrid
Algiers
Cadiz
AZORES
MADEIRA
CANARY IS.
30°
OCEAN
AFRICA
10°E
Captain Argall's Voyages
1609–1626
Voyages 1 Virginia
2 "
3 "
4 "
5 "
6 Algiers
7 Cadiz

Pocahontas

AND HER WORLD

Books by Philip L. Barbour

Kleine Geschichte der westlichen Welt

Boris Godunov *by Alexander Pushkin* (*translator*)

Bartholomew Gosnold (*with Warner F. Gookin*)

The Three Worlds of Captain John Smith

Dimitry, Called the Pretender, Tsar and Great Prince of All Russia, 1605–1606

The Jamestown Voyages under the First Charter, 1606–1609

Pocahontas and Her World

Pocahontas in Her Twenty-first Year

MATOAKA ALS REBECCA FILIA POTENTISS: PRINC: POWHATANI IMP: VIRGINIÆ.
Ætatis suæ 21. A° 1616.
Matoaks als Rebecka daughter to the mighty Prince Powhâtan Emperour of Attanoughskomouck als virginia converted and baptized in the Christian faith, and wife to the wor.ll Mr. Joh: Rolff.
Si: Pass: sculp:
Compton Holland excu

Pocahontas

AND HER WORLD

A Chronicle of America's First Settlement
in Which Is Related the Story of
the Indians and the Englishmen—
Particularly Captain John Smith,
Captain Samuel Argall, and
Master John Rolfe

PHILIP L. BARBOUR

Illustrated

HOUGHTON MIFFLIN COMPANY BOSTON

Second Printing w

Library of Congress
Catalog Card Number: 70–100621

Printed in the United States of America

For

ELIZABETH AND DUDLEY EASBY

Old Friends and Genial Advisers

on Indian Arts and Artifacts

The facts of history are bad enough;

the fictions are, if possible, worse.

HENRY JAMES

Preface

IN AN ARTICLE published not so long since, Philip Young, "the Hemingway man," opened a study of Pocahontas with these lines from Hemingway:

> Were there two sides to Pocahontas?
> Did she have a fourth dimension? *

The question is virtually the *raison-d'être* of this book, although I chanced across Dr. Young's article months after I had started to work.

Wretchedly little is known, historically, about the Indian princess of legend. Yet she has cast a glow across the yellowing pages of manuscripts and books of three and a half centuries ago that seems to answer Hemingway. Her personality was her fourth dimension, as it is with all mankind.

This study is an attempt to present the Pocahontas of history, robbed of many a tawdry poetical embellishment, but framed in what must have been her surroundings, and given life — I hope — by judicious reconstruction and surmise. It is an essay at history, not a capitulation to fantasy.

* Philip Young. "The Mother of us all."

In the eyes of contemporary Englishmen, Pocahontas was not beautiful of face. What her fellow Indians thought, we do not know. But she was her father's "darling," and John Smith's "Nonpareil." The words bespeak character, not erotic beauty. Her eyes surely shone with the deep warmth of compassion and gaiety, and her erect figure must have stood out in the company of the ladies of King James's court. But if she had presence and self-assurance, she lacked the *savoir-faire* of civilized Europe. Hers was certainly the sincerer mold, yet we are only able to see things through her eyes as "through a glass, darkly."

In an effort to come face to face with Pocahontas, the emphasis in this book has been placed on the Indian side of the inevitable conflict which arose when unwanted whitemen first began to settle along the broad, sluggish waters of the James River in Virginia. Nothing has been falsified; nothing has been toned down. But the obvious, though not recorded, reactions of the Indians have been emphasized, perhaps to the disadvantage of the Englishmen. Most of this task had to be accomplished by surmise, "informed guessing." Yet it is my hope that something at least akin to the real woman, Pocahontas, daughter of Powhatan, has emerged.

My thanks are particularly due to three collateral descendants of John Rolfe, Pocahontas' husband: Mr. Clement Rolfe Ingleby, of Collier's Farm, Fernhurst, Surrey; his daughter, Mrs. Alexander J. Stevenson, of West Calder, Midlothian; and Mr. Albert Everard Gunther, a cousin, of Heacham, Norfolk, and London. Without their aid, I would not have known the Rolfe family background, would not have had the opportunity to study the so-called Pocahontas portrait at West Calder or the Rolfe portraits there and in Surrey, and would not have spent delightful hours both at Heacham and in London visiting the Rolfe homestead and discussing the past.

In like manner, there is a debt of gratitude to the Virginia Historical Society and the Jamestown Foundation in the persons of Mr. John M. Jennings and Mr. William M. E. Rachal of the former, and Mr. Parke Rouse, Jr., of the latter, for their help with regard to Pocahontas "relics" in the United States. Dr. William C. Sturtevant, Dr. Wilcomb E. Washburn, and Dr. Daniel J. Reed, of the Smithsonian Institution, have been most hospitably cooperative, and Mr. Thad W. Tate, of the Institute of Early American History and Culture, Williamsburg, Virginia, has shown the same hospitality and helpfulness. And last, but by no means least, Mr. Christian F. Feest, of the Museum für Völkerkunde, Vienna, has gladly given me the benefit of his Indian expertise.

In conclusion, I must add that I am again deeply indebted to the New York Public Library, particularly the Rare Book and Map Divisions, and the British Museum, the Public Record Office, and Somerset House, in London, for their unfailing courtesy and assistance. The Cathedral Archives and Library, Canterbury, have provided hitherto unpublished data regarding the Argall family, and a personal note of thanks is due to Dr. William Urry and his assistant, Mr. P. A. Lyons. Mrs. David B. Quinn, of Liverpool, has kindly supplied a note on Argall; Mr. Edward F. Heite, of the Virginia State Landmarks Commission, has helped unravel the puzzle of where Pocahontas and John Rolfe may have lived; and Mr. Howard A. MacCord, Sr., and other members of the Virginia Archeological Society have been generous in their help on possible Indian sites in Virginia. And Mr. Dewey Scarboro, of Bristol, Virginia, during his year of research abroad, has contributed greatly to a proper conception of the complex character of Sir Thomas Dale. Others who have helped in great ways and small must remain unmentioned lest this preface exceed in length the book it introduces. They have my sincere thanks, also.

Labor Day, 1968
Newtown, Connecticut PHILIP L. BARBOUR

NOTE: Chance had it that after the foregoing went to press, I got to know two charming ladies descended from another branch of the Rolfe family and quite likely from Pocahontas herself, Mrs. Elwin Stock and Mrs. Florence Carson, who went to great trouble to supply information regarding the Pocahontas vase and the English tradition regarding Thomas Rolfe, the son of Pocahontas.

P.L.B.

Contents

	Preface	ix
	Chronology	xix
1.	"In the Gloom and Silence of the Dark and Impenetrable Forest . . ."	1
2.	The Whitemen	8
3.	Pocahontas and Captain John Smith	23
4.	Powhatan and John Smith	36
5.	While Powhatan Watched: the Starving Time	52
6.	Samuel Argall of Kent: Half-idle Onlooker at Jamestown	67
7.	Jamestown Challenges the Indians	82
8.	Pocahontas and Captain Argall	98
9.	John Rolfe Meets Pocahontas	112
10.	Pocahontas' Wedding and Peace with the Indians	128
11.	Peace Within the Colony	138

12. Leaving the Forest Behind 152

13. Pocahontas (and John Smith) in London 165

14. Peace Draws to a Close 178

15. "Like a Death-web Spun . . ." 194

16. The Aftermath 207

17. What Happened to the Three Englishmen in Pocahontas' Life 213

Appendixes

I. Notes on So-called Relics of Powhatan and Pocahontas 231

II. Notes on the Rolfe Family 241

III. John Rolfe's Letter to Sir Thomas Dale Regarding His Marriage to Pocahontas 247

Notes and Comments 255

Bibliography 283

Index 303

Illustrations

Frontispiece

POCAHONTAS IN HER TWENTY-FIRST YEAR

From an engraving by Simon van de Passe, apparently done soon after his "portraictuer" of Captain John Smith, and perhaps at Smith's suggestion. The well-known oil portrait by an unknown artist in the National Portrait Gallery, Smithsonian Institution, Washington, D.C., was most likely copied from the van de Passe engraving. (Courtesy of the Trustees, British Museum.)

following page 168

JOHN SMITH'S ADVENTURES IN DECEMBER, 1607

An anonymous engraving made to illustrate Smith's experiences after his capture and just before Pocahontas "saved" his life, December 28 or 29, 1607. From Pieter van der Aa's *Naaukeurige Versameling* of 1706–1707. (Courtesy of the Rare Book Division, New York Public Library.)

INDIANS DANCING BEFORE MARTIN PRING

Algonkian dances on the shores of Massachusetts Bay in July, 1603. Martin Pring, born in the same year as Captain John Smith, George Percy, Esq., and Captain Samuel Argall, was the first of the three to land in America. The Massachusetts Indians were closely connected with those of Virginia in customs and language and this illustration is as valid for Pocahontas' world as it is for the lands later occupied by the Pilgrims. From Pieter van der Aa's *Naaukeurige Versameling* of 1706–1707. (Courtesy of the Rare Book Division, New York Public Library.)

IAPASSUS AND HIS WIFE PERSUADE POCAHONTAS TO VISIT CAPTAIN ARGALL'S SHIP

Engraving attributed to Georg Keller, of Frankfurt am Main. From Theodore de Bry's *Americae Pars Decima* . . . (Courtesy of the Rare Book Division, New York Public Library.)

POCAHONTAS MEETS TWO OF HER BROTHERS AT MATCHCOT

Engraving attributed to Georg Keller, of Frankfurt am Main. From Theodore de Bry's *Americae Pars Decima* . . . (Courtesy of the Rare Book Division, New York Public Library.)

CAPTAIN SAMUEL ARGALL HARANGUES THE CHICKAHOMINIES

Engraving attributed to Georg Keller, of Frankfurt am Main. From Theodore de Bry's *Americae Pars Decima* . . . (Courtesy of the Rare Book Book Division, New York Public Library.)

LONDON AT THE TIME OF POCAHONTAS' ARRIVAL

The central half of "A Long View of London," drawn and engraved by Claes Jansz. Visscher, the Younger, in 1616. To the extreme left of St. Paul's, three (of four) pinnacles identify the tower of St. Bride's, just to the right of which the Belle Sauvage Inn is hidden by other buildings. St. Mary Overy, now Southwark Cathedral, is in the right foreground, with London Bridge behind and above it, built 1176–1209, demolished 1831–1832. Heads of executed persons can be seen over the gate. (Courtesy of the Trustees, British Museum.)

HEACHAM HALL, RESIDENCE OF THE ROLFE FAMILY

One of the earliest engravings of Heacham Hall, Heacham, Norfolk. The wing is said to have existed in 1617, but the large front building is of later construction. (Print by courtesy of A. E. Gunther, Esq., of Heacham and London.)

HEACHAM CHURCH (ST. MARY'S)

From an old drawing. (Print by courtesy of A. E. Gunther, Esq., of Heacham and London.)

CAPTAIN JOHN SMITH IN HIS THIRTY-SEVENTH YEAR

Captain Smith as he looked when he visited Pocahontas in London. This is one of the best of many surviving prints of the engraving by Simon van de Passe. It appears in the upper left corner of the map of New England included with Smith's *Description of New England* in 1616. The poem is by John Davies of Hereford. (Courtesy of the Trustees, British Museum.)

AN UNIDENTIFIED VIRGINIA INDIAN OF 1645

Drawn from life and engraved in London by Wenceslaus Hollar, of Prague. Next to van de Passe's engraving of Pocahontas, this is the earliest lifelike representation of a Powhatan Indian. Although he was not born until five years after Pocahontas died, this Virginian was surely a representative of his race. (Courtesy of the Rare Book Division, New York Public Library.)

THE POCAHONTAS OF LEGEND

William Ordway Partridge's monument to Pocahontas, between the entrance to Jamestown National Historic Site and the ruins of the old church. Commissioned for the 1607 tricentennial exposition, it was not erected until some years later. A bronze replica, donated to St. George's church, Gravesend, was unveiled on October 5, 1958, in the churchyard, by Mr. John S. Battle, then Governor of Virginia. (Photo by Thomas L. Williams. Courtesy Association for the Preservation of Virginia Antiquities.)

Maps

1. Captain Argall's Voyages *endpapers*
2. Powhatan's "Crescent," The Nucleus of his "Empire" *page 3*

Chronology

1580 January 9. John Smith baptized.
December 4. Samuel Argall baptized.

1584 April–September. First English expedition to North Carolina.

1585–1588 Roanoke colony established and abandoned.

1595–1596 Pocahontas born.

1603 March 24. Death of Queen Elizabeth and accession of King James I.

1607 May 14. Jamestown founded.
December 29(?). Pocahontas meets John Smith.

1609 July 13. Argall's first arrival in Virginia.
October 4(?). Smith sailed back to England.

1610 May 23. John Rolfe arrived in Jamestown, with Gates, Somers, and Newport.

1611 May 12. Sir Thomas Dale, Marshal and Deputy Governor, arrived in Jamestown.

1612 September 17. Argall returned to Virginia. Rolfe planting West Indian tobacco.

1613 April. Argall captured Pocahontas in Potomac country and arrived at Jamestown with her on April 13. Pocahontas later placed with Rev. Alexander Whitaker to learn English and the Christian faith.

1614 April 5(?). Pocahontas, baptized Rebecca, married John Rolfe.

1615 Thomas, son of Pocahontas and John Rolfe, born.

1616 April 21(?). Rolfe family sailed for England with Dale and Argall.

1617 January 6. Pocahontas attended court masque, with the King and Queen present.

March 21. Pocahontas buried at Gravesend.

April 10. Little Thomas Rolfe left at Plymouth in care of Sir Lewis Stukely.

May 15. John Rolfe arrived back in Jamestown with Argall, Acting Governor.

1618 Spring. Powhatan died.

November 18. Virginia Council appointed Yeardley Governor, on receipt of complaints from Virginia.

1619 April 10(?). Argall returned to England.

1622 Early spring. John Rolfe taken sick and died.

March 22. First Virginia Massacre.

June 26. Argall knighted by James I.

1625 March 27. Death of James I and accession of Charles I.

1626 January 24 (25?). Argall died on shipboard.

1631 June 21. John Smith died in London.

1635 Earliest evidence of Thomas Rolfe's return to Virginia.

Pocahontas

AND HER WORLD

CHAPTER 1

"In the Gloom and Silence of the Dark and Impenetrable Forest . . ."[1]

LONG AGO, three shiploads of inquisitive whitemen — Englishmen — came to the shores of Chesapeake Bay in Virginia, and settled on the edge of the primeval North American forest. Hardly aware of the thousands of Indians who roamed and hunted, raised crops and lived, in the vast wilderness beyond, the whitemen planted a tent-village on the banks of the James River, determined to stay.

Before long, one of them — stray and inquisitive — lost himself in the midst of swamps and fallen trees, miles from his tent and his friends. Indian hunters captured him, and took him to their chief. His name was John Smith.

A little girl saved Smith's life — at least, so he thought. And with that act, she became immortal. Her name was Pocahontas.

The tale has been told countless times, always by whitemen. But to see Pocahontas as she was, we must think of her as an Indian, in an Indian setting — not as a Renaissance lady swaddled in a collar, gown, and cuffs, as shown in her only portrait done from life. Pocahontas was a child of the forest. What follows is an attempt to present her in that light.

Prosaically speaking, Pocahontas' people were one of many

tribes in the great family now called Algonkians.[2] Though the Algonkian habitat, or hunting-ground, was enormous, extending over most of northeastern North America, the individual tribes were small and widely scattered. What tied them together was community of language, pattern of life, and religious beliefs.

Accurate pre-Columbian chronology is impossible in America north of Mexico. Nevertheless, archaeological investigations now in progress point to the presence of Algonkian tribes in the lower St. Lawrence Valley at the beginning of the eleventh century, and it seems certain that the ancestors of Pocahontas' tribe tarried somewhere between the Great Lakes and the Gulf of St. Lawrence not many generations later. Then they began to wander southward. A tradition current when the English colonists arrived in Virginia in 1607 claimed that the Indians arrived there three centuries before.

Again, however, no details are known. Still it seems likely that they found other tribes in possession which they pushed back toward the hills; for they established an outpost on the James River, just below the site of modern Richmond, to act as a fort to protect their other villages toward the sea from hostile non-Algonkian tribes to the west. This fort was called Powhatan, and in it, probably in the 1540's, Pocahontas' father was born. At birth, he was given the name of Wahunsonacock.

When he reached manhood, Wahunsonacock inherited or was elected to the chieftaincy of the fort and with it, of five other villages strewn in a crescent down the James River in one direction and along the Pamunkey, now the York, and the Mattaponi in the other. He was then named *Powhatan* after the village, for as the English colonist William Strachey wrote, the "great King" was

> by them called by sundry names, according to his divers places, qualities or honors by himself obtained, either for his valor, his government, or some suchlike goodness.[3]

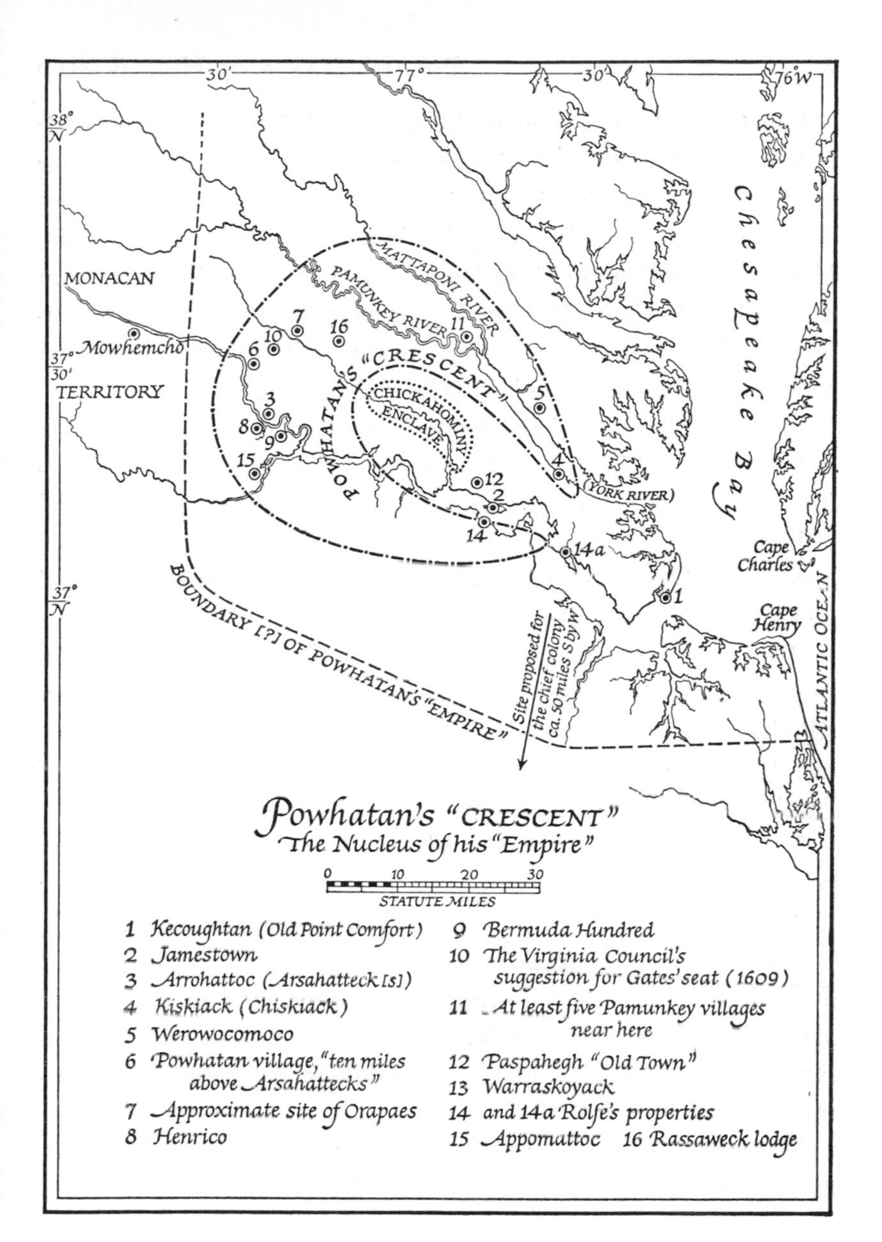
30'
77°
30'
76°W
38° N
37° 30'
37° N
MONACAN
Mowhemcho
TERRITORY
MATTAPONI RIVER
PAMUNKEY RIVER
POWHATAN'S "CRESCENT"
CHICKAHOMINY ENCLAVE
YORK RIVER
Chesapeake Bay
Cape Charles
Cape Henry
ATLANTIC OCEAN
BOUNDARY [?] OF POWHATAN'S "EMPIRE"
Site proposed for the chief colony ca. 50 miles S by W
Powhatan's "CRESCENT"
The Nucleus of his "Empire"
0 10 20 30
STATUTE MILES
1 Kecoughtan (Old Point Comfort)
2 Jamestown
3 Arrohattoc (Arsahatteck[s])
4 Kiskiack (Chiskiack)
5 Werowocomoco
6 Powhatan village, "ten miles above Arsahattecks"
7 Approximate site of Orapaes
8 Henrico
9 Bermuda Hundred
10 The Virginia Council's suggestion for Gates' seat (1609)
11 At least five Pamunkey villages near here
12 Paspahegh "Old Town"
13 Warraskoyack
14 and 14a Rolfe's properties
15 Appomattoc
16 Rassaweck lodge

Strachey and other writers also suggested that Powhatan or his father, or both of them, had come or been driven up from farther south. The implication in this is that Powhatan succeeded his father as chief of the tribe. That is noteworthy, for it hints that the idea of a son following his father as chief had been picked up from the southern Indians. The Powhatans were like many other Algonkians in following a matriarchal system of inheritance, but some sort of monarchy was practiced at least in Florida.[4]

However that may have been, Powhatan did develop into a strong ruler, and his form of government hardened into a despotism. Before long he moved to conquer his neighboring tribes and villages, gradually converting his inherited "confederacy" of six hutments with a total population of perhaps seventeen hundred and fifty souls into an "empire" boasting eight or nine thousand.

Although personal aggrandizement was surely at the root of this, rumors of outside dangers in the form of whitemen were undoubtedly blown up into a real threat by Powhatan's priests and conjurers. More warriors were needed to face the menace. The war cry of "national safety" played into the hands of Powhatan's ambition.

This impulse toward empire was far from unjustified. Twenty years or so before Powhatan was born, several Spanish expeditions had crossed the straits of Florida and skirted the coast as far north, perhaps, as Cape Hatteras. Finding little to attract them, they sailed away. But the French followed in due course, and in 1562 went about planting a colony on St. John's River, Florida. Three years later the Spaniards retaliated by founding St. Augustine and exterminating the French.

Meanwhile, in 1559 or 1560, when Powhatan was in his teens, an obscure Spanish reconnaissance expedition had penetrated Chesapeake Bay. It apparently achieved nothing, but for unexplained reasons a brother of the local petty king surrendered himself to the Spaniards and was taken to Mexico. There he was baptized, with the Viceroy Don Luis de Velasco as his godfather, and named Don

Luis Velasco. Later he went to Spain where Philip II received him, clothed him gallantly, and in time sent him back to America.

In 1570, Don Luis the Indian was chosen to guide a party of Jesuits destined to attempt a mission in his native region. Don Luis' brother received the mission well, but within six months, with Don Luis' connivance, the whole party was wiped out, except for one boy who survived to tell the tale. So thorough was the eradication of the mission that the Spanish government lost interest in further activity in that area. Nevertheless, the incident cannot be ignored in the story of Pocahontas because of the involvement of the Indian chief and his brother. Powhatan was about twenty-five at the time. Was he, too, involved?[5]

The question is impossible to answer. But it can prudently be surmised that Powhatan, at least, became fully aware of the existence of whitemen from across the seas at this time, if he had not run across them before. And from then on at ever briefer intervals until the first permanent English colony was established in 1607, Powhatan was visited and plagued by whitemen: Spanish, French, and English.

Not all of these entered Chesapeake Bay proper. The coast of the Carolinas and Georgia was the scene of much of the activity. But somehow, subsequent developments hint, Powhatan became increasingly uneasy about the ever more obvious sea-borne threat.

In the midst of this, below the Great Dismal Swamp and outside of Powhatan's domain proper, an English colony sent out by Sir Walter Ralegh was established on Roanoke Island in the 1580's. The colossal Spanish punitive expedition against England, known to history as the Invincible Armada, interrupted the dispatch of supplies to Roanoke, but the settlement seems to have been destroyed already. Certainly, the Spanish ship sent to look for it in June, 1588, found only some "debris indicating that a considerable number of people had been" there.[6]

After visiting Chesapeake Bay and kidnapping one of Powhatan's young Indians, the Spanish ship sailed away. Whatever survivors of Roanoke still lingered on seem to have been wiped out by 1590 — wherever they were — and in any case given the *coup de grâce* by Powhatan (so rumor had it) in 1605 or 1606. Then for a dozen years or so, nameless ships and men apparently coasted along the shores of Powhatan's domain. Two of the least shadowy of these incursions were the hinted-at visits of Captain Christopher Newport, of Limehouse, and Captain Bartholomew Gilbert, of Suffolk, both in the early 1600's. But if they came at all, they came, saw, and fled.

A little later, on the basis of what John Smith was told in December, 1607, it may be postulated that a French or French-English ship was prowling in these waters the year before Jamestown was settled. In that event, the hypothetical ship penetrated into the Rappahannock River, where forty-two tiny villages clung to a hundred miles of shoreline.

That these visits troubled Powhatan can hardly be doubted. There are hints in Strachey's *Historie,* written in 1612, that they presaged for him some unforeseeable Thing that boded great ill for his people — even as ill omens had warned the Aztec emperor of the arrival of the Spaniards in Mexico nearly a century before.[7]

In short, at the height of his power, a nameless danger threatened Powhatan. Yet just before those grim times, a ray of light had come to gladden him.

One day, in 1595 or 1596, Powhatan was presented with a baby daughter of so cheerful a nature that she was forthwith named Matoaka, which meant something like "she is playful." He had a favorite daughter already by his dearest wife Winganuske ("lovely woman"). But Matoaka grew in his affections until in time, as William Strachey wrote, he called her, "whom he loved well, Pocahontas, which may signify Little-wanton [playful, frolicsome little girl]." [8]

It was Pocahontas, then, whom Powhatan later chose to intervene for him with the English colonists, especially on that most perplexing of occasions when the life or death of the venturesome Englishman, Captain John Smith, depended on his will. Because this was so, Smith's name has always been associated with Pocahontas', and certainly from *his* point of view, she was indeed the "very Nonpareil" of all Powhatan's nation.

Three hundred years of obscurity had rolled by since Powhatan's tribe left their home in the north. There had been a vast change in that time. They had a firm, capable ruler, despotic though he was. Their food economy was no longer quite so haphazard. They traded with other Indians, perhaps as far away as the Great Lakes. And they had accepted and absorbed many outside influences, especially from the south.

At that juncture, the English arrived. Whether they would remain or not depended on the outcome of the inevitable clash between their will and Powhatan's. Extraordinary, indeed, was the part played in the struggle by the little girl of eleven whose name was Pocahontas.

CHAPTER 2

The Whitemen[1]

POCAHONTAS WAS PROBABLY eight or ten years old when she saw whitemen for the first time. According to an Indian account, a ship of unknown provenance came up the York River to Werowocomoco, in those days Powhatan's place of residence on Purtan Bay. The vessel cast anchor perhaps two miles from shore. And bearded whitemen clambered down into a little boat that had been tied to the ship's stern and rowed over to the village.

Powhatan entertained them suitably, and after a while the ship left. Not many days later, however, word came from a village on the Rappahannock River, some fifty miles away, that the same ship had visited there as well and had again been entertained. But an altercation had ensued, the ship's captain had killed the village chief, several Indians had been captured and taken aboard, and the ship had sailed away.[2]

Nevertheless, the rest of that year and perhaps for two or three more years, peace reigned in tidewater Virginia. And another spring (*cattapeuk*) came, and with it the time for planting. The days were already longer than the nights. Then a messenger paddled up from across the water, bearing alarming news.

Three great ships had appeared in Chesapeake Bay: a very large one, a smaller one, and a stubby one, perhaps half again as long as a war-canoe, but wider and much higher. Some twenty or thirty whitemen had gone ashore in a boat and wandered about. They were some distance from the Chesapeake village, but a handful of the tribe out hunting had seen them. Since the whitemen were too many for the Indians, the latter had not tried to chase them away.

But when night fell and the group started back to their ship's boat, the Indians crept out of the forest, and down from the dunes and attacked, smartly. Two whitemen they knew were wounded. There was a terrible noise from their "thunder-sticks," but it was too dark for the whitemen to aim well. No Indians were harmed. Still, it was a very dangerous encounter, and so with shouts of defiance they retired.

Powhatan must have learned of all this with misgivings. But he evidently decided to wait for a few days before making a move. Not very long before, his young son Pochins had been put in charge of the village of Kecoughtan,[3] across the mouth of the James River from the Chesapeake village, and he was certain that Pochins could take care of the situation if the whitemen crossed over. If not, the numerous and belligerent Nansemonds, who occupied many villages to the west of the Chesapeakes, could be relied on to resist the newcomers with all their strength. By then, Powhatan would have time to consult his priests and elders.

A few days later, just at the full of the moon, Pochins himself sent a message. The three "floating islands," he reported, had halted offshore near Kecoughtan, near what is now Old Point Comfort, and a boat had brought an old man with a gray beard and only one arm to the landing-place, along with several of his companions. Five of Pochins' men had seen them and had started to run away. But the one-armed man had made friendly gestures and had stepped ashore with confidence, putting his hand to his heart.

At this, the Indians encouraged the whitemen to land and conducted them to their village, where Pochins sent a party to meet them with proper reverence. The whitemen stood stiffly as the Indians prostrated themselves on the ground. Then they followed the Indians to the village, where Pochins had mats brought out for his guests to sit on and offered them corn bread and other delicacies.

Although the one-armed man seemed to hesitate — the whitemen called him Captain Newport — Pochins indicated that he and his people welcomed the strangers and wished them to eat, which they then solemnly did. When the whitemen had finished, one of the Indians, at Pochins' command, stepped out of the impassive circle of villagers. He paused briefly before the one-armed man and then began a traditional dance, singing and stamping his feet, toe and heel, while other members of the tribe rose to join him. It was a dance of propitiation, to reap good and repel evil. It was brief.

The whitemen showed their appreciation and pleasure by distributing some rare beads and other tokens. Then they retired to their boat, to return to the three stationary ships.

Pochins trusted that they would sail away. Certainly his men had complied with custom to the best of their ability. At the same time, he had shown by the dance that the village of Kecoughtan would defend itself against all intruders. The whitemen would understand.

With renewed confidence in Pochins' abilities, Powhatan deliberately adopted an attitude of mixed patience and apprehension. He kept himself informed through his spies, invoked the support of the spirits in company with his priests, and kept his council of elders at hand for consultation. So, the days passed.

The whitemen sailed up the great river (the James) slowly, as if studying the shores. At the mouth of the Chickahominy they stopped and landed a boatload of men whom Wowinchopunk, werowance of the Paspahegh Indians, met and entertained. After that, one of his chief men delivered a long and vigorous oration to the party, telling them that they were not wanted. He asked them to go away.

Nevertheless, the whitemen hung around. The petty werowance across the big river invited them over to his village, and they went there in a big canoe — a "shallop" the whitemen called it — which they towed behind one of the big ships. After this visit, the whitemen returned aboard again but remained anchored near the mouth of the Chickahominy.

Two or three days later, a small group of the strangers got in the shallop and sailed far up the big river to the territory of one of Powhatan's principal werowances, Coquonassum, chief of the Appamatucks.

Coquonassum, informed of their approach, stationed a body of his fittest men to stand at the landing-place, waiting for them, armed with bows and arrows, wooden swords studded with sharp bits of stone, and war-tomahawks. Then he placed himself in front of his men, notched an arrow to his bow, and took a pipe of tobacco with his free hand. Sternly he demanded to know what the whitemen wanted, and without waiting for an answer, he told them to be gone.

The whitemen protested some sort of innocence, begging to be allowed to disembark. This was, at last, permitted, but the attitude of Coquonassum and his men discouraged any stay, and the whitemen returned to their boat and sailed back down the river.

Before long, Powhatan heard that the strangers had found a place where they could tie their ships to trees along the shore of a peninsula just below the mouth of the Chickahominy. This done, they unloaded everything and began to put up tents on a site which had been occupied a generation or so before, but had been abandoned except as a Paspahegh tribal hunting-ground. Wowinchopunk was incensed at their boldness.

It was two days, however, before he could gather men from a

neighboring village to augment his own miserable fighting force of only forty braves. When he had assembled an additional sixty, he hid them in the forest. Then he sent word to the whitemen that he would visit them, bring a deer, and entertain them with a feast.

The next day, he ferried his own men across the Chickahominy, joined the hidden force, and suddenly appeared before the half-moon–shaped abatis of boughs on which the strangers were still working. His hundred men matched the strength of the whitemen on shore, man for man. In fact, the latter were too surprised by his sudden arrival to prevent a great body of Indians from getting inside the makeshift fort.

Wowinchopunk then beguilingly invited everybody to lay down their arms and join in a feast. But the whitemen, confused though they were, not only did not lay down their arms, but those who had been working with tools dropped them to go for more arms. Outwitted, Wowinchopunk passed the matter off as a joke, waved his hands before him to show that he would give the visitors all the land they wanted, and repeated his invitation to the feast.

All might have gone well then had not an Indian stolen a hatchet just as the entertainment was about to begin. One of the whitemen saw this and tried to take it back. In so doing, he struck the Indian with it. Another Indian promptly came at the whiteman with his wooden sword.

By then, the whiteman's companions were reaching for muskets and steel swords. Wowinchopunk, no longer able to see any joke, loudly vowed revenge, called his men together, and stalked off, deciding to try for a more successful surprise attack at a better moment.

This was only the beginning of trouble between Wowinchopunk and the whitemen. Neither side trusting the other at all, Wowinchopunk's first move was to test the power of the strangers' weapons, at the same time keeping his eyes open for any advantages to be gained. Another feast was arranged.

This all but fell through because the Indians too plainly wanted to get into the fort. Still, the matter was smoothed over, the feast was celebrated, and feats of arms were displayed. But if the whitemen were startled at the penetrating power of the Indians' arrows, the Indians were in despair over the impenetrability of the visitors' shields. The feast ended with the Indians, once again, leaving in great anger and confusion.

Surprisingly, the whitemen just then chose to divide their forces, sending two dozen men off in their boat. Wowinchopunk hesitated to move against them just then, thinking that this was some sort of trick to outwit him. He kept away from the fort for a few days, keeping himself informed through spies.

The two dozen who had left included the one-armed graybeard, one self-important man in his mid-thirties, who was always very busy, and two younger men, the one slim and highly respected by all the whitemen, the other short, stocky, bearded, and evidently not a man to be trifled with.

As the days passed and information came that the whitemen were far up the river approaching Powhatan village, where another son of Powhatan named Parahunt was werowance, Wowinchopunk took stock of his chances, reflected on the men left in the fort, and began to collect a much bigger force than the hundred warriors he had had before. With two hundred men behind him this time and with four of the white leaders away, he would no longer play games. He would stage an outright attack — by surprise, of course.

According to later Indian reports, Wowinchopunk had four allies in this venture: the werowances of Quiyoughcohannock, Weanoc, Appamatuck, and Kiskiack — all "contracted enemies" of the English, as a friendly Indian put it.[4] Together, the five chiefs had some two hundred and seventy-five men at their disposal, and they controlled the James River on both sides, from a few miles below Powhatan village to as far as Jamestown, with the Kiskiack werowance in command on the south side of the York River, perhaps twenty miles away by the Indian trails. Thus the entire southern horn of Powhatan's crescent was aligned against the intruders.

On Whitsunday, 1607, which of course meant nothing to the Indians, the two dozen Englishmen were far up the James entertaining Parahunt and getting into mischief by setting up a claim to the river and the neighboring territory. Wowinchopunk could easily have known where they were by the next night, though he probably did not know of the claim staked out. Accordingly, he assembled his forces, ferried them across the Chickahominy without being seen, and joined the men from Kiskiack, his only ally back of the English settlement. This was apparently done during the night and early the following morning.

Then, on Tuesday, May 26, the full Indian force made a wild assault on the fort. Many of the whitemen were at work outside when sentries gave the alarm. But the forest lay so near that the English had no time to organize resistance before the Indians reached the abatis.

Bows and arrows were all but winning the skirmish, for pistols and muskets could not be fired as swiftly, when the ship's ordnance opened up. This stopped the Indians; then drove them back. With "a huge noise," as one Englishman put it, they disappeared back into the forest. Several Indians were killed, and many must have been wounded. The English lost a boy, killed outright, and one man who died of his wounds. Otherwise, ten men were wounded. This was the first overt evidence of Wowinchopunk's determination to rid himself of the obstinate trespassers.

The next day, the two dozen explorers returned to the fort. Work was immediately started on stronger fortifications, which kept the men busy for nearly three weeks. Meanwhile, the Indians tried a sneak attack with a small force but were less bold than before. They found the English *pokosacks* ("they burst with violence, like thunder") too dangerous. Still, two days later they attacked again and once more, the day after. One Englishman was killed in these raids.

By then, the palisades around the fort discouraged mass attacks, so that only stray Englishmen, outside the enclosure, suffered wounds. Wowinchopunk, with his spies always watching from the forest, bided his time.

A week after the palisades were completed, the Indians saw the two largest ships sail away. Captain Newport, the graybeard with one arm, directed their departure, and there was much shouting back and forth between him and the sailors with him, and the men left at the fort. Wowinchopunk's spies could have counted a hundred still at the fort — perhaps four or five more than that. It was still too large a force, armed as it was, to encourage running any risks. Besides, it was harvest time — time to work in the fields.

Be that as it may, Powhatan had a slightly younger half-brother who was greatly interested in the whitemen. His name was Opechancanough, and he was reputed to have lived among strange Indians to the south. Possibly he had run across the Spaniards, and in any event he was hostile to the whitemen who had just settled themselves in the Paspahegh territory. His own territory on the Pamunkey River, above modern West Point, was larger than Wowinchopunk's, and his tribe, the Pamunkeys, was the strongest under Powhatan's command.

When the two ships left, then, Opechancanough decided to send a present of a deer to the fort. This would give his men-in-charge an opportunity to ask what had happened to the ships. The white werowance at the fort, another graybeard, named Edward Maria Wingfield, replied that the ships had gone to Croatoan, a village and tribe on the coastal island just south of Cape Hatteras. Although the messengers had surely never heard of the place, they understood it was "not far off." [5] With this meager information they retired, bearing a gift of a hatchet for Opechancanough.

Not long after, Powhatan himself sent a deer, undoubtedly with the same sort of inquiry in mind. He, too, received a hatchet and an evasive answer. It was only then that the whitemen understood that the werowance whom they had known at Powhatan village was not Great Powhatan, but his son.

About the time of the summer full moon, which was July 29 that year, Pippsco, the petty werowance of a village across the river from Jamestown, as the English called their settlement, paddled over with a complaint. A whiteman had stolen one of his canoes. The white werowance investigated, found that it was true, and had the canoe returned immediately. Pippsco then swore by the sun that he would be a special friend of the strangers. Furthermore, when his crop was ripe, he would bring corn to barter. An oath by the sun was sacred, and Pippsco would live up to it. But his aim was subtler. He was in trouble with Powhatan, and he sought the friendship of the powerful English.[6]

Whether or not Wowinchopunk (or Powhatan) knew about this visit, another development at the fort distracted their attention. About two weeks after Pippsco's visit, Wowinchopunk's spies saw that something was wrong. Many Indians by then were bringing their corn and beans to the fort with offers to trade, but few whitemen were around. They tried to find out why from a man named White who had come to live with them. But there were language troubles. All in all, either the absent ships had something to do with it or the whitemen were sick.

Whatever the trouble was, the strangers kept their secret until the weather began to get cooler. A month slipped by. And at last they were seen outside the fort again. Just the same, it was evident that there were fewer of them, and they still did not raise crops, nor were they good hunters. They hardly even knew how to fish. All they wanted to do was barter their little trinkets for food.

About that time the short whiteman with a bushy beard, whom

they had often seen before, told a group of the Indian traders that he was known as John Smith, that he was a captain, or werowance, and that they were to do all their trading with him.[7] He had been made chief of bartering.

John Smith was a hard trader, but he was kind. If there were any little children along with the Indians, he always gave them toys. Indeed, he acted more like a werowance than the man who blustered around with a couple of friends and pointed to himself as the chief.

After that, Smith went trading down the river to Kecoughtan and across to other villages. Only Wowinchopunk remained hostile. Although Powhatan and his brother seemed to be ignoring them, when Smith tried to trade with the Paspahegh villages, he got into fights. Nevertheless, a few days before the frost moon (November 23) he sailed toward the nearest Paspahegh village again. This time he was in a larger boat with eight men. Caught in the mouth of the Chickahominy by the ebb tide, Smith had to drop anchor.

A canoe came out with a few Paspaheghs who wanted to trade. Then a Chickahominy Indian came paddling up and invited Smith to go to *his* village. Despite Paspahegh objections, Smith went along with the Chickahominy Indian by moonlight. After seeing that there might be good trading there, he returned to sleep in his barge.

Taking the barge up the river the next morning, Smith met the Chickahominy Indians for the first time. Trading was excellent. In a few hours the barge was loaded with much-needed food, while the Indians, for their part, revelled in priceless hatchets, bits of copper, and such strange objects as little tinkling bells.

Here in the Chickahominy territory, Smith got his first real experience in trading. His personality, a mixture of firmness and cajolery, appealed to these Indians. For years they had preserved a certain degree of independence from Powhatan by methods similar to Smith's. Furthermore, they were generally more free to act than some of the other Indians, for they were governed by a council of elders, not by a werowance. This permitted John Smith to move at ease amongst them.

Smith made three trips up the Chickahominy in short order. By then, the whitemen had enough to eat for the time being, and the Indians themselves were beginning to run out of corn and beans. Yet Smith returned once more when the thin crescent of the hoarfrost moon first appeared in the west.

Although he had already gone some distance up the river — thirty miles or more — he had not got out of fairly densely populated country. This time it appeared that he wanted to go much farther. Indeed, he soon passed from Chickahominy territory into the hunting-grounds of the Pamunkeys and Youghtanunds and into the heart of Powhatan's empire.

Twenty miles or more above Apokant, the last Chickahominy village, Smith found his progress impeded by shallow water and fallen trees, even though he had hired a canoe from two Indians and had left the barge and all but two of his white companions behind at Apokant. He stopped to reconnoiter and to eat. While the Englishmen and one Indian were preparing lunch, Smith took the other Indian as a guide to explore the terrain.

Unbeknown to Smith, Opechancanough was out hunting in that area with a large body of Pamunkeys. He had not gone far when a small party of hunters learned that two or three whitemen were there, and tracking them down silently, the Pamunkeys soon spotted the English. One Indian shot an arrow which struck Smith's right thigh harmlessly. Smith then saw two other Indians about to notch their arrows and discharged his pistol at them, also harmlessly.

But other Indians soon closed in, while Smith used his guide as a shield to avoid being shot. Nevertheless, arrows sang through the air as two hundred or so hunters came out of the forest. Those in the front rank quickly drew a bead on Smith, but his Indian cried out that Smith was a white werowance. A werowance was not to be killed on the spot. Besides, he wanted peace.

The hunters then laid their bows on the ground, saying that the white werowance must also lay down his weapons. Smith backed away, evidently hoping to make a break for his boat, not far down the creek. A muddy patch was unfortunately behind him, and in he fell, pulling his Indian with him. Unable to extricate himself without help, Smith at last threw his arms on the ground in front of the hunters.

A chain of hands quickly reached out for the white werowance and his Indian and dragged them to firm ground. Releasing the Indian, the hunters then marched Smith back to his canoe. A big fire was burning, and one whiteman lay dead before it; his body full of arrows. The other whiteman and the other Indian had vanished.

Warmed by the fire, Smith asked to be freed. There was no response. Then he demanded to see their werowance. To this they agreed, and shortly led him before Opechancanough, whom Smith remembered as the grave Indian chief he had seen when he went up the James River in May. Opechancanough waited for his prisoner to speak.

Aware that the Indians were always curious about novelties, Smith produced an ivory pocket compass from his doublet and opened a conversation in halting Algonkian by showing how the compass worked, while talking about astronomy in general.[8] Opechancanough, puzzled by the compass needle always pointing in the same direction and by the fact that he could see it but not touch it, decided that Smith possessed a potentially dangerous article. He listened, trying to understand.

After a while, seeing that his men were getting restless, Opechancanough declared that Smith was not to be executed, but to be taken captive to Powhatan. At that, the hunters hurried into a military formation, placed Smith in their midst, and led him off through the forest for nearly two hours. Finally they came to a group of temporary huts set up by the women for the hunters to sleep in. They called the place Rassawek, or "in-between place," because it was between the Chickahominy and Pamunkey Rivers.[9]

Smith was put in one of the larger huts, with a guard, where he was fed and where he slept. In the morning an Indian whom he had befriended at the fort brought him his cloak, which he had left in the canoe, and three women replenished his food. Then Opechancanough visited him, apparently in an effort to find out more about what Smith and his fellow whitemen were doing in Powhatan's country.

Whatever he found out, Opechancanough cannot have been reassured. Nevertheless he answered some of Smith's questions, informing him that there were people dressed like the whitemen five days' march to the south, while a similar distance to the west there was a great "turning of salt water," which Smith thought meant that a great sea or ocean was not far away. Oddly, it was precisely to find out if there were such a sea that Smith had undertaken this fourth Chickahominy voyage.[10]

Thoroughly excited by this news, Smith asked for a messenger to take a piece of paper to the fort, to tell them that he was well and kindly treated. Otherwise, he intimated that the whitemen might send out a posse to investigate and to avenge his capture. His real purpose, however, was to tell briefly what had happened and to relate what Opechancanough had said about other Europeans and about the Pacific Ocean. Furthermore, since Wowinchopunk had turned up at Rassawek and was encouraging Opechancanough to attack the fort, Smith wanted to report this as well.

Opechancanough, not understanding how a piece of paper could carry a detailed message, though symbol-messages were frequently sent by the Indians, agreed to Smith's request. The latter then penned a long letter, at the end of which he asked those at the fort to do certain things when they got the letter which Smith would tell the Indians to expect. Then the runners took off through the bitterest of winter weather. Three days later they returned, convinced that the paper could talk and that their prisoner was a magician as well as a werowance. For the English had behaved exactly as he had said they would.

About this time, Opechancanough took Smith on a march through Pamunkey country for four or five days. Returning then to Rassawek, they dismantled the temporary shelters, packed the venison from the hunt for transportation, and disbanded. Opechancanough was taking Smith with a large body of his own men along to his residence at Menapacant, a couple of miles above modern West Point, on the Pamunkey.

Not long after their arrival, Smith was led to the long-house, where a great fire was lighted. He was given a mat to sit on facing the fire, while another was put beyond it. Then began an Indian abracadabra by seven priests, made up with red, white, and black paint and crowned with feathers and the skins of snakes and weasels. For three days, all day long, these priests danced, chanted, and howled around the fire and around Smith, after which every evening they all dined together.

This gave Smith a chance to ask the meaning of their dancing and chanting, to which they replied that it was to know if he wished them well or ill. The cornmeal they scattered around the fire, the grains of corn, and the little sticks they placed there, they said, represented their country, the sea, and his country. Their country was in the middle. Leaving Smith still far from enlightened, the seven then brought in Smith's bag of gunpowder. They would plant *that* in the spring, they said, to learn what sort of seed it was. With that, the ritual was over.

A day or two later, Smith was led to the Rappahannock River to see if he were the white captain who had killed the werowance and kidnapped some Indians there a year or two before. Since Smith was conspicuously short, the tribe saw that he was not the marauding whiteman and feasted him, making him comfortable for the night.

The next day, Smith and his guards at length set out for Powhatan's residence, Werowocomoco. It took them two days and a night, moving slowly, to reach their destination, during which time Smith repeatedly said that he wanted to go to Powhatan, if he could not go to the fort, and that they were taking him in the wrong direction. The Indians naturally ignored such nonsense, for they were indeed taking him to Powhatan. It was merely that Smith had not yet learned that the Powhatan he had met on the expedition at the end of May was the son of the overlord, not Great Powhatan.

At last, when the moon had already begun to wane, Smith saw a cluster of typical Indian houses surrounding the largest building he had yet seen in Virginia. It was bitter cold, and there was no further need to delay. Powhatan knew that the white werowance was coming and was waiting, robed in Indian majesty. Near him sat his favorite daughter, Pocahontas. Her rôle in the problem of the whitemen was about to begin.

CHAPTER 3

Pocahontas and Captain John Smith

THE FIRST CONFRONTATION of a member of the governing body of the Jamestown settlement and the supreme chief of tidewater Virginia took place on or about December 29, 1607. Other whitemen had faced other North American chiefs before, but the meeting between John Smith and Powhatan was to have consequences no less far-reaching than the reception of Cortés by the Aztec monarch nearly a century before. The difference was in scale, not in import. Powhatan's "palace" was no more than an exaggerated hut, and Smith was alone — a prisoner. Yet it was still a matter of an invading whiteman and of the rightful head of an Indian people, and the outcome was to be fateful in the extreme.

There is no little uncertainty as to just what happened. That is to say, we can only guess at Powhatan's intentions, basing our conjectures on well-attested Indian practices. Then, too, John Smith still had little command of Powhatan's language and certainly did not understand what was going on when he was led in. Nevertheless, his is the only description which is available.

"Arriving at Werowocomoco," he wrote four or five months later, he found

> their Emperour proudly lying upon a bedstead a foot high, upon ten or twelve mats, richly hung with many chains of great pearls about his neck, and covered with a great covering of *Rahaughcums* [raccoon skins]. At his head sat one woman, at his feet another. On each side, sitting upon a mat upon the ground, were ranged his chief men on each side of the fire, ten in a rank, and behind them as many young women, each with a great chain of white beads over their shoulders, their heads painted in red. And Powhatan with such a grave and majestic countenance as drove me into admiration to see such state in a naked savage.[1]

As he entered, all the people — "grim courtiers" Smith called them — gave a mighty shout. Then Opossunoquonuske, werowansqua of Appamatuck, brought water to the Englishman so that he could wash his hands, followed by a woman with a bunch of feathers for a towel. Powhatan welcomed him with words which seemed pleasant enough, and trenchers of food were set before him.

While Smith was eating, the tribal elders held a long consultation with Powhatan. Then two big stones were brought in, and Smith was forcibly stretched out on them. What appeared to be executioners stood over him with clubs ready. A tense, motionless silence descended over the room, while a smoky, flickering blaze illuminated the prostrate victim.

Suddenly, a little girl rushed from Powhatan's side, knelt, and placed her head over Smith's. The executioners released their captive, and the little girl pulled him to his feet. It was the first meeting of John Smith and Pocahontas.

By then, Powhatan's face had relaxed. He spoke at some length, but Smith understood only that they would be friends and that Smith would be free to return to the English fort in four days.

The ceremony of which Smith had been the object was almost certainly a combination of mock execution and salvation, in token of adoption into Powhatan's tribe. Indian boys in their early adolescence were subjected to far more fearful rites when they entered into manhood. They had young braves to "protect" them. In Smith's case, Powhatan himself was possibly his foster-father, but Pocahontas had been chosen to act in his stead.[2] Relations with the dangerous Englishmen were still problematical, and Powhatan must stand aloof.

Smith could not understand, much less know, this. He simply regarded Pocahontas as his savior.

Later — and we have no more accurate description than Smith's befuddled recollections, hampered always by his linguistic shortcomings — later, Powhatan endeavored to learn more about the whitemen. What his half-brother, Opechancanough, had told him about Smith's round box with the magnetic needle and Smith's knowledge of the universe interested him. But what was more important was why the Englishmen had come to his land.

Smith evaded the question with a story of a fight with their enemies, another tribe of whitemen, in which they had been worsted. A storm then drove them to Virginia, he said.

Powhatan next wanted to know why they went up the James River and, more pertinently, why Smith himself had gone so far up the Chickahominy, even beyond where his barge could go.

Smith explained that the whitemen were interested in finding the sea — the salt water beyond the mountains — and that he would supply the details later. What was vital to him just then was that one of his father's children had been slain. He assumed the Monacans had done that. They were Powhatan's enemies, he knew.

Powhatan hesitated briefly. Then he said something about the countries above the rapids, the "falls," five, six, or even eight days away. There the headwaters of the great river were brackish, pounding out of the mountains over stones and rocks. Somewhere beyond there lived the Pocoughtaonacks, a fierce nation that ate men and women, and warred with the people of Moyaones and Potomac who were his subjects.[3]

Smith, in return, was as expansive as his knowledge of Powhatan's language would permit on the power and magnificence of King James, whose subject he was, and on Europe in general. An account of European wars taken from his own experiences followed. In this his penchant for ostentation (and exaggeration) was hampered only by Algonkian syntax. Finally he wound up with words of respect for Captain Newport, the one-armed graybeard, whom he called his father and who he said was Werowance of All the Waters.

Powhatan brought the audience to a conclusion by announcing that Smith was now one of his werowances — in fact, werowance of the village of Capahowasic, an hour downstream by foot or canoe.

Two days later, Powhatan had Smith taken to one of his great houses in the forest, not far off. There he was left alone in a room divided by a hanging mat, where a fire was burning. Some minutes later, from behind the mat a doleful moaning arose that rapidly swelled into a barbaric chant. Whereupon Powhatan emerged, painted black, and followed by a crowd of warriors, also painted black.

Solemnly halting before Smith, the "emperor" told him that they were friends and that he could now return to Jamestown. Powhatan would supply him with guides, and in exchange for his kindnesses would expect Smith to make him a gift of two great "thunder-weapons" and a grindstone. Capahowasic was Smith's whenever he wanted to occupy it, and Smith would forever be as dear to him as his own son Nantaquaus, the brother of Pocahontas.

When Powhatan had retired behind the mat again, Smith's guards conducted him back to Werowocomoco. A squad of Indians was waiting for him — two of them laden with food, one carrying Smith's belongings, and the fourth acting as guide. An hour or less of paddling brought the party to a landing-place across the York and in five hours they could easily have reached the fort. But Powhatan had said that Smith would be free in four days, not three. So they spent the night in one of Powhatan's houses in the forest.

The next morning, not long after sun-up, Smith rejoined his fellow-colonists in the fort. Promptly he showed two demi-culverins, as well as a mill-stone, to his guide, Powhatan's trusty servant Rawhunt. The cannons were too heavy to carry, but the Indians wanted to see them perform. Smith had one of them loaded with stones and fired at a huge tree glistening with snow and icicles.

When the gun roared and the branches came down in a shower of ice the Indians ran away, frightened out of their wits. Calling them back, Smith reassured them. But it was some little time before they regained their courage and accepted a bag of presents for the "emperor," and his women, and children, and another for the messengers themselves. In one of his not infrequent fits of absent-mindedness, Smith forgot about the little girl who he thought had saved his life. True, he was under stress at the time. Yet the omission of Pocahontas' name underlines the always evident fact that he still regarded her as a mere child — just one of Powhatan's children.

No sooner had the Indians left than the reason for Smith's forgetfulness came into the open. Some of the whitemen had already shown their displeasure at his return. Now, one of them threatened to have him hanged for the death of his companions when he was captured. But that night, the second of January, 1608, Captain Newport's long-awaited ship arrived back from London. Newport personally put a stop to such criminal nonsense.

The ship was unloaded the following Monday, January 4. Then, three days later, perhaps because of the confusion, a fire broke out that virtually destroyed Jamestown. Some newcomers lost everything they had; others fared a little better. Although Newport's men lent a hand in rebuilding the settlement, it was not an easy task in the middle of winter, and many of the new arrivals died for lack of shelter.

Just then, Powhatan showed that he had been sincere in saying that Smith was his friend. A present of a deer, bread, and raccoon skins arrived. Four or five days later, he sent another gift, accompanied by Pocahontas and a handful of attendants.

Weeks slipped by. In Jamestown, such was the joy of the old colonists at the arrival of supplies, as well as of new settlers (who brought the total population to well over a hundred), that the mariners were permitted to barter with the Indians at will.

Newport himself began sending valuable gifts to Powhatan, with Pocahontas often, if not always, flitting back and forth with the Indian porters and messengers. Such recklessness with their goods naturally lowered the value of the Englishmen's copper, hatchets, and beads in terms of Indian food supplies and furs. But only Smith seemed to care.

Toward the end of February, Newport decided to take the pinnace around through Chesapeake Bay and up the York River to Werowocomoco. Powhatan had sent repeated word that he would like to meet werowance Smith's "father," the Great White Werowance who was lord of all the waters. Finally he sent the werowance of Kiskiack and his man Namontack to Newport to act as guides. It was then only a matter of waiting for suitable weather.

At last the expedition started out, with Newport commanding, aided by John Smith and a young new member of the Jamestown Council, Matthew Scrivener. They took with them thirty or forty men. When they arrived at Werowocomoco, the whitemen began to be suspicious of Powhatan's designs, and Smith decided to go ashore first, with a company of twenty men in arrow-proof jackets.

In spite of the guides, Smith's party succeeded in getting lost. Pocahontas' brother Nantaquaus came to their aid at last and led them out of a maze of creeks. But there was much petulance and acrimony among the Englishmen before they finished the short march to Powhatan's residence. Outside it, they saw great wooden platters of bread, a symbol of welcome; inside, the assembled Indian court, according to their protocol, shouted loudly with joy and respect.

Powhatan, attired in a huge mantle of skins, lay relaxed on his bed of mats against a leather pillow embroidered with pearls and white beads. His women were seated around him as before, and generally the scene was the same as when Smith first appeared there two months before, but more Indians were in the building, and the atmosphere was friendly.

Smith entered alone. As soon as he had, a crier proclaimed that no-one was to presume to do any of the whitemen any harm. Meanwhile, a place alongside Powhatan was made ready for the visitor. And when all was ready, Smith solemnly presented the "Emperor" with a suit of red woollen cloth, a white greyhound, and a sugar-loaf hat.[4]

Three orators in turn accepted these remarkable gifts on behalf of the supreme ruler and confirmed his perpetual league of friendship with the Englishmen. This accomplished, Smith took his place on the mats, and Powhatan commanded Opossunoquonuske "to give [him] water, a turkey-cock, and bread to eat."

The usual conversational tactics between Smith and Powhatan followed: feint and lunge, parry and riposte — with words. Where was Smith's father, Powhatan asked. And what about the guns he had been promised? Then, where were his companions?

Smith replied with questions about the village Powhatan had given him and asked where the corn was that he had been promised. Powhatan said that Smith would get both, but why did his men not lay down their arms at his feet, as all good subjects should. And so on.

At last Powhatan rose, formally and publicly declaring that Smith was a werowance, that his people should so regard him, and that the whitemen were no longer strangers, or Paspaheghans, but Powhatans.[5] Corn, women, and the country itself, all were to be to the whitemen as they were to the Powhatan people.

With that, Smith took his leave. Powhatan, ever courteous, went to the door with him, noticed that a storm was brewing, and told Nantaquaus and Namontack to take the whitemen to a house where they could spend the night. He even sent a haunch of venison for their supper, despite the fact that all of them had left Powhatan's residence weighted down with food.

That night, Powhatan sent a messenger to invite Smith to dinner with him, with a squad of men to light his way. He was still trying to understand the Englishmen and, especially, to divine how long they would stay. Underneath his attentions there was always the point: how to rid himself of these unwanted people.

The next morning, Powhatan sent for Smith again, this time only to conduct him down to the river-bank. He wanted to show him his canoes, and to explain how he received tribute from the various nations under him — beads from across Chesapeake Bay, and beads, copper, and skins from other regions. Smith must understand that he was lord in his own country.

About that time, Captain Newport was seen disembarking from the pinnace. Powhatan retired to his residence to prepare a suitable welcome while Smith went to join Newport.

Aside from a somewhat ludicrous interlude when Newport's trumpeter frightened the Indians with a sound such as they had never heard before, the usual courtesies were extended on both sides. After these, Newport presented to Powhatan as his son a lad of thirteen named Thomas Savage. (Savage was, in reality, born of a fine old English family from Chester.) He was to stay with Powhatan as a sign of friendship, Newport said. Savage's true task was to learn the language and anything else that might be of use to the colony.

Powhatan returned the courtesy by giving his trusty servant Namontack to Newport, likewise in witness of friendship. His true task was also to learn the language and anything else that might be of use to Powhatan.

After the formalities were over, the whitemen wanted to trade. Although the Indians were more than willing, Powhatan insisted that he would not bargain, personally. It was not for rulers to haggle. Newport was to give him presents freely, and Powhatan would return presents freely. Newport agreed. But John Smith saw in this the ruin of the colony by destroying the market.

Powhatan's attitude was proper, of course. Had not the Aztec emperor refused to barter with the Spaniards? Buying and selling and haggling was the business of petty chiefs, merchants, traders, and the common people, not for exalted rulers. But Smith was right; the colony would starve if the ruler set the rate of exchange.

To save the situation, Smith bethought himself of some blue glass beads he had brought with him. Casually he took a handful out of a bag and flashed them before Powhatan. Powhatan, never having seen anything remotely similar, was enchanted. He offered a basket of corn for them.

Smith demanded, and got, a much larger basket. Suddenly the market for blue glass beads began to get remarkably active. Smith cannily held off, the next day informing Powhatan and his chief men that the beads were made of a most rare substance which took its color from the sky. They were to be worn only by "kings." In this way, Smith obtained from Powhatan, his brother Opechancanough, and perhaps other werowances, quite considerable quantities of corn for a few pounds of beads.

Shortly after, Newport and Smith went trading farther up the river, at least as far as Cinquaoteck and the nearby Menapacant where Smith had stayed a little more than two months before. At Cinquaoteck they traded with Powhatan's half-brothers Opitchapan and Kekataugh and with Opechancanough at Menapacant. Then, having obtained about two hundred and fifty bushels of corn, Newport brought the pinnace back to Jamestown. It was March 9, and a sickle moon hung over the river at sunset. It seemed to augur a new life for the colony.

Four and a half weeks later, Newport set sail for England. Someone, somewhere, had discovered what was thought to be gold-dust in the sands by the river, and that entire month was dedicated to loading the ship with the most promising samples. Despite the protests of Smith and a few others, time was wasted and with it, food. The ship which had come to bring supplies to the colony ended by consuming not only what it had brought but also part of the little the colony had been able to lay in. Smith was particularly annoyed.

However, Powhatan continued to be friendly. Winter was past; the planting season had begun, and some of the Indian surplus could be bartered with the whitemen. So Pocahontas merrily accompanied the parties of Indians that carried food to the fort, and returned with the gewgaws, merrily offered by the English and greedily accepted by the natives in exchange.

During her visits, Pocahontas would blissfully do cart-wheels around the fort, virtually in the nude. Smith found great pleasure in her company, a relief from the grumbling, quarreling colonists, the bulk of whom expected to be housed and fed without lifting a finger in their own behalf. He would trade bits of copper for the white beads called *roanoke* that the Indians made of seashells.[6] Then he would ask Pocahontas to bring little baskets for them. She could make herself a chain, he said.

Pocahontas in turn was fascinated by John Smith. He was good-natured. He was cheerful with her, but he did not laugh at her like many of his companions. He did not laugh at her people, either. He traded pleasantly, unless someone tried to cheat him, and he treated her people with as much regard as his own. Indeed, she could see that there were many of his fellow whitemen whom he neither liked nor trusted.

Not long after the Great Werowance Newport left, more white-men came in a small ship. This caused much activity at the fort. At about the same time, Powhatan sent a present of turkeys. On Newport's departure, he had sent twenty such birds on the understanding that he would get twenty English swords in exchange. Newport had complied.

Now, Powhatan suggested the same sort of exchange to Smith. Smith did not even bother to consult the President of the Council, who was sick anyway. He refused. He was not interested in making the Indians any more dangerous than they already were. Furthermore, he had no swords he wanted to spare under any circumstances.

Powhatan, put out, countered by calling for a systematic effort to obtain the swords by less direct means. The Indians who came to the fort in a steady stream began by trying to steal them. Failing that, they would ambush the colonists at the gate to the fort and take them by force, or they would catch them off guard when they were working outside the palisade. In this way many swords changed hands, to Powhatan's advantage.

To Smith's indescribable disgust, nothing was done about this smartness. The President and the majority of the council, taking literally their orders from London not to "offend" the Indians, sat in their huts or tents and ignored the matter.

This passivity made the Indians bolder. One day, a handful of them went so far as to try to appropriate John Smith's sword. This was a mistake. Smith collected a few men, fell upon the Indians, caught some and imprisoned them in the fort, and soundly thrashed the rest. In the midst of this strong retaliation, however, two of Smith's soldiers went foraging for their personal gain, only to be caught themselves.

Possessed of these hostages, the Indians raced in mass to the gate in an attempt to force Smith to release the seven of their own kind he had caught. That was another mistake.

Smith in short order emerged from the gate to face them with a body of loyal soldiers, armed to the teeth. The fracas that ensued was brief. In less than half an hour, the Indians brought Smith's errant soldiers back and begged him to make peace. They did not even want the Indian prisoners released, they said. And the prisoners in turn blamed it all on Powhatan.

Whatever Smith may have believed about this, Powhatan did move to intercede on behalf of the seven prisoners. He sent Pocahontas to excuse the Indians' behavior and to beg Smith's forgiveness. Through her, he once again assured Smith of his love.

Smith had already punished the men enough, he seems to have thought, but he kept them in prison a day or two more from tactical motives, treating them well to show that they were forgiven. But only after he had made it clear that it was for Pocahontas' sake that their lives were spared and they were freed, did he release them into her custody.

A few days later, on June 2, 1608, the supply ship was ready to return to England. Smith decided to accompany it as far as Cape Henry so that he could privately give the captain a long letter he had written to a friend in London. This letter told what had happened in the colony up to that very date, and he did not want his enemies in the fort to know too much about it. At the same time, he was about to start out on a long survey of the coasts, rivers, and peoples of Chesapeake Bay. He did not care *who* knew that.

Using the two-ton barge that had often taken him on voyages for food, Smith and fourteen companions spent seven weeks sailing and rowing up the bay and the Potomac River. On his way back, at the mouth of the Rappahannock, he was wounded by a dangerous fish, a sting-ray.[7] Although he was treated on the spot, he had to abandon the rest of his exploring and go back to Jamestown.

There he found the colony in an uproar over the misbehavior of the President of the Council. Smith lent a helping hand in removing him from office but refused to accept the post himself. So it was decided to elect a temporary president to govern during the remainder of the ousted President's term, which would expire on September 10.

This accomplished, Smith made a few changes in his party, reduced it to twelve, and finding himself healed of his wound, set out again on July 24. This time, in a determined effort to see if there were any route toward the "great salt water" to the west about which he had heard, he sailed directly north as far as the Susquehanna River. There, among other discoveries, he met a body of Iroquoian Indians from far outside Powhatan's realm.

Smith arrived back from this vastly successful voyage on September 7. Three days later, he was elected and sworn in as President of the Council. Now began a period of new and closer ties with Pocahontas.

CHAPTER 4

Powhatan and John Smith

NO SOONER was John Smith installed as President of the Council than he set to work to reorganize the colony's activities. The construction of a presidential "palace" was stopped, and buildings were put up, instead, to house the supplies which were expected before long. The church was repaired, and a new roof was put on the storehouse. Finally, not only was the shape of the fort revised, but military drill was renewed and the watch reapportioned.

In the midst of all this activity, Captain Newport returned for the second time, bringing evidence of misguided London policies along with the usual additional colonists and supplies. Someone in the royal council for Virginia conceived the notion that Powhatan could be brought to terms and made subject to King James by the simple expedient of sending him a copper crown, a red woollen robe, and an English bedstead to lie on in place of the pile of mats he used for a throne. Newport was consequently instructed to take these and other objects to Virginia and to celebrate a solemn coronation of Powhatan as a subject-king under the overlordship of James I, King of Great Britain, France, and Ireland, and Virginia.

Newport had other commissions, similarly specious but less directly dangerous. Not only was he to search for gold in the unexplored territory above and to the west of Powhatan village, but Poles and "Dutchmen" (probably Germans) were sent over to set up a glass-factory and other manufacturing projects before the colonists had enough to eat and while their "domestic tranquillity" was still so uncertain that few dared leave the stockade unaccompanied. As Smith later said, English agents on the continent could easily buy glass, pitch, and tar in eastern Europe, but only the "Coronation of Powhatan" gave him real concern.

"By whose advice," Smith wrote to the London Council, "you sent him such presents, I know not; but this give me leave to tell you. I fear they will be the confusion of us all ere we hear from you again." [1]

Any semblance of currying favor with Powhatan Smith regarded as certain to produce the opposite of what was expected. It was necessary to do business with him only as equal to equal. Convinced of this, Smith evaded the subject of the ceremony for a short time by suggesting that Powhatan be invited to Jamestown to *receive his presents* — calling them such without hinting at a "coronation." Newport consented but thought that a large force would be needed to take the invitation.

Smith volunteered to act as envoy extraordinary to this end and requested only four Englishmen and the Indian Namontack for companions. (Trusty Namontack had just returned from a brief visit to England.) It was fall, but Jack Frost was still far away in the north. No extraordinary provisions or precautions were required. The Indian trail across the peninsula was open and relatively safe, and once this had been traversed, a canoe to carry the party over the river to Werowocomoco could be found without great trouble.

With Newport's consent, then, that much was accomplished. But when Smith reached Werowocomoco, he found that Powhatan was a day's journey away. There was no remedy but for his "women," as Smith referred to Powhatan's dozen or so wives, to dispatch couriers to summon Powhatan. Meanwhile, the Indians graciously devised an entertainment for their distinguished guest, John Smith, werowance of Capahowasic.

A number of men, women, and children gathered in a field not far from Powhatan's residence. Mats were provided for Smith and his companions, and a fire was lighted. The Englishmen ceremoniously squatted down, cross-legged, in anticipation.

All of a sudden, such a hullabaloo of shrieking came from the ever-present forest that Smith and his four men scrambled to their feet to get their guns. But Pocahontas came running up and assured them that no harm was intended — they could kill her if anything happened, she said. Furthermore, the rest of the audience, the Indians, swore to the jumpy whitemen that it was a show, not a massacre.

The Englishmen sat down again, and then, as Smith wrote,

> thirty young women came naked out of the woods (only covered behind and before with a few green leaves), their bodies all painted, some white, some red, some black, some parti-colored, but every one different. Their leader had a fair pair of stags' horns on her head, and an otter skin at her girdle, another at her arm, a quiver of arrows at her back, and bow and arrows in her hand. The next [had] in her hand a sword; another, a club; another, a pot-stick; all horned alike. The rest, every one with their several devices.

Scurrying up out of the forest, the girls formed a ring around the fire, dancing and screeching "with most excellent ill variety," so far as English ears were concerned. This was interrupted with occasional outbursts which Smith called "infernal passions," only to give place to a solemn dance with singing.

After nearly an hour of this hullabaloo, the group scurried back into the forest. A brief intermission followed, and then all thirty reappeared in their usual dress. Surrounding Smith, the werowance, they coaxed him into a large lodging where they offered themselves to him, as Indian courtesy demanded on such occasions. Smith, whose modesty verged on prudery, refused. But the girls, apparently thinking that it was a matter of personal preference rather than a blanket rejection, then threw themselves at him, one after the other, crying, "Love you not me?"

When the "salutation," as Smith called it, was ended, a feast was set up — enough "for twenty hogs" — consisting of every imaginable Indian dainty. This was accompanied by dancing and general mirth until nightfall, when Smith and his companions were conducted with firebrands to the lodging set aside for them.[2] The next day Powhatan arrived, and Smith returned Namontack, safely back from his long voyage, to him.

While Namontack was in London, the Spanish Ambassador wrote to Philip III of Spain that he was passed off as a son of Powhatan's. It seems more likely, however, that he was treated as an envoy or ambassador, for the Venetian Ambassador reported to *his* government merely that a "chief inhabitant" of Virginia was in London.

In any case, although there is no official record of the title given him by the Virginia Company, it is certain that they made the most of Namontack for publicity purposes, and he became a good friend of the English. It is unfortunate that there is no way of knowing what he told Powhatan and Pocahontas about London. Even more unfortunate for Anglo-Indian relations, he was killed two years later in a brawl with the brother of Powhatan's favorite wife, Winganuske.[3]

Despite the fact that Smith used Namontack as the primary reason for his voyage to Werowocomoco, his true objective was to persuade Powhatan to accompany him to Jamestown to receive the gifts sent from England. In fact, Smith attempted to strengthen his invitation by asserting that the articles had been sent by the King of England himself and by adding an offer of help to Powhatan against his enemies. In addition, Smith again tossed in a long digression on the death of the two men who had gone up the Chickahominy River with him the year before and on the interest of the Englishmen in the great salt sea which he had heard lay to the west.

Powhatan's answer to all this, as reported by John Smith, was:

> If your King has sent me presents, I also am a King, and this is my land. Eight days I will stay [here] to receive them. Your father [Newport] is to come to me, not I to him; nor yet to your fort. Neither will I bite at such a bait. As for the Monacans, I can revenge my own injuries; and as for the Atquanachuck, where you say your brother was slain, it is a contrary way from those parts [where] you suppose it. But for any salt water beyond the mountains, the relations you have from my people are false.[4]

It is evident that Smith's knowledge of Powhatan's language had improved tremendously since the time of their first meeting. Powhatan was now clearly attempting to set matters straight, and Smith seems to have understood. But the myth of the nearby ocean — just across the mountains — did not die. Neither did the Englishmen's confident expectation of eventually luring Powhatan into friendship by offering to help him fight his enemies.

In spite of all, Powhatan remained opposed to the English. His manner was friendly though dignified, and he left no doubt in John Smith's mind, at least, that he intended to remain absolute autocrat of his people. Smith had to return to Jamestown and report that the presents must be taken to Werowocomoco and that the "coronation" must take place there, too. It was the latter that troubled him above all else.

Newport consumed the better part of a day sailing around from Jamestown to Werowocomoco, a distance of a little more than eighty miles. Meanwhile Smith and the other captains among the colonists marched fifteen miles or so to a village nearly opposite Werowocomoco, accompanied by some fifty marksmen. From there they were ferried across the river by canoe. Eventually Newport anchored offshore, and the entire group of Englishmen spent the night divided between Werowocomoco and shipboard. Powhatan was asked to be ready in his residence the next morning.

When all was at last in order, the Englishmen, some of them in glittering armor, marched solemnly through a crowd of half-naked Indians to Powhatan's *machacomoco* ("great house"), followed by Indian porters carrying the presents: a bed, probably of oak or walnut, with its bedding, and other furniture — perhaps a few stools, since chairs were relatively scarce even in England. An Englishman probably carried the ewer and basin for use at meals. These could have been of pewter or brass, hardly of anything more valuable. But they were considered indispensable in English homes in those days for use both before and after eating, since forks were still something of a novelty and fingers supplemented knives and spoons as eating implements. All such things were valued gifts in England itself.[5]

Powhatan accepted these oddities with good grace. But when it came to a scarlet cloak and "apparel," which possibly consisted of a doublet and jacket, a shirt, a pair of hose, and shoes, Powhatan rebelled. Only after Namontack assured him that these confining articles would do him no harm did Powhatan admit to being helped into them. Then came the standstill.

Newport produced the tawdry copper crown which the Virginia Company had had made for Powhatan. Holding it over his head, he told him to kneel so that he could place it on his head. Powhatan, however, as Smith described it, "neither knowing the majesty nor meaning of a crown, nor [of] bending of the knee, endured so many persuasions, examples, and instructions, as tired them all."

And still that proud Indian would not so much as bow his head.

At last, several hands pushed hard on Powhatan's shoulders, and he stooped, ever so little. At that, Newport clapped the crown on him, and the "coronation" was achieved. A pistol was fired to announce the event. And by previous arrangement, the pinnace offshore echoed this with a tremendous volley of shot.

Powhatan started to his feet, throwing off the white hands around him. But with the smiles and respectful attitude of the English leaders reassuring him, he relaxed onto his makeshift divan and with imperturbable mien thanked Newport for his kindness. In reciprocity, he deigned to give his "old shoes" (moccasins) and his mantle to Newport.

Newport then outlined his plan to explore the Monacan country above Powhatan village along the James River. Powhatan had previously blown hot and cold on this subject. Now he blew cold, only. He would contribute absolutely nothing to the proposed expedition, although he was willing that Namontack should go along as a guide. Newport was unable to budge him from this stand.[6]

At length, after presenting Newport with a few bushels of corn, Powhatan indicated that the audience was over. Newport then retired with his captains and his marksmen. Thus, the Virginia Company's instructions to crown Powhatan were obeyed. Perhaps even Newport was disappointed with the result.

In any case, a break between Smith, President of the Council, and Newport, special commissioner for the Company, was already evident. On their return to Jamestown, Newport left the President at the fort with eighty or ninety colonists, to carry out a further order from London: to load the good ship *Mary and Margaret* with something, anything, to show that the colony was prospering — which it was not — while he went up the James with the rest of the council, young Francis West, brother of Lord De La Warr, Lieutenant George Percy, brother of the ninth Earl of Northumberland, and one hundred and twenty picked men. They took with them a knocked-down boat to be put together above the rapids.

Unfortunately, they were unable either to carry the pieces around the rapids or to reassemble them above — it is not clear which — and were compelled to do their exploring and mine hunting on foot. The Monacans, hostile to the Powhatans under any circumstances, were the opposite of cooperative, and the Englishmen had to capture and chain a local Monacan chief to act as guide. They found virtually nothing. The hardships of the march made many of the colonists sick, and in the end they had to turn back after only two and a half days.

By that time, Powhatan had learned of what the Englishmen were doing, and when they passed back through Powhatan village, his son Parahunt refused any sort of help. Indeed, he had had time to hide all his food so that Newport's men could not steal it. The indications were steadily getting stronger that the copper crown had made the Overlord more intransigent than ever.

When the whole colony was again together at the fort, Smith put those who were not sick to work chopping down trees for clapboard and wainscoting, and making "trials" (samples) of pitch, tar, glass, frankincense, and soap-ashes, to be sent as tokens of goodwill to the Virginia Company in London. Of truly profitable things, there were as yet none to send.

The attitude of the Indians naturally also hampered the colony's search for products to defray, if only in part, the cost of the supplies they had to have. Smith, convinced that it was now Powhatan's policy to starve them, went up the Chickahominy River in person since, theretofore, the Chickahominies had been cooperative.

At first, these semi-independent Indians also refused to trade, but upon Smith's insistence, not without implied threats, they unwillingly supplied him with some corn. Lieutenant Percy followed in another barge and collected a similar amount. And Councillor

Scrivener went to Werowocomoco with the pinnace and barges but found the people totally unwilling to trade. Namontack intervened, at last, so that Scrivener got three or four hogsheads of corn. Passing Old Point Comfort on his return he met Newport whose sails were set for England.

The prospects for the two hundred colonists left behind, including Mistress Thomas Forest and her maid, were none too bright. Eighty-nine of them were lame or sick, and Newport, instead of adding to their supplies as the Company had intended, required three hogsheads of the little corn they had for his own voyage home. This forced Smith to set out once again to raid ("barter" he would have called it) the Indians for more supplies.

His first choice was the Nansemond tribe, which had never been friendly. When he got to their territory, he had to make a show of force before they would sell, but he brought back a hundred bushels of corn to Jamestown. Then he sailed up the James to Chawopo (Chippoke Creek), Weanoc, and other localities, where he found neither people nor corn. Still farther upstream he visited the Appamatucks and managed to get a little food, but he returned virtually empty-handed.

Under these circumstances, Smith felt obliged to face Powhatan with an open surprise attack if he would not help feed the colony. The Council, however, refused to go along with this idea, since noone but Captain Waldo agreed with Smith. Apparently the colony was determined to starve unless Providence relieved them.

Smith was of a different nature. Although he was firm, and aggressive when opposed, he treated the Indians more fairly and in a more friendly way than others, but he was not going to let the Indians, on the one hand, and indolence, fatalism, or blind obedience to company orders, on the other, stand between him and nourishment. As he put it, "no persuasions could persuade [him] to starve."

Just what he planned to do, however, must remain buried with Smith. Powhatan himself moved. Then he sent messengers to invite Smith to visit him. He wanted a house built, he said, like the ones he had heard about in Jamestown. So, if Smith would send him men with tools to build such a house, and a grindstone, fifty swords, a cock and a hen, copper, beads, and some guns to boot, he would see that Smith's ship was loaded with corn.

Smith, despite his sometimes excessive caution, accepted the invitation, along with the accompanying "conditions." After witnessing the first Christian marriage in Virginia, that of Mistress Forest's maid and John Laydon, and after presiding at prayers on Sunday, December 25, when there was no minister at Jamestown, Smith dispatched three "Dutchmen" and two Englishmen overland to Werowocomoco to start work on Powhatan's house. Then he asked for volunteers to accompany him in the pinnace and a couple of barges. With Councillor Scrivener appointed as his deputy in Jamestown, Smith sailed with forty-six volunteers on December 29, 1608, through bitter cold, stormy weather.

Delayed by frosty winds and snow, the expedition did not reach Werowocomoco until January 12. No Indian was expecting them. The river was frozen nearly half a mile from shore, and Smith's barge got stuck as the crew tried to maneuver it through the icy mud to the shore. At that, Smith climbed out, calling for his men to follow waist-deep in slime for several hundred yards. Finally taking refuge in the nearest Indian hut, Smith sent to Powhatan for provisions.

The next morning Powhatan received Smith and his men with the usual feast of welcome. This ended, he asked Smith what he was doing there and when he would be gone. He said that he had not sent for Smith, and that he had no corn for him; his own people had none either. Nevertheless, he would give him forty bushels for forty swords.[7]

Smith promptly gave him the lie by pointing to the men who brought the message. He asked Powhatan how he had become so forgetful. Powhatan laughed loudly at this. He would trade, he agreed, but he wanted guns and swords. Other things, such as copper, he would not accept. He could eat his corn, he said, but not the copper.

Smith retaliated by stating that he had forsaken his own interests to supply Powhatan with men to build a house, while Powhatan was seizing his own people's corn merely so that they would have none for the English. He had neither swords nor guns to spare since those he had would keep him from want; and he had no intention of wronging Powhatan, or of stealing. But he concluded his remarks with a broad hint that if Powhatan did not help him out, he might "dissolve that friendship [which] we have mutually promised." In short, he might resort to war.

Powhatan understood. It was a speech an Indian chief of another tribe might have made, if he had the manpower and arms to back it up. Smith, he knew, had that sort of power, despite his want of provisions. He quickly promised to spare what he could to relieve the whitemen. "Yet," he added,

> Captain Smith, some doubt I have of your coming hither, that makes me not so kindly seek to relieve you as I would [like]. For many do inform me your coming is not for trade, but to invade my people and possess my country. [My people] dare not come to bring you corn, seeing you thus armed with your men. To clear us of this fear, leave aboard [the ship] your weapons, for here they are needless, we being all friends and forever Powhatans.

Powhatan's object — to disarm the whitemen — was manifest. It was basic to his make-up and his policy. Smith, understanding this, naturally did not yield. So, the rest of the day was spent in further idle arguing.

The next morning, Powhatan took Smith to inspect his house,

which he was by then in no haste to see completed. The reason for this change in objective was simple. In the space of two or three weeks, the "Dutchmen" sent to build it had discovered that they could live at Werowocomoco with plenty of luxuries, including women. They had also discovered that Powhatan was determined to rid himself of the more than unwelcome Englishmen.

Putting two and two together, despite their scant knowledge of the language, the "Dutchmen" succeeded in winning Powhatan's interest and favor by presenting a picture, which was assuredly pretty accurate, of the plight of the colony: laziness, coupled with disloyalty, and a stalking presence of famine. The way to destroy the colony, they were convinced, was by destroying Smith.

Powhatan, who loved *no* whiteman, undoubtedly listened. Here were ideas that matched his own. Accordingly, it may reasonably be proposed that Powhatan's change of heart regarding Smith's visit is to be ascribed to this treachery on the part of men Smith trusted.

Unaware of the possibility, not to mention the likelihood, of collusion between the "Dutchmen" and Powhatan, Smith renewed his conversation while waiting for corn to be brought from the other villages. Noting that Powhatan prized a copper pot very highly, for instance, Smith put an exorbitant price on it, despite Powhatan's insistence on the divine right of kings not to haggle, but cheerfully agreed to take only part payment at the moment. Later in the year, he said, Powhatan could give him more corn or, say, the country of Monacan. Powhatan, since he did not own Monacan, gladly gave it to Smith — it was the right of kings to give, freely — and went on to philosophize on the matter of Peace and War.

After a cryptic remark about witnessing the death of all his people three times (which Smith obviously did not, and the modern reader cannot, understand), Powhatan soliloquized that he was getting old, and that his brothers and sisters and the latters' sons would in turn succeed him, "ere long." He hoped that their aptitude would be no less than his own, and that Smith would love them as much as he loved Smith. But, he added,

> this bruit from Nansemond, that you are come to destroy my country, so much affrighteth all my people [that] they dare not visit you. What will it avail you to take that perforce [which] you may quietly have with love, or to destroy them that provide you [with] food? What can you get by war, when we can hide our provision and fly to the woods, whereby you must famish, by wronging us, your friends?

Smith knew only too well that without Indian help the colony would starve. His problem, and aim, was to force the Indians to give him food (by barter) without going to war. At the same time, he was well aware, despite Powhatan's words, that his design was simply to get rid of the English. Starvation seemed to be the most feasible way. Meanwhile, Powhatan was talking on; he did not want to be

> forced to fly from all, to lie cold in the woods . . . and be so hunted by you [Smith] that I can neither rest, eat, nor sleep, but my tired men must watch, and if a twig but break, everyone [will] cry "there comes Captain Smith . . ."

Yet in spite of his eloquence, before he finished speaking, Powhatan once again pleaded with Smith to come without guns, without swords, as a friend. And Smith knew that this was only a ruse to get him and the English colony into his, Powhatan's, power.

Smith therefore countered by reminding Powhatan that the Indians were welcome in the fort, bows and arrows, and all. The English, he claimed, were not likely to attack the Indians, unless provoked, for, he said, "had we intended you any hurt, long ere this we could have effected it." They had the advantage in arms, but they had not used it to destroy the Indians. As for the Indians hiding their corn, Smith claimed that he had "a rule to find beyond your knowledge" — a bit of mysticism as unclear to modern ears as it must have been to Powhatan.

By the time the dialogue had reached this point, the Indians were beginning to arrive with corn from neighboring villages. Bartering had commenced. Nevertheless, Powhatan returned to the attack.

Everyone, he said, did what he, Powhatan, desired — except Smith. Yet that same Smith was the werowance above all others whom he had favored. From Smith he got only what Smith would give him, not what he, Powhatan, wanted. At the same time, Smith insisted on having whatever *he* demanded. And with dignity Powhatan remonstrated:

> Captain Newport you call father, and so you call me. But I see, for all us both, you will do what you list, and we must both seek to content you. But if you intend [to be] so friendly as you say, send hence your arms, that I may believe you. For you see the love I bear you doth cause me thus nakedly [to] forget myself.

Smith was not so tired of arguing, perhaps, as he was eager to load his corn and return to Jamestown. He seems to have interrupted the conversation briefly to get some Indians to break the ice offshore at Werowocomoco so that his barge could come near enough for loading. Furthermore, he sent word for some of his men to come ashore "to have surprised the king" — which smacks of some sort of duplicity on Smith's part, possibly provoked by some unrecorded development. But in two minutes he was ready with his answer:

> Powhatan, you must know [that] as I have but one God, I honor but one king. And I live here not as your subject, but as your friend, to pleasure you with what I can. By the gifts you bestow on me you gain more than by trade. Yet would you [but] visit me as

> I [now] do you, you should see [that] it is not our custom to sell our courtesy as a vendible commodity. Bring all your Country with you for your guard. I will not dislike [disapprove] of it as being over-jealous [suspicious]. But to content you, tomorrow I will leave my arms and trust to your promise. I call you father indeed, and as a father you shall see I will love you: but the small care you had of such a child caused my men [to] persuade me to shift [watch out] for myself.

Powhatan had clearly not been unaware of Smith's determination to load the corn and make his way back to Jamestown. Outwitted for the moment, but far from defeated, he also issued instructions. Thus, while Smith was declaiming his love, Powhatan's subjects were preparing a getaway for the "Emperor." As Smith finished and undoubtedly turned to leave, Powhatan himself rose, leaving two or three of his wives to entertain his guest. He slipped out, assembled his other wives, some of his belongings, and several of his children, and disappeared into the wintry forest. As he did so, a body of warriors silently surrounded the residence.

Someone (perhaps John Russell), seeing this, darted in to warn Smith. A glance around was enough. Smith grasped his pistol, sword, and shield and made for the door, followed by Russell. The Indians, whatever their real intentions, scattered before the bearded white fury that charged through their midst.

The panic-stricken population of Werowocomoco cowered as Smith's eight men came up from the river to join him and Russell.[8] The corn was there, but indescribable confusion was there also. Smith himself was uncertain as to what to do next. He was determined to have the corn, but how?

At that juncture, an aged member of Powhatan's council came up with dignified humility. He offered Smith a great bracelet and a chain of pearls. Then he spoke.

He said that Powhatan had fled from fear of the guns. He knew that the ice had been broken and that more of Smith's men would come ashore. He had sent his warriors only to guard the corn for Smith because it could be stolen without Smith's knowing it. He was sorry if anyone were hurt because of Smith's not understanding, and he repeated that he was Smith's friend and would remain so. Smith was to take the corn since it now could be loaded. But if Smith wanted his company, he must send his arms away with the corn.

Then came Indians bringing baskets. They offered to guard the whitemen's arms while the loading went on. But Smith saw in them only "goodly well-appointed fellows, as grim as devils," and said that his men would watch their own arms, while *they* loaded the corn. And so it was. Few words were needed, for the guns were loaded and cocked.

Smith's barges were caught in the ebb-tide, however, and they had to spend the rest of the afternoon and the evening at Werowocomoco. The Indians did what they could to entertain the Englishmen, but the atmosphere was tense. After dark they went away, evidently to procure food for their guests.

Just then, according to one account, Pocahontas slipped in. They had not seen her before that day and thought she had gone away with Powhatan. She said neither yes nor no to their questions, telling Smith only that "great cheer should be sent them" soon, but while they were eating, Powhatan's men would attempt to get their guns and kill them. If that failed, a larger force would come up to attack them. She begged all of them to leave quickly.[9]

If the story is true, Smith gave her some gifts, but she refused them, tears running down her cheeks. If she were seen with whitemen's gifts, she said, Powhatan would kill her. And with that, she vanished into the dark. John Smith and Pocahontas would not meet again for nearly eight years.[10]

CHAPTER 5

While Powhatan Watched: the Starving Time

CAPTAIN JOHN SMITH was uncertain of the real meaning of both Powhatan's flight and Pocahontas' warning. Accordingly, while he welcomed "eight or ten lusty fellows" who came bringing platters of venison and other victuals, he was on his guard — in spite of his men's demonstrations of "such mirth as though we never had suspected or intended anything." [1] But that did not prevent him and his company from feasting while they waited for the return of the high tide.

By about midnight the barge was loaded. The "Dutchmen" were left to work on Powhatan's house, along with Edward Brinton, one of the original colonists, who was detailed to shoot fowl. Powhatan was to be made as comfortable as English ingenuity could make him.

Meanwhile, the pinnace and barges were free of ice. Smith could retire. He had already decided to sail farther up the York the next day instead of returning directly to Jamestown. Since he had had little luck with Powhatan, it would be better to trade for more corn with the Pamunkeys, Opechancanough's people — he was in the neighborhood, and there was no harm in trying.

In the morning, Smith took off in the pinnace. Powhatan, seeing him sail upstream, returned to his residence. Summoning the "Dutchmen" from their work on his house, he sent them to the fort on a smartly planned mission. They were to tell Captain Peter Winne, a new and seemingly artless councillor, that all was well but that the President needed additional arms. Furthermore they, the "Dutchmen," would like "some extraordinary tools and shift of apparel."

This seemed so plausible to the commandant when they arrived at the fort that they were quickly supplied with everything they wanted. But while the Indian porters were being loaded, the "Dutchmen" wasted no time in recruiting six or seven confederates from among the colonists. Life with Powhatan, they said, was "free of the miseries that would happen [to] the colony."

In this way, by the time John Smith reached Opechancanough's village, the "Dutchmen" returned to Werowocomoco "with a great many pikes, pike-heads, pieces [guns], shot, powder, and such like." And the new confederates would soon follow "with a competency of all things they could." The "Dutchmen," be it noted, were undoubtedly woodsmen and glassblowers from the illimitable forests of central Europe — European "savages," so to say. They were more at home with Powhatan than with the citified and stuffy Englishmen, whose language was hardly more comprehensible than Powhatan's.

Meanwhile, for unexplained reasons John Smith had dawdled two or three days in sailing twenty-odd miles. By the time he reached whichever village was then entertaining Opechancanough — there were at least seven within nine miles of modern West Point — that crafty and determined werowance was certainly informed of everything that had happened, and he received the unsuspecting Englishmen with mirthful welcome and Lucullian feasting.

After a couple of days of this, Opechancanough at last agreed to begin to trade. President Smith accordingly, accompanied by such dignitaries as the brother of the Earl of Northumberland, the brother of Lord De La Warr, his loyal aide Master Russell, kinsman of the Earl of Bedford, and others to the number of fifteen, marched the four hundred yards to Opechancanough's residence and found — a deserted village, but for "a lame fellow and a boy." Every house and hut was empty.

To say that Smith was highly incensed is certainly to understate his reaction. Before he did anything rash, however, Opechancanough arrived, followed by a throng of Indians loaded with bows and arrows, but with only "pinching" commodities. And these latter he was so presumptuous as to offer at absurd barter-rates.

Smith, well grasping Opechancanough's meaning, controlled himself, and with a dignity worthy of the gravest Indian, remonstrated:

> Opechancanough, the great love you profess with your tongue seems mere deceit by your actions. Last year, you kindly freighted our ship, but now you have invited me to starve with hunger. You know my want; and I, your plenty: of which, by some means, I must have part. Remember it is fit for kings to keep their promise. Here are my commodities, whereof take your choice. The rest I will proportion fit bargains for your people.

Opechancanough most probably had thought to provoke a skirmish, in which he would have had the advantage. Why he did not remains one of those elusive qualities of his character. He seemed bested, at the moment, and peacefully sold what little he had at the price Smith was willing to pay. Then he promised to return with more Indians, "better provided."

The next day Smith, having first returned to the pinnace and barges, put them under the command of Master William Fettiplace, a loyal and capable gentleman, and returned ashore to Opechancanough's residence with the same fifteen men as before. He found four or five Indians waiting there with great baskets of corn.

Opechancanough then appeared in person, conducted Smith and a few others into the house, and harangued them on the trouble he had taken to keep his promise. But before he had finished, Russell ran in with news that six or seven hundred well-armed Indians had stolen up, occupied the fields, and surrounded the house. Opechancanough, without understanding Russell's words, confirmed their truth by showing signs of fright.

Smith rapidly reassured his companions, pointing out that the difficulty was not so much a matter of the numerical odds against them as of saving the corn as well as their lives. If they started shooting, the Indians would run away with the corn and in addition the peace-loving council in Jamestown would report to London that they had molested the Indians.

Turning then to Opechancanough, whose momentary inaction surely derived from caution recommended by Powhatan, Smith belligerently faced the werowance, a span or more taller than himself. He said that he saw through Opechancanough's plot to murder him but that it was not necessary for the Indians and the Englishmen to get involved. He suggested, instead, a man-to-man fight between the two leaders. There was an island in the river nearby where the two of them could have it out, with his own body as naked as Opechancanough's. And the winner would be lord over "all our men."

Otherwise, he added with increasing aggressiveness,

> draw all your men into the field. If you have not enough, take time to fetch more, and bring what number you will, so [long as] every one bring[s] a basket of corn. Against all which, I will stake the value in copper.

And he added a veiled threat that there would be a fight if this did not work out. Then "the conqueror [would] take all."

Opechancanough consulted with his elders, after which he evasively told Smith that he would receive a great present at the door of the house, if he would go with him. Smith instantly saw that this was a ruse to "draw him without the door, where the present was guarded with at the least two hundred men."

Shouting to four of his gentlemen to guard the house and the door from the inside, in a towering rage Smith seized the werowance by his long lock of hair, shoved his pistol against his ribs, and pushed him out before his assembled people. There, he gave the tribe the best tongue-lashing he could, considering his limited knowledge of their language.

Smith's meaning was clear. He intended to obtain corn, and corn he got. The ship being loaded, he was then ready to sail. He had "paid for" the corn with such gifts as he saw proper, and as he wrote, "Whatsoever we gave them, they seemed well contented with it." Powhatan had spoken truly when he said to Smith, "You will have whatever you demand."

On or about January 22, 1609, when John Smith concluded his trading at Opechancanough's residence, a colonist by the name of Richard Wiffin came up unexpectedly in a canoe. Seeking Smith out, he quickly told him of a great tragedy at Jamestown. Matthew Scrivener, the acting president in Smith's absence, had attempted to cross the James in a skiff during a storm, in company with Captain Waldo, Bartholomew Gosnold's brother Anthony, and eight others. A gust of wind overturned the skiff, and in the cold every one of them was drowned.

Wiffin himself had had great trouble in reaching Smith. In fact, he did not know what to do when he got to Werowocomoco and found Smith gone, but Pocahontas had protected him. When Powhatan attempted to have him killed, she hid him and then threw the would-be murderers off the scent by lying about the direction he had taken. Bribes had done the rest. Wiffin reached Smith, thirty miles away, in three days.

Smith kept the news to himself until he went on board that night. The next morning, however, instead of going back to Jamestown, he sent two gentlemen with a message to Captain Winne, presumably to tell him to take charge while he himself continued trading, by necessity so far as the colony was concerned, and now by constraint so far as the Indians were concerned. It is true that this policy kept the colony from starving. But it could not but turn the Indians' resentment gradually into hatred.

The only Indian who seems to have understood, or at least sympathized, was the little girl named Pocahontas. She was twelve by then, at most thirteen. Her handsprings in Jamestown were a thing of the past because she had to wear something approximating a dress. But Powhatan seems to have curtailed even her visits. For the time being at least, if not for all time, the whitemen were to be shunned.

Powhatan himself, after some vacillation, bundled up his lares and penates, his granary, and his treasury and moved to the relative security of Orapaks.[2] Werowocomoco was far too easy of access to the importunate whitemen in Jamestown. Orapaks was secure — lost in the forest somewhere between the source of the Chickahominy and the Youghtanund, now called the Pamunkey River — so secure, in fact, that no whiteman seems ever to have found it.

The retreat to Orapaks showed that Powhatan realized he could not defeat the whitemen. It also was a signal that he did not intend to unite with them, though he did intend to keep himself informed. Even Pocahontas knew what was going on in Jamestown. If it was difficult, improper, or even impossible under the circumstances for her to visit the fort, she did not, as later events show, lose interest in her "godson," President John Smith.

Meanwhile Indian spies were kept busy. No sooner had Smith returned to the fort than they began reporting that the whitemen were working harder than ever at the fort. Houses were built, a new roof was put on the building they called the church, and a small fort or blockhouse was erected at the Jamestown end of the narrow strip of land that connected Jamestown with the mainland.

At the mainland end of the same strip about a mile from the fort, furthermore, a group of small, new buildings housed an enormous amount of activity, with much fire and smoke issuing from the largest. This was the glass-house, where the colony was attempting to produce articles of glass, but there can be little doubt that the Indians felt it was a temple or workshop of a whiteman's demon.

For the first time, the whitemen were planting corn and beans in quantity, which seemed to mean that they planned firmly to stay — a disturbing thought to Powhatan. Yet at the same time he as well as his people found other aspects of the whitemen's culture at least estimable. Exotic forms of wildlife had been trained, for instance, and the whitemen had brought from across the water hundreds of strange birds which could not fly but which waddled and pecked in the fields and by the houses and which were delicious eating. There were also great sleek animals, much bigger than a muskrat, that lolled and grunted around the fort until most of them were ferried over to "Hog Island." Then, too, the whitemen spent many hours sawing trees lengthwise to make what they called "clapboard." There was no conceivable way that these strips of wood could be warped into making a canoe, but the whitemen dedicated hours and days to shaping them. Why?

Whatever the reason, it seemed that the English were indeed productively busy, although many of them were evidently unhappy. Friends of the "Dutchmen" who were building the house for Powhatan sent tools and swords to the Indians as well as some guns and shot. Through these men, Powhatan learned much about the discontent at the fort. Some of the whitemen even wanted to get rid of werowance Smith. Powhatan sent forty Indians to help them.

But Smith turned the tables on them, and in the resulting fray captured the werowance of Paspahegh whom Smith then offered to release if Powhatan would send back the "Dutchmen." They, he said, were the cause of all the trouble. The "Dutchmen," not surprisingly, refused to return; Powhatan, for reasons of his own, refused to force them. And finally the negligence of a guard allowed the werowance to escape.

Another skirmish followed, with little damage to the Indians except for a house that was burnt and two canoes which were taken as prizes. For some reason, Smith got very angry then and raided the Paspahegh village and surrounding fields. The Paspaheghs thereupon sent "a stout young man" to protest. He so eloquently pleaded the cause of the werowance that Smith finally gave in, and there was peace between him and the Paspaheghs as long as Smith remained in Jamestown.

Although minor troubles continued, this time with the Chickahominies, Smith smoothed things over in the end, and for several weeks the whitemen could work in peace — at least, such of them as would work. Then suddenly the orderly busyness in and around the fort stopped. The whitemen ran to and fro, somewhat like their birds that could not fly, and gathered together to chatter and wave their arms.

Soon, nearly two dozen whitemen sailed down to the mouth of the James River and camped near Kecoughtan, for no apparent reason, and without doing anything when they got there. Five or six dozen or more followed down the other side of the river, to the oyster banks, and stayed there. And another five dozen went up the James to Powhatan village to live for a while on berries and acorns.

The Indians usually did the same thing at that season of the year, until the new crops were ready, but since they had given the whitemen a great deal of corn, why did they have to search so madly for food? And why was Captain Smith protesting so violently? Or was he encouraging them?

Eventually, a number of the whitemen asked for Indian hospitality. The village chiefs would have welcomed them in any case, as their ancient customs required, but just then they had a better reason. Their guests could satisfy their curiosity. And in this way, the Indians, including Powhatan, learned that all the corn in the fort had been ruined by dampness — the whitemen being hopelessly careless and ignorant — or devoured by pestiferous little beasts, rats, which they had brought with them.

Powhatan spent most of his time at Orapaks. There he learned not only about the near-famine among the whitemen but about the incessant quarrels that plagued them. He knew that the men Smith had given him to build his house were disloyal to Smith, but he was convinced that whitemen had no loyalties at all. Still, he would continue to treat the workmen well so long as they continued to work well.

Then a small ship arrived from across the great salt water, bringing supplies and later going to fish in Chesapeake Bay. All the whitemen then returned to Jamestown, and Smith showed how happy he was to welcome the captain of the new ship, a man about the same age as Captain Smith named Samuel Argall.

A month later, several big ships arrived, though not all at the same time. And after they came, there were many, many whitemen at the fort and much, much confusion. Soon after that, three or four days before the last full moon of summer, Captain Argall sailed away again, and by the time the moon was full, Captain Smith went up to the rapids and negotiated with Parahunt to sell him Powhatan village. The whitemen needed room.

Parahunt agreed, it being hopeless to resist, and Smith gave him copper and left a white lad with him in token of good faith and to learn the Indian language. But there was still dissension and confusion at the fort and wherever the whitemen were. Those at the "Falls" misbehaved in such fashion that Parahunt said they were more dangerous than their traditional enemies, the Monacans. Smith tried to make peace for them but failed.

Returning to Jamestown, Smith was badly injured by an explosion of gunpowder. For some days both whitemen and Indians wondered if he would live. Then all the ships, save one or two, sailed away again, leaving at least five hundred men behind. As a precaution Powhatan sent spies to see what was going on.

Soon word reached him that there was a new President (or werowance) at Jamestown. Captain Smith, some said, was dead. Others said he had sailed away in one of the ships. All Powhatan knew was that he was no longer there.

Pocahontas knew it, too, and though she had seen little of Smith since winter, she had always hoped for better times and for peace. Now that he was gone, there was an emptiness in her life. But she could still hope — probably even Powhatan hoped — that Smith might return.

Meanwhile, the unremitting ferment in the fort gathered head, and the danger for Powhatan and the Indians in general redoubled. No matter what Pocahontas said then, Powhatan determined to eliminate the troublesome Englishmen. Since open war would be suicidal, he would instead have his men snipe, ambush, deceive, and assassinate. The gradual eradication of the poisonous colony was his only salvation.

November 1, 1609, came, and with it, another full moon glowed bright and clear. The colony's agony was about to begin.

Smith had indeed returned to England about four weeks before, although the Indians did not know it for certain. The faction in the fort which had tried to supplant him as president, even while Smith's term had a month to run, eventually lost out in the struggle for power. Conservative forces insisted on George Percy, brother of the Earl of Northumberland, as Smith's successor, apparently because of his social rank and his uninterrupted presence in the colony since its foundation. On Smith's departure, Percy was installed as President.

About two weeks later, the new President sent a body of men to Old Point Comfort to build a fort and try to live on fish. About the same time another original colonist, Captain John Martin, returned from Nansemond, where he had taken a body of men to live off the land, because he feared "to be surprised by the Indians," Percy wrote. Jamestown was safer.

But in leaving his post and duty, Martin deserted a group of men which he left under a young lieutenant. Mutiny broke out immediately and seventeen men ran away, never to be heard of again. Soon, in the Indian attack Martin had feared, the lieutenant and all the remaining men were murdered.

Meanwhile, with Smith gone, the outpost he had established at Powhatan village had been moved a quarter of a mile down to the shore of the James. The lad Smith had left with the Indians, Henry Spelman by name, then asked to "see our English," and to "fetch such things" as he had left behind. Aged fourteen or so, Henry had left England "in displeasure of [his] friends," to use his own words, and unquestionably had a streak of waywardness in his character.

But George Percy had already ordered the outpost evacuated. The lieutenant in charge, Francis West, hastened to obey for obvious reasons. With some of his men dead already, apparently of malnutrition, others died on the way back. Still, Henry Spelman survived to reach Jamestown; but shortly thereafter decided to go back to live with the Indians, "by reason that victuals were scarce with us."

Percy then appointed a Captain Tucker to take stock of the food supplies which, according to Percy, "at a poor allowance of half a can of meal a day amounted unto three months' provision." Knowing that he could not expect relief from England in that time, additional food had to be obtained. Percy therefore sent another early colonist, Captain Ratcliffe, to Powhatan to bargain for victuals. Under the circumstances and considering the character of Ratcliffe, he might as well have sent him to the gallows.

Taking a company of men and "Powhatan's son and daughter" with him, Ratcliffe boarded the pinnace and steered up the Pamunkey River. (The identity of the "son and daughter" is a complete mystery.)[3] When the party arrived, Powhatan, dissembling, extended the customary Algonkian hospitality to his guests and seemed willing to trade.

Discipline being even scarcer than food in the colony, the hungry men wandered off anywhere they thought they could get something to eat. Ratcliffe allowed the "son and daughter" to go ashore, although Percy sent them as hostages to ensure the party's safety, and before long the English were completely off guard. Then the "sly old king" struck. Of about thirty men, only one Jeffrey Shortridge lived to tell the tale.[4] From this account, Percy was able to write to his brother that Ratcliffe was captured alive and that Powhatan

> caused him to be bound unto a tree, naked, with a fire before [him]. And by women his flesh was scraped from his bones with mussel shells, and before his face thrown into the fire. And so for want of circumspection [he] miserably perished.

An anonymous report adds that it was at this time that Pocahontas saved Henry Spelman, who "lived many years after by her means, amongst the Potomacs."[5] Spelman's own account, however, indicates that he was not with Powhatan at the time but was sixteen miles away at Youghtanund. When Powhatan joined him there, he noticed that the "King" seemed "declined" in affection for him, and later he found a way to escape and live with the Potomacs. Since he had some trouble getting away, it may be that Pocahontas helped him then, not before. Curiously, Spelman did not mention Pocahontas at all in the crudely written "Relation of Virginea" which he penned in England in about 1613.[6]

The situation in Jamestown was getting desperate. After sending a replacement for Ratcliffe to Old Point Comfort, Percy dispatched Francis West to the Potomac tribe with about three dozen men in an attempt to trade for food. There, young West succeeded in acquiring a quantity of "maize and grain," but for no known reason he dealt truculently with the Indians, even cutting off the heads of two.

As the pinnace passed Old Point Comfort on its way back, the captain in charge shouted to West to make haste, that Jamestown was starving. West and his men then astoundingly hoisted sail "and shaped their course directly for England." Percy blamed this on the men's "persuasion" or "enforcement," adding:

> a world of miseries ensued . . . in so much that some to satisfy their hunger have robbed the store, for the which I caused them to be executed. Then, having fed upon horses and other beasts as long as they lasted, we were glad to make shift with [such] vermin as dogs, cats, rats, and mice.

In a later report of some thirty survivors of those grim times, the lack of food was blamed squarely on the Treasurer of the Virginia Company, Sir Thomas Smythe, under whose government insufficient supplies were sent from England. John Smith, on the other hand, complained to Smythe, blaming the shortages on Newport's overoptimistic reports. Those who lived through the starving time showed what *they* thought:

> so miserable was our estate that the happiest day that ever some of them hoped to see was when the Indians had killed a mare — they wishing whilst she was boiling that Sir Thomas Smythe was upon her back in the kettle.[7]

Indeed, as Percy wrote, famine loomed "ghastly and pale in

every face." Some searched the woods for serpents and snakes to eat and dug the earth for roots, only to be cut off and slain by the Indians. Nothing, he added, was spared, and men did

> things which seem incredible, as to dig up corpses out of graves and to eat them — and some have licked up the blood which hath fallen from their weak fellows. And amongst the rest, this was most lamentable, that one of our colony murdered his wife, ripped the child out of her womb and threw it into the river, and after chopped the mother in pieces and salted her for his food, the same not being discovered before he had eaten part thereof.

Before this man could be executed, President Percy had to extract a confession from him by torture — having hung, Percy explained, "by the thumbs with weights at his feet a quarter of an hour before he would confess the same." The execution, according to the thirty surviviors, was by being burned, presumably alive.

Such was the state of the colony at Jamestown as winter turned into spring. They had but one boat and one canoe left, but fishing could start. Yet when the boat accidentally broke loose and drifted downstream, no-one would take the canoe and chase it. Captain Martin, instead of going himself, commanded "some" to go fetch it, but the presence of Percy with his sword drawn was needed before anyone would bother. They would rather starve than move.

Many of the men, Percy said, ran away to the Indians to live and were never heard of again. Perhaps it was just as well. They would probably have been put to death under the laws of the times. In fact, only such things as Captain Tucker's building another boat with his own hands "did keep us from killing one of another."

About this time, Percy went down the river to Old Point Comfort to find out how the men in the little fort there had survived the winter, "as also to have been revenged of the savages at Kecoughtan [nearby] who had treacherously slain divers of our men." To his amazement, he found those at the Point in good health, with such a store of seafood that they had enough to keep their hogs alive.

Their plan, they said, was to keep "some of the better sort alive and with their two pinnaces to have returned for England."

Percy remonstrated vigorously with the captain "for not regarding our miseries and wants at all" and told him he would bring the Jamestown colonists there to recuperate, half of them at a time.[8] But by the very next tide they saw two pinnaces coming into the river.

Not knowing but what they might be Spanish, a watch was set all night, but in the morning they spotted a boat coming from one of them. It announced that "Sir Thomas Gates and Sir George Somers were come in those pinnaces, which by their great industry they had builded in the Bermudas."

The men at Old Point Comfort received this news "with no small joy." The boat then returned for Gates and Somers and "divers others," who soon came ashore. And, Percy added,

> the next tide [they all] went up to Jamestown, where they might read a lecture of misery in our people's faces, and perceive the scarcity of victuals, and understand the malice of the savages, who, knowing our weakness, had divers times assaulted us without the fort.—Of five hundred men we had only left about sixty, the rest being either starved through famine, or cut off by the savages.

The blame for their ills was thus always thrust upon the Indians, whose territory they had occupied and whose rights they refused to recognize.

So ended the winter of 1609–1610, the first after the departure of Captain John Smith. Another Captain, of almost exactly the same age, now enters the picture. He is the Samuel Argall who had paid a brief visit to Jamestown during the summer of 1609. His story must be told, and it will be seen that he was similar to Smith in many respects. Peace and trade between redman and whiteman would soon return.

CHAPTER 6

Samuel Argall of Kent: Half-idle Onlooker at Jamestown

PRACTICALLY EVERYBODY has heard of King Canute the Dane who ruled England but not the waves of the sea. It was very likely that during his reign, early in the eleventh century, the Scandinavian family of Argall arrived and established themselves in Norfolk, or thereabouts. The name, Arkil in old Danish, seems to have meant "eagle," but this is uncertain and relatively unimportant. The essential fact is that the Argalls eventually established themselves a little farther to the south, in the county of Kent, where the ownership of land was traditionally of primary importance.

What specifically happened to the Argall family for the first five hundred years of their presence in southeastern England is almost totally unrecorded. But late in the reign of King Henry VIII an obscure gentleman of London, John Argall by name, acquired a coat of arms (emblem of gentility) and died, leaving a son Thomas. Thomas had already married a Cornish heiress, Margaret Tallakarne.[1]

Between the year of Henry VIII's death, 1547, and his own death, 1563, Thomas Argall acquired the manor of East Sutton, near Maidstone, Kent, from one Richard Covert, as well as a "capital messuage," or residence, called Kenchill, between there and the port of Rye, and the manor of Walthamstow Bedyk, Essex, near London. The last mentioned was a part of the great Walthamstow estate owned by the earl of Northumbria before 1066. After a brief interlude in other hands, the great tithes of the manor reverted to the Argalls where they remained from 1600 until 1663.

Finally, Thomas Argall owned other properties in Kent, as well as in three parishes in London, and in Bedfordshire and Buckinghamshire to the northwest, and Hampshire and Dorset to the southwest. Land tenure was important to Thomas Argall.

Thomas and his wife had five sons and one daughter. The eldest son was Richard, born about 1536. Richard succeeded to his father's estate, including Walthamstow Bedyk, except for the Dorset properties which went to his younger brothers when Thomas died in 1563.

Richard Argall was not then married, to judge by his father's will, but his next younger brother was. Nevertheless, sometime before 1574 he married Mary Scott, daughter of Sir Reginald Scott, of Scot's Hall and Nettlestead, Kent.[2] Sir Reginald was an important man in the county for he was descended from a younger brother of King John Baliol of Scotland who had established himself in Kent in the thirteenth century. Furthermore, he first married Emmeline Kemp, of another ancient Kentish family, and then added up-to-date social luster by taking as his second wife, Mary Tuke, daughter of Sir Bryan Tuke, secretary to Cardinal Wolsey and later to King Henry VIII. All of these relatives and connections played an important part in the career of Samuel Argall, onlooker and then vital participant in the Jamestown colony.

Richard Argall and his wife Mary Scott Argall had fifteen sons and daughters, of whom Samuel was the eighth and last son, although he had three younger sisters. Coming so far down the line, he could look forward to little by way of inheritance. Still, the mortality rate was high in those days, and he could reasonably expect a few bequests, if he outlived any of his brothers.

Samuel Argall was baptized on December 4, 1580, and was therefore about eleven months younger than Captain John Smith. He was not yet eight years old when his father died, in the year of the Armada. Two years later, his older sister Mary married Reginald Kemp, a nephew of the Emmeline Kemp mentioned before. About the same time, or shortly thereafter, their mother, Mary Scott Argall, chose for her second husband one Lawrence Washington, of Maidstone, a collateral ancestor of President George Washington.

Samuel Argall probably attended the grammar school at Maidstone, half a dozen miles from East Sutton, but he may also have been tutored at home. Whatever his educational background, however, it is clear that his surroundings counted more. With the exception of some "kinsmen" who were in London more often than on their estates in Kent, all of Samuel's friends and relatives were landowners who were economically tied to the soil in one way or another.

It is not surprising, then, that the surviving letters and reports from Samuel's goose-quill point to a practical mind — tidy is perhaps a better word — and this is borne out by his general behavior. He was, in addition, observant by nature, and, despite the career he seems to have stumbled into, he was far less aggressive than many of his contemporaries.

Under the protective and animating pennants of the Argalls, Scotts, Kemps, and other Kentish families firmly planted in centuries-old land tenure and service to the kingdom, Samuel grew up with little personal wealth, but with vast opportunity. His older brothers inherited and acquired property, and his sisters married well. To make a name for himself, however, and to vie with an unrememberable horde of relatives, Samuel had to strike out on his own.

By his father's will, Samuel had an annuity of thirty pounds a year (that is, just about enough to live on modestly) plus "certain property rights" after he was eighteen.[3] He does not seem to have attended either Oxford, where his uncle John had received his M.A., or Cambridge. Instead of attending a university, young men of his type and family often sought a career in the Dutch wars of independence from Spain.

That this is precisely what Samuel did is hinted at in a report on the fortifications at Berg, now Rheinberg, southeast of Cleves. Sir William Browne, Lieutenant Governor of Flushing, sent this report to the Governor with a comment that it was written by "Lieutenant Argull." The letter was dated in mid-June, 1601. Two and a half years later, the same Lieutenant Argull asked Browne to recommend him for "preferment." [4]

It was just about this time, as Samuel Argall later testified before the court of the Virginia Company, that he had met one John Bargrave, Esq., who by his own testimony served in the wars in the Netherlands.[5] John Bargrave was two years older than Argall and came from the village of Patrixbourne, some thirty miles east of Argall's home at East Sutton. Furthermore, Bargrave had a brother who later became owner or part-owner of a ship.

This has direct bearing on Samuel Argall because his later activities demand that he have had some experience both as a soldier and a sailor. In fact, he became an expert navigator, and his own words imply that Bargrave was not without influence in his career. John Smith, as it happens, was in the Netherlands learning to be a soldier at about the same time as Argall seems to have been there, but he went to the trouble of writing something about it. Samuel Argall unfortunately did not.

For the next five years, if "Argull" was Argall, there is no word of what he was doing. Then about 1608, by his own statement again, he got in touch with his cousin-by-marriage, Sir Thomas Smythe. Sir Thomas had been acting as treasurer of the Virginia Company since 1606 or 1607, and was Governor of the East India

Company and a powerful influence in the Levant Company as well. He was a logical person for an ambitious young man almost twenty-eight to turn to.

It can in any case be reasonably assumed that, regardless of the conjectural service in the Netherlands, Argall spent some time on a ship in his youth. This may have been with Bargrave or his brother. It may even have been in the service of the East India or Levant Company, or the Muscovy Company, wherein Sir Thomas Smythe's voice was far from still or small. Above all, it may have kept him out of England during most of those five years.

If so, Argall would have heard little about the project for establishing a colony in Virginia until he got back. (That had happened to John Smith four years before, when the project was still unborn.) But the first ships had sailed, as we know, late in 1606, and the first reports from the colony had arrived in England as July turned to August in 1607. And things were going well or ill according to whom you listened to.

Then, in April, 1608, one of the patentees for the colony, Sir Thomas Gates, was released temporarily from service in the Netherlands, with an eye to sending him to Virginia. Before the end of the year a plan was afoot to reorganize the administration of the controversial colony, and a new charter was drawn up. With the King's consent, direct control of the company was removed from the Crown's responsibility to be placed in private hands, under license from the Crown.[6]

Sir Thomas Smythe was officially named head of the reorganized company with the title of Treasurer. Plans were made for a large expedition to be sent to Virginia under Sir Thomas West, Lord De La Warr. A last-minute change "for personal reasons" put Gates in charge as De La Warr's deputy, and preparations went on "apace," which means none too fast — at the pace of a man walking.

To speed things up a little for the future, it was decided that immediate steps should be taken to shorten the duration of the transatlantic voyage, and at the same time explore the possibilities of avoiding conflict with Spain, either verbal or military, by keeping as far as convenient from the Canary Islands and the West Indies. Chosen to make just such a trial voyage was none other than Sir Thomas Smythe's cousin, Samuel Argall, now officially entitled "Captain."

It is evident that Argall would not have been picked to seek out a new, and faster, route to Virginia if he had not had experience as a navigator. His commission, as later printed, was, after avoiding all danger of encroaching on Spanish territory,

> to attempt a direct and clear passage, by leaving the Canaries to the east, and from thence to run in a straight western course, or some point [of the compass] near thereunto.

While this indicated that Argall was considered an intelligent navigator, there was a further instruction

> to make an experience [observation] of the winds and currents which have affrighted all undertakers [explorers] by the north [route].[7]

In short, the Virginia Council employed Argall to test a new route scientifically, politically, and economically, as a result of which

> there would grow to us [colony-minded Englishmen] much security, and ease, and all occasion of offence [to Spain] removed, and we [of the Company] should husband and save a moiety of the charge in victual and freight [hire of the ship] which was expended and lost in the southern passage [previously followed].

Nevertheless, when it came to the implementation of this commission, it was not the council which supplied the ship to Argall, but an individual: an obscure merchant named John Cornelius, who was an associate of Sir Thomas Smythe in at least the East India and Virginia Companies. By this arrangement, Argall was to "truck with the colony and fish for sturgeon (including caviar)," apparently for Master Cornelius's benefit.[8]

There would be nothing remarkable about this, although it was the first time a private ship would arrive at Jamestown, if it were not for Smith's comment upon Argall's arrival:

> God having seen our misery sufficient, sent in Captain Argall to fish for sturgeon with a ship well furnished with wine and biscuit, which, though it was not sent us, such were our occasions [needs] we took it at a price.[9]

If the "wine and biscuit" were not for the colony, were they for the Indians? Or did Cornelius merely intend to make a profit at the expense of the colonists?

However that was, Argall arrived in Jamestown on July 13, 1609, after a voyage of nine weeks and six days. He had been becalmed fourteen days but had found no contrary currents or other impediments on the new route. The voyage could be made in seven weeks, he claimed, thereby abundantly fulfilling the Company's hopes.

In the colony, Argall was received with open arms and bursting hearts, for he brought word that there was a new charter, which promised more support than the colonists had ever had, and that a great supply fleet was being organized under Lord De La Warr. Only Captain John Smith was unconvinced. London had already shown great capacity for doing the wrong thing, especially so far as the Indians were concerned.

It seems that Argall, in addition to fishing in Chesapeake Bay, was kept busy for some time in and around Jamestown.[10] Then in mid-August, four weeks after his arrival, the first ships of the great supply fleet arrived, and he was detained by the quarreling that broke out between Smith and his followers, on the one side, and on the other by the group of returning colonists under Smith's arch-foe, Captain Gabriel Archer. At last, on August 31, Archer signed a letter to an unknown addressee (undoubtedly some member of the London Council) summarizing the misfortunes of the voyage and of the colony,[11] and Argall got away. The story of what followed has been told.

How long it took Argall to return from Jamestown to London is not known. All that is certain is that he had arrived in England by November 9 and reported to the Virginia Council that the route he followed was practicable and fast, that fishing would be profitable, and that the colony was in "necessity and distress . . . for want of victual." It is only proper to add that Sir Thomas Smythe and the Council blamed the "want of victual," not on their own bad planning, but squarely on "the misgovernment of the [local] Commanders."[12]

Argall's success, including his obvious abstention from taking sides in the passionate quarreling in Jamestown, won him the hearty support and approval of the London Council. Lord De La Warr, the Lord Governor and Captain General, who should have set sail in May, was now scheduled to depart "by the last of January [1610]."[13]

Within three weeks of Argall's semi-triumphal return, however, and before November 30, the horrifying news reached London of the loss of the flagship of the great fleet, with all the chief officers and their commissions on board.[14] The Virginia Council hastily published a twenty-six-page brochure, *A true and sincere declaration of the purpose of the plantation begun in Virginia,* which was entered for publication on December 14. (If other matters had been attended to with equal speed, the colony might have prospered more conspicuously.) It explained all, hoped for the best, and asked for more colonists: ministers, surgeons, and druggists, and artisans of all sorts, from armorers and bakers to turners and vine-dressers.

The disaster, even though everyone hoped that the flagship would eventually turn up, delayed the departure of Lord De La Warr. Instead of a single ship to carry him, a fleet of three was assembled, fitted out with supplies, and filled with a hundred and fifty new colonists to replace a like number presumably lost in the flagship. Samuel Argall was put in command of Lord De La Warr's ship, the *De La Warr.* And after the inevitable minor delays of the times, the little fleet sailed from Cowes, Isle of Wight, on April 1, 1610. Despite contrary winds, they sighted the coast of Virginia nine weeks and two days later.

Argall reached the James River with the Governor General just in time to prevent the settlement from being abandoned.[15] Had he been delayed a day or two longer, it is not inconceivable that Jamestown would have followed Roanoke into oblivion and that America, north of Florida, would have been left to the slowly emerging Indian nations who had so successfully fought off Spanish forays. As it turned out, Powhatan and Pocahontas, along with Massasoit and King Philip, took their places among the millions who have been overwhelmed by technological, but not necessarily human, superiority. The tide turned against the Indians.

On June 10, 1610, Lord De La Warr had his standard-bearer Anthony Scott publicly read his commission — Anthony was surely a cousin of Samuel Argall — and in due course himself appointed his Council. Beginning with Sir Thomas Gates, named Lieutenant General, Sir George Somers, named Admiral, and Christopher Newport, now Vice Admiral, De La Warr appointed the following to significant posts: William Strachey, Recorder (and future author of a *Historie of Travell into Virginia Britan-*

nia); George Percy, Captain of James Fort (he was not only brother of the Earl of Northumberland but brother-in-law of Lord De La Warr's first cousin); Sir Ferdinand Wainman, Master of the Ordnance (a first cousin); Edward Brewster, Captain of De La Warr's own company (son of one of the original colonists); and, among others, two captains of companies, Samuel Argall and George Yeardley.[16]

With all this organization — a peer in command, three knights on the Council, and a glittering array of captains — Virginia became a very different place from the starving colony Argall had found under Captain John Smith in July, 1609; very different, indeed, from the decimated relic of only three weeks before.

The day after this imposing proceeding, which must have been observed by bewildered Indian eyes, Admiral Sir George Somers proposed to the colonial Council that he should return to Bermuda to "fetch six months' provision of flesh and fish, and some live hogs to store our colony again."

The Lord Governor gave him a commission to that end on June 15. Samuel Argall was again called upon and on Tuesday, June 19, the Admiral and the Captain sailed their respective ships from Jamestown with the outgoing tide. On Friday they left Cape Henry astern. With good luck, they might return by the end of August.

Meanwhile, the previous Sunday, De La Warr had sent ship's master Robert Tindall, on leave from being gunner to Prince Henry Frederick of Great Britain, to search for fish in lower Chesapeake Bay. Gates had sent his longboat fishing for seven days on end, three or four weeks before, without success. Tindall had no better luck in fourteen days. Yet Argall had fished successfully in those same waters almost exactly a year before. William Strachey wrote laconically of these efforts: "Let the blame of this lie where it is, both upon our nets, and the unskilfulness of our men to lay them."

And the Indians?

After the near death of the colony during the "starving time," 1609–1610, spies had seen the arrival of Gates, Somers, and Newport, with a hundred and fifty colonists, just when it seemed to them that the plague of whitemen was abating. Powhatan quickly issued a command to all his subjects not to trade with them, "but to endanger and assault any boat upon the river, or straggler out of the fort by land." [17]

The orders were obeyed, with flexibility. After killing two careless colonists almost before they had landed, various Indians came visiting the fort to trade, but in trading to spy and to cheat. They spied on the colonists, and cheated the mariners, who sneaked out at night to barter for skins of otters, beavers, bears, raccoons, or anything else that could be sold in London. Powhatan's policy worked well. And there can be little doubt that he rejoiced when he saw Gates pack up the entire colony and sail away on June 7.

But before Gates got out of the river, De La Warr arrived, and all of them went back up the river to reestablish the fort. Still, the colony did not thrive. The Indians watched hopefully.

Nearly a month later Gates discovered on a trip to Old Point Comfort that the longboat belonging to the fort there had been blown across the mouth of the James, where it was aground below Warraskoyack, and he sent a man over to recover it. Indians from nearby, seeing him reach shore, slipped up, seized him, led him into the woods, and killed him.

Gates had thought of, and tried, making peace with the unrepentant Indians, but this was too much. Three days after the episode of the longboat, on July 10, he went in force to Kecoughtan, four miles from the English fort at the point, attacked, and took it without loss. The werowance, Powhatan's son Pochins, was not there, but all the inhabitants fled, leaving behind "a few baskets of old wheat [corn], and some other[s] of peas and beans, a little tobacco, and some few women's girdles of silk, of the grass-silk . . ."

With hostility again overt, De La Warr felt obliged to send an embassy to Powhatan with an ultimatum. Powhatan was to see that all weapons, tools, and the like which had been stolen before De La Warr's arrival were returned, and to give "an universal order" to his subjects to refrain from hostile acts, otherwise "the Lord Governor and Captain General" would be "compelled . . . to offend him." In other words, he would have to go to war.

In answer, Powhatan sent word "that either we should depart his country, or confine ourselves to Jamestown only . . . or otherwise he would give a command to his people to kill us, and do unto us all that mischief which they at their pleasure could." In conclusion, he demanded that De La Warr send him "a coach and three horses, for he had understood by the Indians which were in England how such was the state of the great werowances and lords in England, to ride and visit other great men."

Lord De La Warr, whose grandmother was a cousin of that High and Mighty Princess, Queen Elizabeth, was incensed over this impertinence. But he was even more disturbed by the continual Indian harassment of the fort, the glass-house, and the colonists in person. Any who went out gathering strawberries and such natural delicacies were likely to be ambushed and killed.

At last two Paspaheghans were captured, one of whom had done more mischief than any other one Indian. This one the Lord Governor commanded should have his right hand struck off with a sword, and at the same time he sent to Powhatan a stern message repeating his demands. In fact, he warned the Indian ruler that unless he obeyed the English Lord Governor, he would find all his fields burned and ravaged.

Soon after, as Gates and Newport were preparing to return to England with letters and reports, as well as such freight of local natural commodities as were by then available, a body of English soldier-laborers captured the werowance of Warraskoyack. The werowance, presumably under duress, allowed his son to be sent to England.[18]

That same day, July 15, 1610, General Gates and Vice Admiral Newport, in all the panoply of important pretension, boarded their respective ships and entrusted themselves to the mercies of wind and sea.

But the unregenerate heathens who owned the place still persisted in their efforts to reject the intruders. The Lord Governor, by then virtually confined to his ship and his bed by physical and mental distempers, decided to cast off the pretence of kindness and understanding conducive to converting the Indians to Christianity. He summoned George Percy, Esq., and commanded him to take revenge — not on Powhatan, but on the Paspaheghs and Chickahominies, who were vulnerable because they were neighbors.

Percy chose for a guide an Indian named Kemps, who had long since given full notice of his unreliability and inclination toward treachery to Indian and whiteman alike. Shipping Kemps and his men to a landing-place three miles from the Paspahegh village, Percy tied Kemps to his provost-marshal, lined up his seventy men in battle array "placing a captain or lieutenant at every file," and set out to attack a village which numbered forty naked Indian warriors at most.

Kemps, out of racial loyalty, first tried to lead the company astray, but Percy noticed this and beat the right path into his head with a cudgel. When they were near the village, Percy gave orders to surround the place and let none escape, but to make no noise until he arrived "with the colors" — a hint of Percy's military past involving the Netherlands and possibly Ireland. Upon that event, Captain William West, a relative of the Lord Governor, was to fire a pistol.

All went as prearranged. The English attacked, killed fifteen or sixteen Indians, and put the rest to flight. Then, as Percy later wrote to his brother the Earl,

> I caused my drum to beat, and drew all my soldiers to the colors, my lieutenant bringing with him the Queen and her children and one Indian prisoners, for the which I taxed [reproved] him because he had spared them.
>
> His answer was that, Having them now in my custody, I might do with them as I pleased. Upon the same, I caused the Indian's head to be cut off.

Percy next ordered the men to burn the village and cut down the corn — an incredible if all too characteristic move, when the English were so short of food! Then he marched the Queen and her, as yet, spared children to his boat. No sooner were they aboard, however, than the soldiers complained that they should have been killed. So, Percy went on to write,

> a council being called, it was agreed upon to put the children to death, the which was effected by throwing them overboard and shooting out their brains in the water. Yet for all this cruelty, the soldiers were not well pleased. And I had much to do to save the Queen's life for that time.

Two miles farther down the river, Percy landed his deputy, Captain Davis, for the purpose of cutting down more corn, and burning more houses, "temples and idols." This was quickly accomplished, and Percy was pompously rowed downstream to the ship where Lord De La Warr was resting.

Percy himself was so tired, with cause, that he sent Davis to report to His Lordship. That nobleman sent back word that he was "discontent" because the Queen was spared, and thought it was best to burn her alive. Percy replied that he had seen enough bloodshed for one day; he did "not hold it fitting" to burn her, but "either by shot or sword to give her a quicker dispatch."

Captain Davis thereupon took the Queen ashore with two soldiers and put her to the sword in the forest.

In Werowocomoco Powhatan may well have murmured to his favorite daughter, "Captain Smith, that bold trader but our friend, has indeed gone."

And Pocahontas' answer may have been, "They tell me he is dead."

CHAPTER 7

Jamestown Challenges the Indians

IN THE INTERIM, as we know, Sir George Somers and Captain Argall had set sail for Bermuda in two pinnaces.

The tiny archipelago only a year before had been described as:

> the dangerous and dreaded Island, or rather Islands, of the Bermudas . . . [which] be so terrible to all that ever touched on them, and such tempests, thunders, and other fearful objects are seen and heard about them, that they be called commonly "The Devil's Islands," and are feared and avoided of all sea travellers alive, above any other place in the world.[1]

Now, the Virginians called them the "fortunate" islands, and they were sought after "for the better relief, and good of the colony."

The weather was bad, and the two doughty mariners did not get out of Chesapeake Bay until June 23. Three weeks later, they were still tacking this way and that in the general latitude of Bermuda without sighting it. Puzzled, Argall hailed Somers, who had been to Bermuda and presumably knew where it was. Somers, running out of water as well as nautical "guidelines," proposed that they try for Cape Cod, seven hundred odd miles to the north-northwest.

On July 25 the pinnaces were miraculously still together, and soundings indicated that land must be near. Argall's log argued that they had sailed two hundred and eighteen leagues from where they had decided to look for Cape Cod — that is, six hundred and fifty-four statute miles. According to their instruments they were at about 42° north latitude, which, judging by their charts, meant that they were to the east of Cape Cod. Finding the fishing good, both captains furled sails to stock up with food. Then, before noon, July 26, Somers sent word to Argall "that he would set sail, and stand in for the river of Sagadahoc [Kennebec, Maine]; whose directions I [Argall] followed." [2]

That was the last Captain Argall saw of Admiral Somers. Weather of all kinds, mostly foggy, separated the ships. Somers eventually found Bermuda, where he died in November from "a surfeit in eating of a pig." [3] Argall wore and tacked until he reached "a small rocky island" lying in 44° north latitude. Still unidentifiable, this island was almost certainly one of the many off Penobscot Bay, somewhat to the east of Sagadahoc.

After fishing and waiting for Somers for some time, Argall at last decided, on August 12, to turn back to Jamestown. He passed near Cape Cod, without touching land, and continued to the south with many deviations of course, until he sighted and "came to an anchor in nine fathoms in a very great Bay," where he found "great store of people which were very kind." The date was August 27, 1610. Henry Hudson had been there just a year before, but as yet the bay had no name.

Samuel Argall remedied the oversight by naming his "discovery" after Lord De La Warr. And that same night when a propitious wind came up, which Argall decided to take advantage of, he shaped his course for Cape Charles and Chesapeake Bay. Contrary winds and unexplored shoals off the coast of what is now called Maryland delayed him a good deal. But at last, just after sunset on

August 31, he "came to an anchor under Cape Charles . . . and rode there all night."

Back at Jamestown a day or two later, Argall found that Sir Ferdinando Wainman was dead, and learned of Percy's raid on the Paspaheghs. Then, on the heels of his arrival, Lord De La Warr ordered another punitive expedition against the unfortunate Indians.

As has been mentioned, the aged werowance of Warraskoyack, Tackonekintaco, had been captured by Captain Newport some time before, along with his son. He had been released only after promising to supply provisions in August, or thereabouts. Leaving his nephew as further guaranty of performance, Tackonekintaco returned to his village.

The nephew, then, although held in fetters on board the ship *De La Warr,* found a chance to elude his guard and jump overboard. He was never seen again. Yet the Indians, according to Strachey,

> would oftentimes afterwards mock us, and call to us for him, and at length make a great laughter, and tell us he was come home . . .[4]

However it was, Tackonekintaco thereupon refused to live up to his agreement with the Lord Governor, and the latter sent his own company under Captain Edward Brewster to Warraskoyack. (Edward was probably the son of the William Brewster who had been killed by Indians three years before.) Samuel Argall went along with "some seamen." They were sent to show that his lordship was not to be trifled with.

But it was not all that easy to victimize the Indians. They had seen the Lord Governor's hand at work on the Paspaheghs. So, when the English war-barges started across the twenty miles of water to their village, they took to their heels. The only revenge available to Argall was to burn two Warraskoyack villages, along with their mats, wooden dishes, pots, and what not, and to cut down and waste their corn. This, of course, deprived the colony of the food it so desperately needed. But Argall, though not malicious, was a man who obeyed orders, especially from the King's own representative, the nobleman who, as it happened, had married Argall's brother-in-law's niece.[5]

The Indians, looking at all these matters in another light, continued what the whitemen called their "malice," their active ill-will. But somehow one of them innocently dared enter the fort, where once they had been more than welcome, bearing corn for trade. He was apprehended, probably for a spy. And the Lord Governor, who needed the corn he brought, caused him "to have his hand cut off, and so sent him unto his fellows to give them warning." [6] Warning, it would seem, that the whitemen intended to exterminate them — and starve.

Only by dint of revenge and arson, it appeared, the colony persisted in the face of Indian opposition. Lord De La Warr commanded the destruction of the Indians' corn to weaken them and keep them away, but it was the English who sickened for lack of what they had destroyed. In the end, the Lord Governor himself suffered. In his own words:

> the flux surprised me, . . . then the cramp assaulted my weak body; and afterwards the gout . . . that, making my body through weakness unable to stir . . . drew upon me the disease called the scurvy . . . till I was upon the point to leave the world.[7]

The long period of jockeying for position had obviously come to a halt, if not to an end. Indian resistance was turning into open hostility, to match white aggressiveness. Surely keenly aware by that time of the genocidal intentions of the white rulers, the Indians retreated into the sanctuary of the forest, husbanded their resources in men and food, and bided the outcome of the English frenzy in silence. Convinced that the Englishmen would destroy themselves by famine, they chose a path they thought would lead to an eventual victory at arms over a debilitated opponent.

True, the doors of the future loomed obscurely before them. In the obscurity they could not read the warning Fate had placed there: "Through me you march toward everlasting grief. Before you enter, leave all hope behind." Artlessly, innocently, Pocahontas' people strode into the nighttime of their race.

Not long after the episode of the Indian losing his hand for entering the fort with corn, there was a conspiracy among some of the Englishmen, by no means for the first time, to run away with a seaworthy bark. Caught, the man who was adjudged ringleader was sentenced to death by hanging. The rope broke, and the Lord Governor issued a reprieve. It was a sign from Above, he said. If it was, the Lord Governor had misunderstood it. The victim died of his injuries anyway.[8]

Two days later, the Governor sent a party up the James to search for the iron mines whose existence had been reported by Captain Newport more than a year before. He was confident that he had the Indians under control. At an Appamatuck village, the party was called ashore by honey-tongued Indians who offered food and entertainment. Two days later, the entire English party was dead, except for Thomas Dowse, a laborer. Dowse escaped by using the boat's rudder as a shield.

Thereupon, apparently out of sheer defiance, Lord De La Warr decided to go up to the "Falls" himself. Evidently on the site of Powhatan village, abandoned since John Smith had bought it from Parahunt, De La Warr established a fort "for their defence and shelter" during the winter. He envisioned extensive exploration for various coveted minerals to be undertaken the following spring. His kinsman George Percy was left at Jamestown with full powers to act in his lordship's absence.

The werowance of Paspahegh promptly decided to investigate. He had far from forgotten the brutal murder of Paspahegh women and children a month or two before. Accompanied by a small force, he got as far as the blockhouse, less than half a mile from the fort.

Hearing of this, Percy issued orders to try to capture Wowinchopunk alive. John Waller, one of the original colonists, boldly caught hold of him, but more Indians appeared out of nowhere, "sending their arrows freely amongst our men." At that, the werowance, struggling to escape, was thrust through with a sword but was still alive when his men got the better of the colonists and carried him off to die. Such was the sordid end of "one of the mightiest and strongest savages that Powhatan had under him." [9]

Peaceful trade, the while, had been rendered impossible in the environs of Jamestown by the intransigence of both sides. The colony still lacked food, and about Christmastime, 1610, Samuel Argall — perhaps divining where the real fault lay — got permission to try trafficking with the Indians along the shores of the Potomac. No purposeful reconnoitering had been carried out there since John Smith's day.

The results of this sensible suggestion were reported by Lord De La Warr in his *Short Relation . . . to the . . . Counsell of Virginia,* which was published the following year in London:

> The last discovery, during my continual sickness, was by Captain Argall, who hath found a trade with Potomac (a king as great as Powhatan, who still remains our enemy, though not able to do us hurt).[10]

How great a werowance the Potomac chief was is somewhat uncertain. He was evidently on good terms with Powhatan, perhaps through acting as an intermediary in trade with Indians farther to the north and west or perhaps through payment of tribute. His brother Iapassus (which could mean "little Buffalo") was in any case friendly with Powhatan while willing also to become friendly with the whitemen. It was Iapassus who received Captain Argall. With him was Henry Spelman, the boy who had been left with Powhatan's son by Captain John Smith in 1609.

Henry had gone to live with Powhatan himself when Percy took over in Jamestown. Later Powhatan had sent him to live at Youghtanund. While he was there, probably in the spring of 1610, the werowance of Potomac visited Powhatan in that village and made much of both Henry and another white boy, Thomas Savage. In the end, after various adventures and misadventures, Henry made his way alone to the werowance of Potomac, and thus he lived in a village a few miles below modern Quantico until Argall arrived.

Argall came seeking trade. Henry Spelman by then spoke Powhatan's language reasonably fluently. The outcome of this combination was that Spelman regained his freedom in short order (Argall's stock of copper had something to do with that), and Argall contrived to purchase some four hundred bushels of corn, beans, and peas "besides many kinds of furs" — all for the value of forty shillings, or a little more. Four hundred bushels of wheat alone could have cost thirty times that amount in England. All in all, it was a happy encounter for Iapassus, Spelman, and Argall.[11] Neither the first mentioned nor the last could have foreseen, however, what would happen on the occasion of their next encounter. They merely parted most amicably. "The devil with Powhatan," they seem to have said among one another.

In the interim, the Lord Governor was getting sicker and sicker, day by day. At last, he held a long consultation at Powhatan village, otherwise known as La Warr's Fort, with friends and advisers, and "resolved by general consent and persuasion" to take ship for the West Indies, where the island of Nevis boasted of medicinal hot-springs. He thereupon returned to Jamestown to order his affairs.

Then, on March 28, 1611, he turned the reins of government over to George Percy, commended himself to God and Captain Argall's seamanship, and sailed away.[12] Not yet thirty-four, Thomas West, Baron De La Warr, was permanently damaged in health.

Hardly had he left, with George Percy in radiant uniform at shipside, than Indian spies near the blockhouse spotted the lieutenant-in-charge going out of the fort, accompanied only by a small number of men — as Percy wrote, "showing more valor than will, more fury than judgment." The spies gave a noiseless alarm, and a shower of arrows ended the careers of every one of the English party.

Then, deliberately, the Indians "did so acclaim, shout and halloo in triumph" that fifty colonists ran out of the fort, armed to the teeth. The Indians only fled. But their intent was clear. Crying, "Paspahegh, Paspahegh!" they showed whose death was avenged. George Percy sent a messenger posthaste to catch Lord De La Warr and inform him of the affray, but he was gone. Not long after, Captain Robert Adams arrived from England with a fresh supply of men and victuals, and the information that the Marshal-elect of Virginia, Sir Thomas Dale, was on his way to take charge of the colony's defence. Sir Thomas would act also in the capacity of Deputy Governor when occasion demanded.[13]

The military discipline which John Smith had labored to inculcate on the colony from within was soon imposed from without. With it came an impenitent hostility to the Indians, however, which Smith had considered unwise and disadvantageous. Indeed, with Smith gone, no Englishman seemed to give thought to what today is called "peaceful coexistence." The voices of caution, reason, and justice had fled.

Sir Thomas Dale roared into the colony on May 12 like an avenging angel, smiting redman and whiteman alike. After landing with Captain Newport at Old Point Comfort, he spent two days surveying conditions. Apparently before he had even looked into the facts, he flew into a rage. Grabbing Newport by the beard, he threatened to hang him on the charges of misleading the Council in London by false reports of nonexistent prosperity in the colony, even as John Smith had accused Newport of doing.[14]

"Was it meant," Dale demanded, "that the people here in Virginia should feed upon trees?" And he set to work to make Old Point Comfort and its fort, or forts, functional.

A week later, he bore down on Jamestown. After attending a church service (it was a Sunday), he had the Secretary of the Council, William Strachey, read his commission as Deputy Governor as well as Marshal, and George Percy promptly resigned his temporary appointment,[15] only to be immediately named Captain of the Fort.

On May 22, Dale issued a Draconian legal code, of which he was at most co-author but with which he was evidently in full sympathy. Almost anything from murder to blasphemy to stealing an ear of corn was punishable by death. Three days after thus establishing law and order, he sent Captain Adams back to England with reports and letters, while he began the search for a better site than Jamestown for the colony's chief seat.[16]

Sir Thomas Dale had brought with him three hundred new colonists, in addition to, as Percy put it, "great store of armor, munition, victuals, and other provision." He saw to it straight away that these people went to work. Then, with equal promptness, he made manifest his attitude toward the Indians. Without apparent provocation, he himself led a hundred well-armed whitemen against the Nansemonds. In this raid he risked his own life, an arrow just missing his eye, and both Francis West and John Martin were wounded. But Dale had brought with him long-unused armor from the Tower of London which offered protection against bows and arrows — almost forgotten weapons in "civilized warfare."

Many Indians were killed and badly hurt. The rest "much wondered" at the whitemen's impenetrable mail, a novelty they had not seen before; no longer did the whitemen fall when an arrow struck them. When the Indians saw this, as Percy wrote,

> they did fall into their exorcisms, conjurations and charms, throwing fire up into the skies, running up and down with rattles, and making many diabolical gestures with many negromantic spells and incantations, imagining thereby to cause rain to fall from the clouds, to extinguish and put out our men's matches [for the matchlock muskets] and to wet and spoil their powder.

All to no avail. The Englishmen cut down their corn, burned their houses, and sailed away with many prisoners.

Dale's razzia was followed, for unexplained reasons, by more "invasions and excursions upon the savages," the most notable of which occurred at the time Dale planned an expedition to the "Falls" at Richmond, late in June or early in July.[17]

A week before the exploring party's start, Powhatan sent messengers to Jamestown forbidding any such trespass and demanding the return of two Indian prisoners, apparently recently taken. Otherwise, he intimated that he would cripple the men with "drink" (poison must have been meant) and then kill them. He even gave them six or seven days warning.

Dale took the warning as a huge joke and sent back a comparable threat of punishment. Then, when it suited his convenience without returning any prisoners he set out for the "Falls," well armed. What happened during the expedition is best described by the young minister and voluntary missionary in Virginia, the Rev. Alexander Whitaker, son of the famous Puritan who had been a canon of Canterbury.

> Trenches had been dug around the camp, and one night when the men were at prayers around a fire, a strange noise was heard coming out of the corn . . . like an Indian *"hup hup"* with an *"Oho Oho."*

> Some say that they saw one like an Indian leap over the fire and run into the corn with the same noise. At the which our men were confusedly amazed. They could speak nothing but "*Oho Oho.*"

Then they seized the barrel instead of the butt of their arms to shoot at the invisible enemy.

The confusion lasted a quarter of an hour but no harm was done except for two or three that were knocked down when they rushed out. It was as if they had awaked from a dream. Finding no enemy, they retired again for the night.

Whitaker also added to the story of the raid on the Nansemond Indians, although it is not clear that he was present, saying that it was Powhatan's brother-in-law Machumps who predicted rain and that the conjurations did produce "exceeding thunder and lightning and much rain within five miles," but not close enough to wet their powder. Furthermore, he wrote that some of the chiefs whom they had captured

> and bound with strong irons and kept with great watch have strayed from us without our knowledge. All which things make me think that there be great witches amongst them, and they very faithful with the devil.

Alexander Whitaker was an intelligent, well-educated man, possessed of few prejudices beyond those inspired by his strict Calvinism. If such a man was ready to fall prey to the fear caused by the impenetrable forest and the silent Indian, it is small wonder that the less privileged elements often acted completely irrationally.

Shortly after these experiences, apparently about the middle of June, a Spanish caravel from Cuba entered Chesapeake Bay. It had come to spy out the English settlement and was under the command of Alcalde Don Diego de Molina. Going ashore with his ensign and his pilot, an Englishman, Don Diego was surprised by a party from the fort at Old Point Comfort.

The captain of the fort sent a pilot to the caravel to bring it in, but to his amazement he soon saw the sails hoisted and the ship sail away with the pilot. The captured Spaniards and their renegade English pilot were then taken to Jamestown as prisoners. An exchange of presumptuousnesses ensued between Don Diego and Sir Thomas Dale, during which the Spaniards claimed that the ship had sailed and entered the bay in good faith. The English were certain, however, that the motives of the voyage were questionable.

In any event, Don Diego, his ensign, and the renegade pilot remained in Jamestown for five years, until 1616 when Don Diego returned to Europe under circumstances as extraordinary as they were unforeseen. Meanwhile, he entertained himself with unremitting espionage.[18]

The arrival of such distinguished guests as the Spanish prisoners, coupled with a sense for the need of social as well as political stability under a knight with the rank of marshal, served to remind George Percy, Captain of James Fort, of his own social prestige. Learning that a ship would soon carry a report from Marshal Dale to the treasurer and council in London, Percy seized a quill and in his careful hand wrote a letter to his "singular good Lord and Brother, The Earl of Northumberland."

He regretted that his existence in Jamestown had cost his brother so much already (over £432 the year before, or more than half his mother's yearly allowance!) but he certainly had not wasted any money. Now, however, he had to request further financial assistance, "it standing upon [his] reputation (being Governor of James Town) to keep a continual and daily table for Gentlemen of fashion about [him]." To this letter he attached bills which, according to surviving records, amounted to £74 3*s.* 8*d.* — almost equal to the annual stipend of the Earl's distinguished mathematician, Thomas Hariot.[19]

Not content with that, however, it appears that Captain Percy ordered sent to him from London a number of articles of clothing, including £6 18*s.* worth of gold lace and a Dutch beaver hat that cost £2 16*s.*, for a total of £14 3*s.* 6*d.*. This sartorial splendor was to be worn in a starving village clinging to the edge of a primeval forest. In modern terms, it would be comparable to sending over a thousand dollars worth of dress suits, top hats, and patent leather pumps to the chief archeologist in a camp in the Brazilian "green hell."

By the same ship that carried George Percy's request for "suitable clothing," and so on, went Dale's letter dated August 17 (as was Percy's), informing Lord Salisbury, King James' Principal Secretary of State, of the internment of Don Diego and his two companions and proposing a number of reforms in the administration of the colony as well as architectural improvements. The latter included the erection of four additional forts, by means of which, he wrote,

> I should so overmaster the subtle, mischievous Great Powhatan, that I should leave him either no room in his country to harbor in, or draw him to a firm association with ourselves.

Dale's idea was basically the same as John Smith's: the fortification and firm control of the peninsula between the James and York Rivers, from the neighborhood of modern Richmond to Chesapeake Bay. He planned to fortify Kecoughtan (already possessed of two tiny forts), to take over the Indian village of Kiskiack and fortify it, to build a new town and fort in Arrohattoc country (already thought of in London), and to make permanent the twice established-and-abandoned fort at Powhatan village. The new town was to be called Henrico after Prince Henry, "protector and patron of Virginia."

But the ship that was to bear Dale's letter, along with other correspondence, dispatches, and the like, as well as the former Secretary of the Colony, William Strachey, had not gotten away from Jamestown when a frightened sentry at the outermost fort at Old Point Comfort reported sighting a flotilla of nine ships, great and small, bearing down on the mouth of the James.

Dale was speedily advised, and forty men were sent headlong "to discover what they were." At the same time, not unreasonably afraid that these were Spanish ships alerted by the one that had brought Don Diego, he called a council to decide whether to wait at the fort or to arm their own ships and face the enemy. "There was no running," George Percy explained, for the only place to run to was the dangerous asylum of Powhatan's empire.

By this time, however, word reached Jamestown that the ships constituted Governor Gates' fleet. Dale relinquished his title of Deputy Governor to revert to that of Marshal of Virginia, the colony was once again reorganized, and firm plans were made for the foundation of Henrico. To that end, early in September Dale set out by boat up the James, while his company commander, Captain Brewster, led "most of his men overland." As Percy described the undertaking,

> Captain Brewster in his march was divers times assaulted and encountered by the savages, being sent from Powhatan, having for their leader one Munetute [Nemattanon], commonly called amongst us "Jack of the Feathers" by reason that he used to come into the field all covered over with feathers and swan's wings fastened unto his shoulders as though he meant to fly.

Brewster joined Dale at the appointed place, on what is today called Farrar's Island but was then a tongue of land enclosed in a great bend in the river. Indians swarmed all over the proposed site, and it was only after many a skirmish that the colonists were able to find a suitable spot and begin to build their fort. Even then, the Indians hindered the work as much as they could, wounding many whitemen with their arrows and killing some of those who ventured outside the hastily constructed palisade.

In spite of steady progress, not a few colonists deserted Dale due to the endemic laziness that had been the curse of the colony since the day Edward Maria Wingfield first ordered the three original ships unloaded. Dale's punishment for such of those as were retrieved for the colony was severe. In Percy's words:

> Some he appointed to be hanged. Some burned. Some to be broken upon wheels. Others to be staked, and some to be shot to death. All these extreme and cruel tortures he used and inflicted upon them to terrify the rest for [from?] attempting the like. And some which robbed the store, he caused them to be bound fast unto trees and so starved them to death.

While this was going on in the neighborhood of the new town of Henrico, Governor Gates ran the colony in Jamestown, and Indians began to frequent the fort once more, bringing various food products. But the spirit of trade that had existed four years before was gone. Gates, in fact, was so convinced that the Indians came not to trade but to spy, that he had some of the would-be traders apprehended and put to death "for a terror to the rest to cause them to desist from their subtle practices."

By then, George Percy had been in Virginia almost five years. Whether it was because of the behavior of the new administration, of his own recurring sickness, or of some suggestion from home, the fact is that suddenly, on April 22, 1612, he "set sail in the ship named the *Trial.*" His voyage was not easy, but at length the *Trial* came to anchor in Dover Road just in time to meet Captain Samuel Argall's ship heading for Virginia again. A few days later, on July 23, Argall hoisted anchor and Percy "took post-horse, and from thence rode to London."

Argall held a new variety of commission this time. The Virginia venture had received its third charter from the King on March 12, expanding the territorial limits of the colony and strengthening the executive powers of the company and its treasure. The Company Council had already learned that a French group had sent out a ship to start a plantation on what had been the North Virginia Company's authorized area for settlement. With the North Virginia Company in the doldrums, the South Virginia Company's Council interpreted their third charter broadly and gave Captain Argall a commission to "displace" the French.

Argall's ship was the *Treasurer,* one hundred and thirty tons, manned by a crew of sixty, and mounting fourteen guns. It was owned by Sir Robert Rich, the son of the extremely wealthy third Baron Rich and his wife the Lady Penelope, sister of the famous second Earl of Essex. The Lady Penelope had been divorced by Lord Rich for adultery with Lord Mountjoy and had died two years later, in 1607. Even before that, she had courted the attentions of Sir Philip Sidney. In short, young Sir Robert Rich came of a conspicuous family.[20]

When Samuel Argall first met Sir Robert is not clear, but there are hints that he had already bought an interest in the *Treasurer.* In any case, an association between Argall and young Rich, seven years his junior, existed by 1612, and for Argall it was to prove valuable.

CHAPTER 8

Pocahontas and Captain Argall

SAMUEL ARGALL reached Old Point Comfort on this, his third, voyage about September 17, 1612. Three years had passed since the end of John Smith's presidency. That meant that three years (and more) had passed since Pocahontas had visited Jamestown. That something had gone wrong there, she could not but know.

A swarm of uncomprehending newcomers had arrived and with them, a handful of former colonists, returning not to be friendly but to be self-important, greedy, and unpleasant. Upon their return, Captain Smith had left. The one bond, tenuous as it was, between Pocahontas' people, herself, and the blustering whitemen was broken. Whether Smith lived or, as some reported, was dead, he was no longer in command. He was no longer in Jamestown.

Then had come the winter of the "starving time." And before the full of the Goose Moon late in March, 1610, it seems that Pocahontas realized that the days of friendly, playful association with the whitemen at the fort were over. She had reached the threshold of adult life.

An Indian "private captain," to use the words of a not unfriendly

Englishman, came on the scene, and Pocahontas married him that year. Nothing is known about him beyond the name he is said to have had, Kocoum.[1] And after that a curtain of silence fell over Pocahontas, not to be lifted for many months.

At the same time, Powhatan, deluded of his hope that the colony would wither away or collapse, set his mind on a war of attrition. Up to then stray whitemen had not been precisely safe — other than those who deliberately sought Indian protection or hospitality — but now Indian spies saw to it that they were in mortal danger. If no Indian was to be safe in the hands of the English, then no Englishman was to be spared if caught.

Where Powhatan was living at this time is not precisely known. The James River area of his "empire" was forfeited to the intruders. Since his son Pochins was driven out of Kecoughtan, since Wowinchopunk, werowance of Paspahegh, was murdered in his struggle for freedom, and since Powhatan village was sold to the whitemen by his son Parahunt, Powhatan had only one village on the peninsula between the James and the York which he could call his: Kiskiack. How long would *it* be secure from the white plunderers and murderers?

Powhatan could not know of Dale's project to take over all the territory from modern Richmond to Old Point Comfort, but he must have known that his personal saftey lay elsewhere. He may have resided at Orapaks, as in John Smith's day. Or he may have retired to some other village, as a later event indicates. But this much is certain. Pocahontas was spending some time in the Potomac country—perhaps Kocoum was of that tribe. Her visits or life there were to have vast significance in the history of her people.

Samuel Argall had sailed up the Potomac when Lord De La Warr was in Virginia, as we have seen, and now that Pocahontas was sixteen he was again westward bound across the great salt water. He had learned that the only Indians who would still exchange their food and skins for gewgaws were the Potomacs. Evidently it would not be long before he returned to trade.

After his first voyage, Argall had expressed the opinion that Virginia could be reached in seven weeks by the route he had tested. On his third voyage he virtually proved this. After leaving the coast of England on July 23, he "fell with the coast of Virginia in the latitude of forty degrees" on September 12, arriving at Old Point Comfort five days later.[2]

Although reports reaching London just before he left suggested that the colony would "fall to the ground of itself," [3] he found it in unexpectedly good shape. With a will, Argall spent six weeks first putting the colony's small "navy" in shape and then helping Marshal Dale fleece the Indians of their food supplies.

The pickings were slim, and for a second time Dale barely escaped being killed. But it seemed to occur to nobody that continued raids, murder, and arson in the cornfields hardly encouraged agricultural production outside the colony. Yet such people as Gates, Dale, and Argall well knew that the "beastly idleness" of the colonists would not grow food inside their domain. Argall, however, was a strict believer in discipline, whichever way it worked. And in this instance he properly carried out Dale's orders.

With these primary designs accomplished and during the first week in November, Argall took Dale down the James and out beyond Cape Charles, at the suggestion of Sir Thomas Gates, to inspect the island originally named by and for Captain John Smith but renamed Sir Thomas Smythe's Island in honor of the Treasurer of the Virginia Company. The object of the visit to "Smyths Iles" was to obtain Dale's opinion of a proposal to station some men there. By the end of the week, the explorers were back in Jamestown. Though Dale's report was highly favorable, nothing came of the idea.

With winter approaching, the seemingly unexorcizable demon,

Famine, gave warning of its annual visit. John Smith had long before issued an edict that he who would not work should not eat, but that had been a dead letter since his departure. The thing for the colonists to do was not to provide for themselves but to raid the Indians.

Samuel Argall, apparently voluntarily, revived the practice of trading voyages, however, and on the first day of December he set sail from Old Point Comfort for the Potomac River. His men, he stated, were "in as good health, as at [his] arrival."

Back in July, 1608, Smith had reported that there were signs of minerals on or near the upper Potomac. In fact, even before that first Potomac voyage, an Indian had told Captain Newport that "a glistering metal" was got from the Indians there, which Newport thought must be half silver. Smith himself had found what he considered to be an antimony mine. And two years later, following in Smith's wake in December, 1610, Argall seems to have rediscovered the antimony mine and found a lead mine as well.[4]

In December, 1612, however, corn was Argall's objective. Paying no attention to the mines or the natural wonders of the Potomac, Argall delayed little in finding Iapassus, who was on a hunting expedition. He invited the werowance aboard his ship, as he later wrote to his lifelong friend Nicholas Hawes. Iapassus immediately accepted,

> seeming to be very glad of my coming, and [he] told me that all the Indians there were my very great friends, and that they had [a] good store of corn for me, which they provided the year before, which we found to be true.

Thereupon Argall sailed his ship to a spot near Iapassus' town, Pastancie,[5] put together a shallop to ferry the corn from the shore to the ship, and when the loading was finished, concluded a peace with various chiefs, exchanging hostages. This was on the first of

January, 1613. A month later, the corn reached Old Point Comfort. All of Argall's voyages were filled with bursts of speed followed by unexplained dilatoriness.

When he got back to the colony, Argall delivered eight hundred bushels of corn to the storehouses, reserving three hundred for his own men — the sort of consideration that kept his men loyal, contented, and well.

Argall next put his men to work felling timber to build a frigate. When this was well along, "half finished" he wrote, he left the job to the carpenters, ordered his company aboard the *Treasurer,* and on March 19 started back to the Potomac. This time, corn was not his sole interest.

Argall reported that he explored as far as the head of the river, "which is about sixty-five leagues into the land, and navigable for any ship," or one hundred and ninety-five statute miles. Since it is about one hundred and ninety miles from the head of navigation of the Potomac, at Washington, to the mouth of the Chesapeake Bay, it is seen that Argall's estimate is professionally pretty accurate.

Instead of attempting to go around the falls, which today extend some distance upstream from Potomac Heights, and to march farther into the country, Argall returned a short distance downstream. At an unknown point there, he disembarked and took a body of men on a march. This seems to have led him through the wooded and well-watered country to the west and south of the Potomac, from Aquia Creek toward Fredericksburg. There, he wrote, he

> found great store of cattle as big as kine, of which the Indians that were my guides killed a couple which we found to be very good and wholesome meat; in regard [appearance] they are heavy, slow, and not so wild as other beasts of the wilderness.

This is one of the very rare mentions of bison in Virginia in those days or, indeed, for years to come.[6]

Argall found another mine but did not specify of what mineral. Also, the Indians showed him a kind of earth which they ate to comfort an upset stomach. Finally, he came across a spring of mineral water that tasted of alum and was good and wholesome, and three other sorts of earth, one of which was similar to the then much prized *terra sigillata*.[7] But all of these matters pale in significance as he opens a new paragraph in his letter:

> Whilst I was in this business, I was told by certain Indians, my friends, that the Great Powhatan's daughter Pokahuntis was with the great King Patowomeck, whither I presently repaired, resolving to possess myself of her by any stratagem that I could use, for the ransoming of so many Englishmen as were prisoners with Powhatan; as also to get such arms and tools as he and other Indians had got by murder and stealing from others of our nation, with some quantity of corn for the Colony's relief.

Whatever the colors one chooses to paint the picture of Argall's action, his words not only ring true but lucidly show that nothing more vicious was in his mind than acquiring a hostage worth a great deal by way of ransom. The caution he employed in carrying out his plan furthermore reflects, for all its calculated callousness, a quick and active mind, not by any means lacking in knowledge of human weaknesses or, on the other hand, in kindness.

By this bold stroke, Argall meant to accomplish what Sir Thomas Dale had wanted two thousand men to effect two years before: a check on Powhatan's hostility. And he was going about it in a fashion reminiscent of John Smith. Not wholesale slaughter, but a quick, unexpected move, and a hostage. With Pocahontas in the hands of the English, Powhatan would think well before repeating the treacherous massacre of Captain John Sicklemore, alias Ratcliffe, and his men, in the winter of 1609.

Back aboard his ship, Argall steered directly to Pastancie —

whose location we no longer know. He dropped anchor nearby and quickly sent a messenger in the ship's boat asking Iapassus to come and bring James Swift, the ensign whom he "had left as a pledge of our love and truce" the voyage before. Swift was an investor in the Virginia Company who had been shipwrecked with Gates on Bermuda.

Iapassus promptly brought Swift aboard. Argall welcomed them solemnly. Formalities concluded, however, the English captain surprised the werowance by not immediately suggesting further barter of goods and food. Instead, undoubtedly aided by Swift's knowledge of Potomac speech, Argall mentioned the presence of Pocahontas at Iapassus' brother's residence. Although he had never seen her, he pointed out to Iapassus that she was of vital importance in re-establishing friendship between the Indians and the English. In fact, without too much circumlocution, he announced that if Iapassus "did not betray Pokahuntis unto my hands, we would no longer be brothers nor friends."

Iapassus remonstrated that such a betrayal would bring Powhatan and all his army down upon him and his people. Argall countered by promising in that event to join with him against Powhatan. At that point, from motives that smacked little of loyalty or personal disinterestedness, Iapassus excused himself to go and consult with his brother, whose residence evidently was not far away.

It seems from what Ralph Hamor, the young clerk of the Council in Jamestown, later learned that Argall in the same breath explained

> that in ransom of her he might redeem some of our Englishmen and arms, now in possession of her father, promising to use her with all fair and gentle entreaty [treatment].[8]

Hamor's account did not go on to mention Iapassus' visit to his brother, the "great King" of the Potomacs, but Argall's statement that he did seek his approval makes such a visit plausible. In fact, the Potomacs were less despotically ruled than the Powhatans, and the Potomac chief undoubtedly felt obliged to consult his council of elders.

The visit itself remaining largely hypothetical, there is of course no hint anywhere of what was discussed. Nevertheless, there were two pertinent factors which could well have influenced any decision. Powhatan's control over the Potomacs was clearly little more than nominal and friendly. Already that tribe had willingly traded with the English, despite Powhatan's evident interdiction of such activities.

The other factor, intimately connected, could have been that the trading was countenanced because of the geographical location of the Potomac nation. The Potomacs were the most remote of all his subject-and-tributary peoples from Powhatan's Werowocomoco residence. This not only weakened his control but put them in the position of a buffer people protecting his northern flank against the non-Algonkian Indians who roamed nearby.

These tribes or nations, including the feared Massawomecks, were not only powerful but also had valuable products of the hinterland to exchange for what the bayshore and the seashore had to offer. But the self-confident whitemen who wanted to hold Pocahontas in ransom had even more exotic goods to trade — goods that came from a barely imaginable "outside." These things could improve the Potomacs' trading position with the non-Algonkians. If the Potomac trade could be expanded and at the same time protected by so efficient a power as Argall's, there might be much to gain, and virtually nothing to lose, by acceding to Argall's request. On the other hand, such broad considerations may not have entered into the matter at all. Such concepts of trade may not have been developed. And Iapassus' actions may have been inspired by nothing more profound than thoughts of personal gain.

In any case, Iapassus and Argall put their heads together to work out a course of action. In Ralph Hamor's words:

> It chanced [that] Powhatan's delight and darling, his daughter Pocahontas (whose name hath even been spread in England by the title of Nonpareil of Virginia) in her princely progress, if I may so term it, took some pleasure . . . to be among her friends at Potomac (as it seemeth by the relation I had), employed thither as shopkeepers to a fair, to exchange some of her father's commodities for theirs . . .

Pocahontas had remained "at Potomac" for some three months, or longer. Argall had turned up on his December, 1612, voyage just about the time of her arrival. Learning of this, Pocahontas had felt a certain ill-defined longing to see Englishmen again, and let it be known that she would gladly meet them. By then winter had turned to spring, and the English were again in the neighborhood. Iapassus, aware of all this, suggested that he could take advantage of Pocahontas' desire and bring about a meeting.

Such was the story. Whether it was true or made up to accomodate Argall cannot be determined. However it was, Iapassus made up his mind to use his wife as the instrument for carrying out his plan; "which sex," Hamor commented, "have ever been most powerful in beguiling enticements."

The wife would meet Pocahontas and bring her down to the shore, along with Iapassus. Argall would be in his boat. Iapassus' wife would feign a great desire to go aboard the ship lying out in the stream, especially because it had been there more than once before and beause she had never visited it. And the rest would be left to the spur of the moment.

All went well. Pocahontas accompanied Iapassus and his wife to the boat, where Argall stood looking perhaps not a little like John Smith — at least, they were the same age, and undoubtedly Argall had as much of a beard as Smith. Iapassus' wife gave voice to her wish to go aboard the ship. He pretended that he was angry at such a request, for it was not proper for a woman to go aboard alone. The wife thereupon began to weep, noisily. Iapassus, "seeming to pity those counterfeit tears," then told her she could go, providing Pocahontas was willing to go with her.

Pocahontas at first refused. She certainly knew that her father would not approve. But Iapassus' wife between tears and prayers finally won her over. The daughter of Powhatan at last permitted Captain Argall to help her into his boat. Iapassus and his wife followed.

Once on shipboard, Argall was a kind and attentive host. He ordered a supper prepared, showed his guests around the ship, and conversed merrily with all. When they had feasted, the gunner's room was offered to Pocahontas for her to rest in, and Iapassus and his wife went to talk with Argall, explaining how they had arranged all that he wanted. Argall rewarded them with a small copper kettle and "some other less valuable toys [gewgaws] so highly by him [Iapassus] esteemed that doubtless he would have betrayed his own father for them." After that, they also retired for a nap.

Pocahontas had suspected nothing when she was offered the courtesy of a couch for a brief rest. Yet before long she began to take alarm, got up while the others were still resting, and urged Iapassus and his wife to take her ashore.

Argall then stepped in. He informed Pocahontas that her father

> had then eight of our Englishmen, many swords and other tools which he had at several times by treacherous murdering our men taken from them, which, though of no use to him, he would not redeliver, [and for that reason] he would reserve [keep] Pocahontas [aboard].

He agreed to Iapassus and his wife going ashore.

Pocahontas lapsed into deep thought. Though she was unaware of Iapassus' double-dealing, she was annoyed and concerned. Iapassus, sensing what was wrong, claimed that he was to blame for her being thus captured, but Pocahontas seemed to disregard him. Argall, too, was troubled by the dignified resentment shown by Pocahontas, and he resorted to extraordinary courtesy in an attempt to win her over. Just how, we do not know.

It may only be surmised on the basis of subsequent events that Argall pointed out that Pocahontas would be his noble guest — a princess, not a prisoner. She would be honored. And she would be in a position to bring back friendship and faith between Powhatan and the English. It was not so much the matter of the eight English prisoners in Powhatan's hands or of the swords and tools. It was something deeper, more permanent.

At last, Pocahontas bade Iapassus and his wife adieu and remained aboard. She did not stir from her cabin to watch them being rowed away.

Captain Argall then dispatched an Indian runner to Powhatan through seventy-five miles, or so, of forest. The Indian, according to Argall's own account, was to let Powhatan clearly know

> that I had taken his daughter. And if he would send home the Englishmen whom he detained in slavery, with such arms and tools as the Indians had gotten and stolen, and also a great quantity of corn — that then he should have his daughter restored. Otherwise not.

The messenger returned without delay, stating that Great Powhatan was much grieved by this, but

> that he desired me to use his daughter well, and bring my ship into his harbor [Werowocomoco?], and there he would give me my demands; which being performed, I should deliver him his daughter, and we should be friends.

It was April 13, 1613, by then, and Argall decided to hasten back to Jamestown. Rumor would already have reached Dale's ears. Argall did not want his action misunderstood or, above all, repudiated. The colony still suffered from factions and disruptive dislikes, and the success of any undertaking might depend on who got the Governor's or the Marshal's ear and approval first. In fact, Argall had already been somewhat rash in proposing terms to Powhatan which in fact could be proposed only by the Governor or his deputy.

Although there appears to be no contemporary evidence as to the manner in which Pocahontas was received in Jamestown, it is likely that she was treated with respect and kindness. To be sure, Powhatan was considered a "savage," but he was also an "emperor" in his own country. Individuals might manhandle him, if they got a chance, but Gates can hardly have violated the sacred codes dealing with rank. Pocahontas was the daughter of the ruler of the land. She was therefore a princess.

At the same time Pocahontas was a prisoner, Don Diego de Molina, an *alcalde,* was also a prisoner. Both had very great freedom within the colony. Yet in the case of Pocahontas, Dale was especially charged with the responsibility for her because Jamestown, where she was first detained, was surrounded by her own people. There were no Spaniards in the offing who might rescue Don Diego. On this basis, it may be imagined that Pocahontas was watched much more closely.

Gates seems to have confirmed Argall's conditions in a message to Powhatan, but there was no immediate answer. Argall consequently returned to Old Point Comfort to finish work on his frigate.

Explaining that he was planning a lengthy fishing voyage outside the bay, as he termed his objective, Argall put his ship's-master in charge of a gang to overhaul the *Treasurer,* while his lieutenant commanded a shore gang engaged in felling timber and cleaving planks to build a fishing boat.

The frigate, when it was finished, was put under Argall's ensign, Swift, to fish off Cape Charles and transport the catch to "Henry's Town" on Cape Henry, opposite, for the relief of the men employed there. When this was all functioning with military precision, Argall himself took off with a fourth gang to explore the eastern shore of Chesapeake Bay. No-one had done this systematically since John Smith's voyages of the summer of 1608.

While Argall never had the ethnological interest in the Indians which was characteristic of Smith, on this occasion he did report that they were generally friendly and that there were a great many of them. The friendliness, he said, was due to his treatment of the Potomacs. If this was true, it is only further evidence of the wisdom of Smith's policy of trade, accompanied by military strictness and personal kindness. From the Indian point of view, here was at last another whiteman whom they could understand.

Argall explored the eastern shore "some forty leagues [one hundred and twenty statute miles] northward," probably as far as Kent Island, below modern Annapolis and the Chesapeake Bay Bridge. His most important discovery was perhaps the possibility of making salt on some of the islands, but he also observed, as had Smith before him, the wealth of fish and shellfish still untouched there. He then returned to Old Point Comfort and his ship. It was May 12.

By the middle of the following week, Don Diego de Molina had written a letter to the Spanish Ambassador in London, and since Argall's and Molina's letters were received by July 20, a ship must have sailed by the middle of June, or so. Furthermore, a surviving fragment of a letter from Dale to Sir Thomas Smythe is dated June, but neither Molina's nor Dale's mentions Pocahontas — only Argall's. All that is known is that from resignation to her fate, she gradually came to welcome her new role in the relations between the colony and her people. When this change came about cannot be determined, but later events show that it did come.

Sometime during the next twelve months, probably nearer the beginning than the end, Alexander Whitaker, minister and missionary, took Pocahontas under his wing and, at the request of Sir Thomas Dale, began her instruction in the Christian faith. Either because of that, or because of her captivity which showed her the pious behavior of a handful of whitemen, Pocahontas clearly saw what Fate wanted of her. This happened during the remaining months of the year 1613. About that same time, a third Englishman entered her life: Master John Rolfe.

CHAPTER 9

John Rolfe Meets Pocahontas

LEGEND AND FAMILY TRADITIONS have combined to "establish" the village of Heacham, in Norfolk, as the ancestral home of John Rolfe. According to surviving village records, a Eustace Rolfe of Heacham, yeoman, had a son baptized John on October 13, 1562. John in turn married a Dorothy Mason, three years his junior, had twin sons (Eustace and John) who were baptized on May 6, 1585, and another son baptized Edward on February 22, 1591. Eustace died at the age of three, and John Rolfe, Sr., followed him to the grave in 1594. By then the latter was ranked as a gentleman.

John Rolfe, Jr., has for many years been considered to have been the John Rolfe who went to Virginia — largely, perhaps, because the age is right and because no other suitable John Rolfe has turned up in existing records. If there is no firm evidence to prove that they were the same person, there is nothing to disprove it either. Probably the best that can be said is that, if the John Rolfe of Virginia was not the John Rolfe of Heacham, an astounding amount of inventiveness has been brought into action to build up the legend.[1]

Indeed, the fact that prodigious energy has been employed not to show some noble descent but merely to establish the identity of so un-unique an individual as the son of a young Norfolk self-made gentleman falls little short of constituting presumptive proof. The legend, therefore, with its supporting tradition, will here be accepted as history.

The Rolfes of Heacham have been described as a family in which intellectual capacity has been less of a feature than character and persistence. The Rolfes were sturdy and able, not brainy. And John Rolfe's father's epitaph hints at the type of man the son would be: "He increased his property by merchandise. By exporting and importing such things as England abounded in, or needed, he was of the greatest service . . ."

In mid-May, 1609, John Rolfe of Virginia stepped into the historic scene when he boarded the *Sea Adventure* (or *Sea Venture*) with Sir Thomas Gates, Sir George Somers, Captain Christopher Newport, William Strachey, Esq., and a company of perhaps a hundred and fifty other men, women, and children. With John Rolfe went his wife, whose name is not recorded.[2]

The most astounding fact about the departure of the *Sea Adventure* was the mix-up that arose, even before she sailed. Although King James' Council for the reorganized "Company of Adventurers and Planters in Virginia" had specified that the three chief officers of the fleet — Gates, the Governor, Somers, the Admiral, and Newport, the Vice Admiral — should take their several commissions with them and "be divided into several ships," [3] it appears that Gates wanted Newport to captain the flagship. This put two of the leaders in one ship, against orders. Then Sir George Somers joined the fleet at Plymouth and apparently refused to be accorded less importance than his subordinate, Newport. He would sail in the flagship, too.

The Council, amazingly, knew more about the perils of the deep than the "absolute Governor," Gates, and the two distinguished navigators — the one ranked as an admiral, the other considered the most experienced English navigator so far as American waters were concerned. These three forgot, or ignored, the Council's wise words about "the mortality and uncertainty of human life." [4] As a result, the infant colony suffered its first great disaster, the "starving time," already described.

The flagship was separated from the rest of the fleet on Monday, July 24, the eve of St. James' Day. The circumstances were vividly set forth by William Strachey in a long missive addressed to an "Excellent Lady," [5] possibly Dame Sara Smythe, the wife of Sir Thomas. He wrote, in part,

> the clouds gathering thick upon us, and the winds singing and whistling most unusually . . . a dreadful storm and hideous began to blow from out the northeast, which swelling and roaring as it were by fits, some hours with more violence than others, at length did beat all light from heaven, which like a hell of darkness turned black upon us, so much the more fuller of horror . . . as who was most armed and best prepared was not a little shaken . . . For four and twenty hours the storm in a restless tumult had blown so exceedingly as [that] we could not apprehend in our imaginations any possibility of greater violence, yet did we still find it not only more terrible but more constant, fury added to fury, and one storm urging a second more outrageous than the former . . . What shall I say? Winds and seas were as mad as fury and rage could make them.

Tuesday morning, a leak was discovered, to add to the misery of the terrified colonists. Gates promptly divided the hundred and forty or so men aboard into three groups to man the pumps. Each one, from the Governor down, "took the bucket or pump for one hour, and rested another." And for three days in darkness as great by day as by night, this struggle for survival continued.

Thursday night, St. Elmo's fire danced over the shrouds, but it did not light them "any whit the more to our known way." The helmsman steered this way and that, striving only to keep the ship afloat, until by Friday morning most of those aboard were ready to shut the hatches, commend themselves to God, and leave the ship to the mercy of the sea.

It was ten or eleven that morning, July 28, when Sir George Somers, straining his eyes as light began to penetrate the gloom, suddenly cried "Land!" Gates then commanded the helmsman to bear up, while the boatswain frantically threw the lead to determine the depth of the water.

Somehow they got the ship into relatively smooth water, a mile or less from shore, but discovered that it would be impossible to beach her. She ran on a reef, still some thirteen hundred yards from the coast. There, by dint of manning the ship's boats, the entire company got ashore.

They had reached "the dangerous and dreaded island, or rather islands, of Bermuda," which were in those days so feared that they were called the Devil's Islands. But to the great surprise of all, Bermuda was found to be a delightful place, with abundant food, fish, fowl, fruit, and even wild hogs left there before by shipwrecked Spaniards. The only problem was: how to get to Virginia. The *Sea Adventure* was hopelessly lost.

Nevertheless, within a month of their landing, the longboat had been refashioned into a pinnace, and Master's Mate Henry Ravens[6] was ready and willing to attempt a voyage to Chesapeake Bay, which he estimated to be a hundred and forty leagues away. (It was, in fact, about two hundred and twenty leagues to Cape Hatteras, or six hundred and sixty statute miles, with Jamestown a good deal farther.)

Ravens took off with six sailors. After some trouble getting past the coral reefs, the boat at last vanished over the horizon on Friday, the seventh of September.

It would be full moon a day or two later, and Ravens promised "if he lived and arrived safe there, to return unto us the next [following] new moon with the pinnace belonging to the colony there," Strachey wrote. Governor Gates commanded fires prepared as beacons for his return, "but two moons were wasted upon the promontory," in vain. The bold mate and his men were never heard of again.

Meanwhile, a determined shipwright, Richard Frobisher, of Gravesend, and most probably a collateral descendant of the great Sir Martin Frobisher, was already at work building a pinnace out of raw material available on the island. This little boat had reached such a stage of construction by the end of November that Gates, at Frobisher's request, granted special help to him to build another, so that all the colonists might be transported to Virginia. By then, all hope of Ravens' return had vanished.

During those same months of waiting and building, a mutiny broke out. A small group of religious enthusiasts and malcontents resolved to have no part in expediting the work on the first pinnace. They preferred to take possession of another island and to settle there. This canker was not rooted out until mid-March, 1610. It only serves to illustrate the sort of thing that made English colonization so unbelievably complicated.

The rest of the colony backed, and obeyed, their Governor, as was both proper and sensible. John Rolfe's wife gave birth to a daughter who was christened Bermuda, with Mistress Alexander Horton, Captain Newport, and William Strachey as godparents. Six weeks later a boy was born to Edward Eason and his wife, and he was named Bermudas. The little boy survived, but Bermuda Rolfe evidently died before John Rolfe and his wife reached Virginia.

At length, the two pinnaces were ready. They were named the *Deliverance* and the *Patience.* Then for several days the wind was contrary, but on May 10, 1610, the two vessels were cautiously sailed through the narrow exit from the harbor, clear of the "Devil's Island." Ten days later, the night breeze brought odors of land. And about eleven o'clock the next morning they sailed before an easy gale into Chesapeake Bay.

But for the brief fame attendant on the birth of their daughter, John Rolfe and his wife faded into total obscurity for at least a year after they left Bermuda. His wife, never mentioned by name, died, perhaps soon after the survivors from Bermuda reached Jamestown. Rolfe, we know, dedicated himself to work in the colony and especially to the improvement of the quality of tobacco grown there. He seems to have been an avid smoker. And he was, like his father, interested in providing "such things as England . . . needed."

Although there is no direct record of it, Rolfe seems to have succeeded in getting some tobacco seeds from Trinidad in 1611. This type of tobacco was far more palatable than the course, rough native leaf. Rolfe planted and tended, and with the industry and persistence which is said to have characterized his family, he thus made "trial" of these seeds. Indeed, by 1612 he was able to ship some of his product to England.[7]

Before long the native Virginia tobacco had virtually disappeared from the English-held part of Virginia, as a result of Rolfe's efforts. At the same time, it may be said that the colony was saved economically. Even before Rolfe's "trial," Robert Harcourt, would-be colonizer of Guyana, had held that tobacco would "bring as great a benefit and profit to the undertakers as ever the Spaniards gained by the best and richest silver-mine in all their Indies." But these ideas did not appear in *print* until 1613. It is doubtful that Rolfe was inspired by them.

Meanwhile, on May 12, 1611, Marshal Dale had arrived from England, bringing with him, among many others, the Rev. Alexander Whitaker. Dale was to be Acting Governor in the absence of

Lord De La Warr. Whitaker, as has been mentioned, was a missionary at heart. Seeking closer contact with the "savages," he proposed to attempt to convert them to the "True Faith." To accomplish this, he established himself at Henrico, Dale's new foundation.

It was to Alexander Whitaker, then, that Dale entrusted Pocahontas for training in the Christian religion. Whether this was because he did not want Pocahontas in Jamestown or because of personal preferences cannot be known. Certainly, Whitaker was more articulate than Richard Buck, who had baptized Bermuda Rolfe and was the minister at Jamestown. Perhaps his religious zeal for the conversion of Indians was greater. Or, it may merely have been that Buck was Gates' man, and Dale found Whitaker more congenial in one way or another.

By contemporary calculation, it was eighty miles by water from Jamestown to Henrico, Whitaker's parish. By modern measurements, it would be about fifty-five miles, though differences in the river-channel could add something. The details are unimportant. It should only be remembered that it was not an afternoon's outing to go from Jamestown to Dale's "model city."

Nevertheless, it was obviously not long after Pocahontas' arrival at Henrico that John Rolfe met her. It may be that Rolfe experimented with his tobacco seeds in the neighborhood, for it is known that there was a "great quantity of corn ground impaled" at Henrico and even more at Bermuda Nether Hundred, five miles downstream. In any event, it seems certain that John Rolfe visited Henrico by about July, 1613.

It was at that time that Powhatan sent word to Gates that "whensoever we pleased to deliver his daughter, he would give us in satisfaction of his injuries done to us, and for the rest of our pieces broken and stolen from him, 500 bushels of corn, and be forever friends with us." With the message, and in token of good faith, came seven white prisoners, each armed with a broken musket.[8]

Gates sent back word that Pocahontas was very well and was being treated with all kindness. Indeed, she would continue to be so treated however Powhatan dealt with Gates. At the same time, it was incomprehensible to him that the rest of the stolen arms had been lost or, in turn, stolen from Powhatan. So, the English would not return Pocahontas until these weapons were given up. When they were and when Pocahontas was delivered back to Powhatan, they would leave it up to him whether he would establish peace or continue to play the enemy.

Months passed without an answer. Meanwhile, Samuel Argall was ready to sail on his "fishing trip," the real object of which was then made clear.

As long before as 1609, the great colonial propagandist, Richard Hakluyt the preacher, had published a translation of a work which described the colonial activities of France in what is now the Bay of Fundy area. In 1612, about the time Argall sailed from England, Marc Lescarbot's *Relation dernière* was published with more recent details. The London Council learned from these publications and passed on word to both Gates and Dale that French religious activities were on the upsurge in that part of Canada. And if they needed further confirmation, this was to be had from Huguenots and other friendly Protestants.

Since the English "North Virginia" colony, in Maine, had been abandoned in 1609, no Englishmen were nearby to deter French colonists from occupying the region, which, incidentally, lay outside the limits set out in King James' Virginia charters. Nevertheless, a French establishment on the doorstep of the abandoned northern colony was not to be accepted complacently.

Samuel Argall, a thoroughly capable pilot, commander, and soldier, was therefore dispatched to remove these French colonies, by force if necessary. Argall received a commission from Gates (or Dale), without which he undoubtedly would not have undertaken the voyage. His flagship, the *Treasurer,* with its full complement of men, arms, and armor, had just been overhauled, and he also had a fishing ship.[9]

While this expedition was in preparation, unbeknown to Gates, Dale, and Argall, a wealthy and deeply religious French noblewoman had begun to interest herself in establishing a specific "foundation for the maintenance of the [Canadian] missionaries." She was Madame Antoinette de Pons, Marquise de Guercheville, and wife of Charles du Plessis, Duc de Liancourt and Governor of Paris. Being rich, Madame la Marquise was still interested in money — more money. Therefore, while she was backing the Jesuits in the confused situation in the infant French colonial enterprise by supplying funds for missions, she also sent ships to trade with the Indians. All they had were furs of all sorts, but furs were valuable and brought good prices in the French market.[10]

The upshot of the Canadian complications, which need not be entered into here, was that Madame la Marquise appointed a courtier named René Le Coq de la Saussaye to act as her lieutenant in the establishment of a new French colony in what was called Acadia — virtually synonymous with the Nova Scotia of more modern times. La Saussaye, as he is commonly called, landed and "took possession" of the North American coast in that region in the name of Madame, on May 16, 1613. That is to say, he omitted Port Royal from his claim, since it was already in existence, but he abstracted two Jesuit Fathers therefrom to accompany him while he set up his new colony. Then he sailed to modern Frenchman Bay, on the eastern side of Mount Desert Island, Maine.

La Saussaye seems to have been obtuse, from more than one point of view. He erected no fortifications but went to work on an agricultural project. Six weeks after his arrival, he learned from friendly Indians that an English warship was fishing off the coast only forty to fifty miles to the southwest. La Saussaye went on planting corn and vegetables. Then, the Friday following the Indians' visit, which was July 2 according to the French (new style) calendar, the warship appeared in the bay.

It was the *Treasurer.* Captain Argall, in turn, had been told by friendly Indians that there were Frenchmen not far away. Conceivably, the "friendly" Indians hoped that the whitemen would exterminate one another.

Nearly all the French colonizers were on shore. Given such an opportunity, Argall sensibly seized their ship first and landed afterward. La Saussaye fled into the forest. As a result, Argall could occupy the camp, too, without resistance. With it, he made a point of locating La Saussaye's private chest. This he calmly had opened by a skilled locksmith, extracted such of the documents in it as might be useful, and had it shut and locked again.

La Saussaye came back after a while, asserting that he was there by right and that he was under the protection of the French King, eleven-year-old Louis XIII. Argall politely asked for his papers. La Saussaye, of course, could find none, for they were in Argall's pocket. Argall, taking advantage of the man's confusion, sternly declared then that La Saussaye was nothing but a pirate, pilfering articles in a land rightly claimed by James I of England under the terms of the Charters of Virginia.

Not wanting to burden himself with all thirty Frenchmen, however, Argall agreed to grant La Saussaye the choice of having a pinnace to take him and his men to France, of traveling in Argall's own ship to Newfoundland, where they might find a French ship, or finally, of having a shallop in which he could find his way back to Port Royal with as many men as he chose to take with him. The rest Argall would conduct to Virginia.

La Saussaye chose the last of the alternatives. He asked for one of the Jesuit Fathers, accepted the gift of the shallop, and sailed off with about half of his men. Two other Fathers, Pierre Biard and Jacques Quentin, along with the French ship-captain and the other half of the group, went aboard Argall's *Treasurer.*

They reached Jamestown promptly, only to find that Marshal Dale regarded them as criminals. As Father Biard later wrote, the Marshal "spoke of nothing but ropes and gallows, and hanging every one of us."

Argall, however, on the basis of the friendship which had sprung up between the Frenchmen and himself, and of his promised word that they would be returned safely to France, protested with such effect that Dale gave in.[11] As a result, the Jamestown Colony, tiny as it was, could boast the presence of a numerous and variegated group of prisoners. The French, first in number, came to fifteen men, including two Jesuit fathers and a ship-captain. Then there were two Spaniards, one of minor distinction, and a pretended Spaniard who was a renegade English pilot. And finally, most important of all, the Indian Princess, Pocahontas.

For Dale to have yielded to Argall is not only witness to Argall's character but also to Dale's perspicacity. He needed Argall. In short, the considerations which outweighed all others for Dale were almost certainly that he now knew that at least two French settlements still survived in "North Virginia," that Argall was the man clearly indicated to sail back to dislodge and destroy them, and that the Frenchmen would be needed to show the way.

As soon, therefore, as the *Treasurer* could be unloaded (of fish and possibly furs) and once more fitted out for the voyage and the French ship and tiny bark also be made ready, Argall sailed away again. The season was well advanced. Speed was essential.

According to his commission, Argall's first task was to obliterate La Saussaye's would-be colony. This accomplished, he set up a cross on the site, claiming it for King James. Then he steered for the two colonies on the Bay of Fundy, well over two hundred miles to the northeast. Whether or not the Frenchmen helped him find them is surely an academic question. Argall had already rifled La Saussaye's chest, with its charts and instructions as well as the royal commission authorizing his expedition.

Argall stopped briefly at Sainte-Croix, on the Bay of Fundy. He razed what remained of the old settlement but found no loot worth taking beyond a stock of salt for preserving fish. Then he crossed over to Port-Royal, where he was conceivably the last person the French colonists expected to see. Young Charles de Biencourt, son of the Lieutenant Governor of Acadia, had been left in charge at Port-Royal. Inexperienced — he was barely twenty-one — and more concerned about his food supply than his defences, Biencourt had taken off with some Indians to forage when Argall hove into sight. There was not even a sentinel to halt him.

Not knowing where the French captain was, or his people, Argall leisurely pillaged the settlement thoroughly. He slaughtered some of the cattle for his immediate use and carried aboard ship as many live animals as he could. He burned and then uprooted the fields, destroyed houses, and virtually erased the place from the map. His mission accomplished, he was ready to sail away when whom should he see but Charles de Biencourt, returning with supplies.

Argall met the young Frenchman, apparently alone. Immediately, he placed the blame for his actions on the Jesuits. They, he said, had caused the Governor of Virginia to order his expedition. Biencourt indignantly asked him then to turn over Father Biard to French justice. He would be hanged, he said. Argall refused.

Leaving Biencourt and his men to spend a winter of frightful hardship, Argall sailed for Jamestown on November 9, 1613, according to Father Biard. He still had three vessels. Two days later, the eve of St. Martin's Day, a fierce storm blew up, separating them. The tiny bark was never heard from again. The captured French ship, under Argall's lieutenant William Turner, and with the two Jesuits aboard, fought the wind for more than two weeks trying to follow Argall but finally gave up and sailed for the Azores and, eventually, England. Argall himself stood for Jamestown in the *Treasurer.*

Father Biard, who was not along, later said that Argall's return voyage took "three weeks or thereabouts." Although there is no way of knowing where he got his information, the estimate was surely not far wrong. Biard, however, clearly did not know that Argall most probably sailed into New York Bay on the way. There he is said to have visited a "pretended Dutch Governor" on what must have been Manhattan Island.[12] Whatever the details of the supposed meeting, ten years or so later Argall was concerned about the Dutch being there again.

After Argall's ship got to Jamestown, all was evidently calm for two months or so. In the meantime, the same Captain Adams of previous Jamestown voyages had returned there early in 1614 with a cargo of silkworms and letters (as well as much-needed food supplies) and was ready to sail again. Sir Thomas Gates had been on a leave of absence from command in the Netherlands and at that time decided to avail himself of the chance to return, partly to collect back pay. With him he was willing to take one of the French prisoners, M. La Motte-le-Vilin. He left the colony's affairs to Sir Thomas Dale to administer as Deputy Governor with full authority.

Apparently within a matter of days after the ship left, Dale was ready with a new plan to reduce the Indians to his will. He "put himself into Captain Argall's ship," as he phrased it in a letter, packed a hundred and fifty men into the newly built frigate, and accompanied by "other boats" sailed around into the York River to

Powhatan's old residence, Werowocomoco. There, he explained, Powhatan "can in two or three days, draw a thousand men together" — a bit of exaggeration worthy of John Smith at his best. With him he carried Pocahontas! [13]

It was a day or two after the apocalyptic advent of this fleet before the Indians sent anyone to ask what they wanted. Dale replied with military starch that he had brought Powhatan's daughter, Pocahontas, who would be returned to him if he would comply with the conditions which had been agreed on months before: the surrender of stolen tools, arms, and so on and the return of captive Englishmen.

The Indians, whoever they were, demanded time to send to Powhatan for instructions. Dale agreed, and hostages were exchanged to ensure compliance. The next day, however, word came that Powhatan was three days' journey away but that his brother Opechancanough was nearby. They would deliver Dale's message to him. Whatever Opechancanough did or said, they vowed, Powhatan would confirm.

Dale refused this offer. The hostages were returned on both sides, after a minor altercation. Then there was further delay.

Dale, suspicious of all this, decided on direct action. He landed a party. The Indians shot at the whitemen. The whitemen returned fire, killed some Indians, wounded others, marched inland, and burned houses and stole what corn they could find. Then they spent the night on shore.

In the morning, Dale took his fleet farther upstream. The Indians sent men to follow them who called out to know where they were going. Dale let them know that the English would burn everything if they did not fulfil their engagement about the men, arms, and corn. At that, the Indians promised to do what Dale wanted the very next day. Dale then agreed to go ashore again and wait.

At that point Pocahontas disembarked. Going toward the Indians, as Dale described it, she

> would not talk to any of them, scarce[ly] to them of the best sort, and to them only, [saying] that if her father had loved her, he would not value her less than old swords, pieces [guns], or axes: wherefore she should still dwell with the English men, who loved her.

At last a messenger arrived from Powhatan, declaring that the guns, swords, and tools would be brought to Jamestown within fifteen days, along with some corn. Furthermore, Powhatan said that his daughter should be Dale's child and always live with him so that they would always be friends.

In addition, he mentioned some of his people and neighboring Kings whom he wanted included in the general peace. And he promised that any runaway Englishmen would be returned to Jamestown and that if any of his men stole anything or killed cattle, he would send them, too, to Jamestown to be punished as the Englishmen saw fit. Dale at last accepted these terms and returned to Jamestown.

In due time, the arms and tools were brought back and baskets of corn began to reach the colony. Even Opechancanough was reconciled, in appearance at least. He "desired [Dale] would call him friend, that he might call [Dale] so." Declaring that he, Opechancanough, was a great captain and fighter, he averred that Dale was that as well. Therefore he loved him, and Dale's friends would be his friends. So, to use Dale's own words,

> the bargain was made, and every eight or ten days, I have messages and presents from him, that he much desireth to continue friendship.

Thus peace was established between Powhatan and the English

early in the spring of 1614. And it was Pocahontas' speech and her attitude and her faith in the English which made it possible.

Is it too much to suggest that at that time, in Pocahontas' mind, "the English" were summed up in the person of John Rolfe?

CHAPTER 10

Pocahontas' Wedding and Peace with the Indians

IT HAD BEEN nearly a year since Samuel Argall had brought Pocahontas to Jamestown. During that time, as has been mentioned, John Rolfe met her and fell in love with her.

But Rolfe was a Calvinist, even a strict one. To marry a "strange wife" would incur the "heavy displeasure" of Almighty God. Was not the tenth chapter of *Ezra* a great preachment against marrying outside one's race?

Still, John Rolfe's heart seems to have paid little heed to the dictates of his head with regard to the strict interpretation of the Word of God. As a result, his mind gradually began to seek ways to circumvent the Lord's displeasure. Would it not, as one letter of Rolfe's struggled to say, "be an act pleasing to God and beneficial to ourselves, if I were to marry and bring to Christ this poor heathen?" [1]

So, in time, possibly before the end of the year 1613, Rolfe set himself to the task of clarifying his thoughts by writing a long and open letter to the Deputy Governor, Sir Thomas Dale.[2] It was a matter, he wrote,

> of no small moment concerning my own particular, which here I impart unto you, and which toucheth me so nearly as the tender-

> ness of my Salvation. Howbeit, I freely subject myself to your grave and mature judgment, deliberation, approbation, and determination . . . either persuading me to desist, or encouraging me to persist herein with a religious fear and godly care . . .

After this and much more by way of preamble, Rolfe wrestled, by way of the written word, with his conscience, considered graphically the "dreadful Day of Judgment" and "the unbridled desire of carnal affection," and expounded at length his plan to undertake

> so weighty a matter . . . for the good of the plantation, the honor of our country, for the glory of God, for mine own salvation, and for the converting to the true knowledge of God and Jesus Christ an unbelieving creature, namely Pohahuntas, to whom my heart and best thoughts are and have been a long time so entangled and enthralled in so intricate a labyrinth, that I was even a-wearied to unwind myself thereout . . .

Rolfe acknowledged that he was aware of what had happened to the sons of Levi and Israel, and of the wicked instigations of "him who seeketh and delighteth in man's destruction," considering that after all he was in love with "one whose education hath been rude, her manners barbarous, her generation cursed, and so discrepant in all nutriture [rearing] from myself."

This was obviously the work of the devil. But when he thought he had won out against such temptations, another "more gracious temptation" had even aroused him from sleep at night to say that he had neglected "to perform the duty of a good Christian." And this happened "even when she hath been farthest separated from me."

"Why dost thou not endeavor to make her a Christian?" the voice of the "more gracious temptation" asked. For, in addition to her "great appearance of love" for him, she desired "to be taught and instructed in the knowledge of God." Indeed, there were the promises of "the Holy Prophet Daniel to the righteous," which bring many to that very thing.

But marriage? Rolfe at length got around to mentioning this clearly.

And with the aid of Calvin's *Institutions,* with the chapter and verse cited, he reached the involved conclusion that an unbelieving wife is sanctified by a believing husband. Even such children as they might have would be holy, though only one parent were faithful. They would "differ from the unclean seed of idolatry."

To conclude, after tossing in a few Latin quotations for greater emphasis, John Rolfe submitted himself to Marshal Dale, for God's glory, Dale's honor, their country's good, the plantation's benefit, and the converting of an irregenerate to regeneration. All this with the purely implied purpose of getting official permission to marry the girl!

A final paragraph opened then with Rolfe's defiance of "the vulgar sort" who might see in his "godly labor" nothing but a means of satisfying his sexual appetite.

This was absurd, he stated, for he "might satisfy such desire . . . with Christians more pleasing to the eye," and with less fear of an offence "unlawfully committed." He could obviously obtain a match in his own country to his "great content." But he determined on this course as a duty imposed on him by the Almighty. Not doubting of Dale's gracious acceptance, he closed the letter

> beseeching Almighty God to rain down upon you such plenitude of his heavenly graces as your heart can wish and desire. And so I rest. At your command most willing to be disposed.
>
> JO: ROLFE

This epistle addressed to the [Deputy] Governor covers four foolscap pages and is not simple to read, despite the clear handwriting.[3] It obviously has a strange ring to modern ears, and some historians have seen little love and a vast amount of religious rationalization in it. Yet one recent writer has correctly observed that just "such were the extravangances and complexities of the contemporary evangelical mind." [4]

There is nothing to indicate that Sir Thomas Dale was particularly qualified to unravel the theological problem. As Deputy Governor, however, he had authority to give his consent to the marriage. This he did, "well approving," as Ralph Hamor put it. And Hamor was in a position to know, for he was the bearer of Rolfe's letter to Dale.[5]

Immediately thereafter, Pocahontas' brothers were informed of the impending wedding, as requested by John Rolfe. Otherwise, according to Hamor, they "would not have departed their river without other conditions." The Indians had no more reason to trust the English than the English the Indians.

In this way, Powhatan learned that Pocahontas was ready and willing to marry John Rolfe, though there seems to exist no record anywhere that says that she *was* willing. Furthermore, what happened to Kocoum, if there was such a person, is not known. Divorce existed among the Algonkian Indians, and Powhatan himself could presumably have dissolved the marriage if he thought proper. As it was, he only dispatched word of his consent, promptly.

Ten days later, Powhatan sent "an old uncle" of Pocahontas', named Opachisco, "to give her as his deputy in the church, and two of his sons to see the marriage solemnized."

This event, unique in the annals of Virginia, took place about April 5, 1614. It was followed by an equally unique, if short-lived, era. For the English, Hamor wrote,

> ever since . . . have had friendly commerce and trade, not only with Powhatan himself, but also with his subjects round about us; so as now I see no reason why the colony should not thrive apace.

Sir Thomas Dale himself had this to say about the marriage in a letter:

> Powhatan's daughter I caused to be carefully instructed in Christian religion, who after she had made some good progress therein renounced publicly her country['s] idolatry, openly confessed her Christian faith, was, as she desired, baptized, and is since married to an English gentleman of good understanding.[6]

Dale, be it said, had already been convinced as a military man that "the God of battles" had a "helping hand" in producing peace with the Indians, for his army had swept over the unfortunate people like the car of Juggernaut — killing, burning, and spoliating. So he mostly saw in Pocahontas' wedding an "other knot to bind this peace the stronger." Nevertheless, he was most contented with the happy conclusion:

> Her father and friends gave approbation to it, and her uncle gave her to him in the church. She lives civilly and lovingly with him [Rolfe], and I trust will increase in goodness, as the knowledge of God increaseth in her. She will go into England with me, and were it but the gaining of this one soul I will think my time, toil, and present stay well spent.

Alexander Whitaker, likewise, attributed the peace to Dale's military prowess and ruthlessness — a strange attitude, perhaps, for a minister. On June 18, the same day as Dale wrote his letter, Whitaker wrote to his cousin, William Gouge, minister of the Blackfriars' church in London:

> Sir Thomas Dale, our religious and valiant Governor, hath now brought that to pass which never before could be effected. For by war upon our enemies and kind usage of our friends, he hath brought them to seek peace of us, which is made, and they dare not break. But that which is best, one Pocahontas or Matoa, the

> daughter of Powhatan, is married to an honest and discreet English gentleman, Master Rolfe, and that after she had openly renounced her country['s] idolatry, confessed the faith of Jesus Christ, and was baptized; which thing Sir Thomas Dale had labored a long time to ground in her.[7]

The couple seems to have been married by the Rev. Richard Buck, a staunch Puritan, in Jamestown.[8] Rolfe owned property across the James River, near John Smith's New Fort, and also downstream on what is now Mulberry Island. Where the new couple set up housekeeping does not seem to be recorded.

However it was, peace being at last achieved with Powhatan, Deputy Governor Dale decided to make certain of the friendship of another body of Indians, the semi-independent Chickahominies, who were not only near neighbors but also a powerful people.

Fortunately, the Chickahominies made the first move. They had learned of the marriage and the peace concluded between Dale and Powhatan and did not want to be left friendless in the face of such a combination.

Two Chickahominy representatives arrived at Dale's residence bearing "two fat bucks for present to our King" — as Dale was "reputed and termed amongst them." Prompted by their cockarouses and a variety of motives, they offered themselves "and service" to him.

At the same time, they admitted that the Chickahominies and the English had at times been enemies. Now they were ready to "become not only our trusty friends, but even King James's subjects and tributaries." In token of which they were ready to "relinquish their old name of Chickahominies, and take upon them, as they call us, the name of Tossantessas" — a distortion of a common Indian name for the English, the meaning of which is far from precisely established, perhaps "strangers."

The Chickahominies, who had survived for unnumbered generations without an autocrat, then added that they entreated Sir Thomas Dale, as a deputy of King James, to become their "supreme head, king, and governor." But with a flourish of practicality seldom to be found among King James' subjects, they suggested that they would like, when King James did not need them, "to enjoy their own laws and liberties . . . to be governed as formerly by eight of the elders and principal men among them."

Sir Thomas agreed to think the matter over, adding that on such-and-such a day he would send some of his men "to propose certain conditions unto them." If they accepted these, he would agree to be their werowance. In token of good faith he then offered them a quantity of copper in return for the venison they had brought. This they refused. It was a free gift. At that, Dale dismissed them.

Something was evidently in the wind. A mere seven years had slipped by since the English had settled on an all-but island in Paspahegh territory. Yet Powhatan himself had already decided to ally his people with them by marriage. Could the Chickahominies risk not following suit?

They clearly could not copy Powhatan's procedure, for they had no "royal family" to supply a marital alliance. They were a democracy. And in the democratic spirit, they chose to negotiate. They were strong enough in number to yield on many trivial points, provided they could still preserve some semblance of independence. After all, they had had experience with this sort of thing for many, many winters with Powhatan and had succeeded reasonably well. The Chickahominy cockarouses might therefore well doubt that the unpredictable English would be likely to prove more intractable than the despot across the York River from them, one of whose residences was at the head of the river they called their own. Such, more or less, must have been the Chickahominy motives.

Dale's motives were simpler, and his action quite direct. A few days after receiving the Chickahominy proposal, he put Samuel Argall in charge of a barge and the recently built frigate, along with fifty men well armed. Then, taking personal command, he conducted the expedition up the Chickahominy, with its ticklish shoals and marshes. Nearly ten miles upstream the river became narrow, though deep enough for the boats, and bent sharply to the west. There were cattail swamps and bogs on both sides of the river.[9]

After another sharp bend, higher ground was visible, and on it stood scores of Indians, waving and hallooing. Dale sent a messenger ashore to tell them to be quick, for he had but little time. At that, the Indians sent runners and canoe-men to bring their elders, their cockarouses, to meet the barge. And Dale and Argall made themselves comfortable for the night.

The next morning, Dale decided to remain on board, hiding from the Indians for some unexplained reason. He sent Argall as his deputy to discuss the proposed truce or treaty. As soon as Argall landed and met the cockarouses, there began long discourses on both sides.

In the end, Argall summed up the whitemen's terms, but in what language or how, the records do not state. He was conciliatory, though firm. The "great white werowance," he said, had accepted their offer of peace and friendship and had sent him to confirm this. "All former injuries on both sides" would be "set apart and forgotten." But there were conditions — six of them.

First, the Chickahominies should call themselves *Tossantessas,* that is, "Englishmen," and they would become subjects of King James and his deputy, Governor Dale.

Second, they should not kill any men or cattle belonging to the colony, and they would agree to bring back any men or cattle which strayed into their territory.

Third, they should be ready to supply three or four hundred archers upon demand, to aid the English

> against the Spaniards, whose name is odious amongst them, for Powhatan's father was driven by them from the West Indies into those parts . . .

a noteworthy requirement, which may well have been totally incomprehensible to the cockarouses. And these three or four hundred archers should be ready to help against other Indians, too.

Fourth, they should not approach or attempt to enter the fort without identifying themselves, after which they would at all times be welcome.

Fifth, each and every one of their fighting men (here much overestimated at five hundred) should bring two bushels of corn at the beginning of their harvest, for which they would receive a like number of iron "tomahawks," or small hatchets.

And lastly, the eight cockarouses would each receive a red coat every year as a livery, along with a copper medallion of King James on a copper chain, and would be known as King James' "noble men" (surely not "noblemen"!). On their side, they would be then responsible for the behavior of their people and the maintenance of the treaty.

These conditions were assented to, one by one, with great shouts and much noise. Then the cockarouses explained everything in detail to the tribesmen no less than three times: first to the old men, then to the young men, and finally to the women and children.

The benefits of these conditions were especially explained, for the Chickahominies wanted to know not only that the English would protect them from Powhatan but also that they would profit by trade with the English.

Ralph Hamor, in reporting on the discussions, stressed the fear of Powhatan rather than the other aspects of the agreement. Yet if fear was the prime mover in the Chickahominy decision, it is far more likely that it was fear of the English themselves.

When all of this speech-making was finished, Argall produced eight great copper medallions (without King James' effigy) and eight great tomahawks, and presented them to the eight cockarouses. They, in turn, reciprocated with venison, turkeys, fresh fish, baskets, mats, and whatnot. This was the signal for unstinted trading to begin. The formal assembly was over. In Hamor's words:

> Then every man brought to sell to our men skins, bowls, mats, baskets, tobacco, etc., and became as familiar amongst us as if they had been Englishmen indeed.

It is almost certainly to this treaty that John Rolfe referred when he wrote in 1616 that it

> still continued so firm, that our people yearly plant and reap quietly, and travel in the woods a-fowling and a-hunting as freely and securely from fear of danger or treachery as in England.[10]

Yet it was the marriage of Pocahontas that brought the peace. The treaty with the Chickahominies was its inevitable result.

CHAPTER 11

Peace Within the Colony

WHATEVER THE REASON for Dale's not revealing his presence during the conclusion of the treaty, the barge and the frigate sailed back to Jamestown with the Deputy Governor still concealed. Argall by then was making plans to return to England. There were letters to take, including reports on the Spanish and French prisoners, and Ralph Hamor and three Frenchmen were to go along. Before leaving, however, Hamor wanted to get a glimpse of the fearsome monarch named Powhatan. And Dale not only permitted him to go but even added a curious mission for his benefit.

Hamor was to take young Thomas Savage, then about nineteen,[1] as an interpreter, along with two Indian guides to seek out Powhatan and

> to deal with him, [to see] if by any means I [Hamor] might procure a daughter of his, who (Pocahontas being already in our possession) is generally reported to be his delight, and darling, and surely he esteemeth her as his own soul, for surer pledge of peace.

The party left "the Bermudas," now called Bermuda Hundred, early Sunday morning, May 15.[2] While it is impossible to trace the route they followed, the distance amounted to sixty miles, according to their calculations, and they reached their objective the next night about midnight. This would seem to be pretty fast marching along trails that wound mostly through dense forest.

Be that as it may, when they arrived on the shore of the Pamunkey River, they shouted for a canoe to ferry them over to Powhatan's residence at Matchcot — almost certainly the village called Maskunt through which Captain John Smith had been taken when he was a prisoner in December, 1607.[3] Commenting on this long trek, Hamor underlined the happy state of relations then existing between the Indians and the whitemen by stressing that they slept one night out in the open, "fearless and without danger," which would have been impossible even a year before.

When they reached the other side of the Pamunkey, Powhatan himself came to the landing-place to greet them, recognizing Thomas Savage immediately. First recalling that Savage had deserted him without his permission and that his own servant Namontack had never been returned by the English (though he had appeared briefly for Powhatan's "coronation"),[4] Powhatan turned to Hamor,

> and his first salutation, without any words at all, was about my neck; and with his hand he felt round about it, so as I might have imagined he would have cut my throat, but that I knew he durst not . . .

Then he asked Hamor where "the chain of pearl" was. Hamor knew nothing about a "chain of pearl."

Powhatan explained that he had sent it to Dale on the latter's arrival as a present. Then when peace had been concluded, at the time of Pocahontas' marriage, Dale had voluntarily sent word that if he authorized any emissary to him, the emissary would wear that chain, and Powhatan would know that he was Dale's representative. Otherwise, he was to send the emissary back to Dale.

Hamor did not know quite what to say. At that time he did not know that Dale had made such an arrangement and had given the chain to his page to deliver to Hamor. But the page forgot it, leaving Hamor in total ignorance of the matter. Hamor, nevertheless, was equal to the occasion. He said that Dale intended the chain to be used only when he sent a representative on some urgent matter, without advance notice and without any Indian guide. In his case, Dale had given him two Indian guides, one of whom was one of Powhatan's own councillors. *They* were testimony, he said. No mute chain was needed.

With that Powhatan was contented and escorted Hamor and Savage and their guides to his residence, "not full a stone's cast from the waterside." The two Englishmen entered after Powhatan, who sat himself on his mat, with a comely young woman on either side of him — his queens at the moment. Outside, a hundred archers stood on guard.

The ceremonial tobacco pipe was filled and lighted. Powhatan puffed it solemnly, then offered it to Hamor. When Hamor had returned the courtesy, the pipe was laid by, and Powhatan inquired about Dale's health. Satisfied on that score, he then asked about Pocahontas, "her marriage, his unknown son [Rolfe], and how they liked, lived and loved together."

Hamor answered that his daughter was so contented that she "would not change her life to return to live with him."

At this, Powhatan laughed heartily, saying that he was very glad of it. "Now proceed," he went on, "to deliver the cause of your unexpected coming."

Hamor objected that his message was private, to be delivered without anyone present excepting the member of Powhatan's council who had been his guide. Thereupon Powhatan dismissed everyone but kept his two queens by his side.

Hamor began, through Thomas Savage, by offering various gifts which Dale had sent to his "brother," the Indian ruler. This accomplished, and the gifts accepted, Hamor came down to the point:

> The bruit [tidings] of the exquisite perfection of your youngest daughter, being famous through all your territories, hath come to the hearing of your brother, Sir Thomas Dale, who for this purpose hath addressed me hither, to entreat you by that brotherly friendship you make profession of, to permit her (with me) to return unto him, partly for the desire which himself hath, and partly for the desire her sister hath, to see her, of whom, if fame hath not been prodigal, as like enough it hath not, your brother (by your favor) would gladly make his nearest companion, wife and bedfellow . . .

Powhatan attempted several times to interrupt, but Hamor begged him to wait until he had finished. Dale wanted him to add that he expected to live the rest of his life in Virginia and would like to see a closer union between himself and his brother.

When he had at last finished, Powhatan was more than ready with an answer. First remarking that Dale had been anything but proper in his gifts, which were far from being as "ample" as he was accustomed to — Captain Newport had been much more gracious — he continued dryly:

> But to the purpose: my daughter whom my brother desireth I sold within these few days to be wife to a great werowance for two bushels of roanoke, and it is true she is already gone with him, three days' journey from me.

Hamor quickly protested that Powhatan was so great a monarch that he could give back the beads and recall his daughter. After all Dale could give him treble the price for her.

Powhatan broke in, as Hamor recorded it, that his daughter was as dear as life itself to him and that none of his many children delighted him as much. If he did not see her often, he could not live. If she lived with the English, he added pointedly, he could not see her at all,

> having with himself resolved upon no terms whatsoever to put himself into our hands, or come amongst us, and therefore entreated me to urge that suit no further, but return his brother this answer: I desire no firmer assurance of his friendship than his promise, which he hath already made . . .

Powhatan had been irritated from the moment Hamor mentioned the matter of his daughter. Now he was wound up. The English already had one of his daughters, he lectured. She was a pledge. It was not brotherly of Dale to ask for another. And even if Dale had no pledge at all, he had nothing to fear. Too many Englishmen and Indians had already been killed. Powhatan would not cause the death of any more. And if the Englishmen caused *him* any further grief, he would merely move still farther away.

It was late; Powhatan at length concluded. The business was settled. He summoned a man to bring them bread, and he offered them a little wine which Newport had given him half a dozen years before. Then at his command they were escorted to a house to sleep.

Hardly had they stretched their limbs on the sleeping mats, however, than a battalion of fleas set to work. Tired as they were from the long march, both Hamor and Savage had to pick up their mats, shake them, and take them out of doors to sleep in the open.

In the morning, Powhatan came personally to escort the two of them to his residence, where they breakfasted. Hunters had been sent out already to procure venison and turkeys for their supper and by ten o'clock had returned well laden. (Hamor evidently was outside the residence watching.) About then, despite Hamor's confused chronology, it seems that an Englishman came to the village who had been surprised by some Indians near Fort Henry three years before and led off. Hearing of Hamor's and Savage's presence there, he looked them up and begged to be taken back to the colony. By then, Hamor noted, between his Indian clothes and his tanned complexion, the Englishman could not be distinguished from an Indian but by his "tongue."

Hamor immediately went with him to Powhatan, saying that the Indians had long since told them that this man had fallen sick and died. But because he had not, he must now be taken back. If not, Dale would undoubtedly send for him.

Powhatan took no pains to conceal his anger. The English had one of his daughters, he said, and he was not unhappy over that. But, he went on,

> you can no sooner see or know of any Englishman's being with me, but you must have him away, or else break peace and friendship. If you must needs have him, he shall go with you, but I will send no guides along with you, so as if any ill befall you by the way, thank yourselves.

Hamor replied that he knew the way, without a guide, but that Dale would have "just occasion to distrust his [Powhatan's] love if he returned him [Hamor] without guides" or if anything happened to him en route. At that, Powhatan turned away "in passion and discontentment."

At suppertime Powhatan sent for Hamor to give him some provisions but said nothing about his going back to the colony. Nevertheless about midnight he came to him and Savage to tell them that their guide would be ready to leave early in the morning. In addition, Powhatan recited a list of articles he would like to have from Dale: copper, a shaving knife, bone combs, a grindstone, fishhooks or a seine, a cleaving-froe for lath, and a cat and a dog. In return, he would give Dale a supply of skins.

Insisting that Hamor repeat the list several times, Powhatan seemed to set great store by the punctilious carrying out of this mission. Even the next morning he repeated what he wanted, at the same time giving Hamor and Savage a buck-skin each. Then, on the way to their canoe, he solemnly told Hamor, "I hope this [answer to Dale] will give him good satisfaction. If it do not, I will go three days journey farther from him, and never see Englishmen more." But he agreed to receive further emissaries from Dale and to treat them well.

Hamor left with the conviction that Powhatan sincerely wanted to preserve the peace. Whether the captive Englishman accompanied him and Savage to "the Bermudas" is apparently not recorded. Still, special significance attaches to this visit of Hamor's. It was the last time Powhatan received an Englishman in audience.

While Hamor was away, Dale uncovered a new attempt at subverting the colony. There had been two already during his term of office — for the colonists generally were an unruly lot — but the one of the summer of 1614 was more serious. One Edward Coles and a man named Kitchin, with three others who composed the guard of Don Diego de Molina, slipped away at Molina's behest to try to reach the Spanish settlements in Florida, more than four hundred miles to the south.

They had traveled five days' journey before the Indians sent after them by Dale caught up with them and brought them back to Jamestown. There they were promptly executed. The charge was that they had let a prisoner of war go (an odd way of saying that they had quit guarding him), for there was no law against their deserting *overland.* Gates and Dale, who to all purposes drew up the code of laws for Virginia, had not dreamed that anyone would be so desperate as to try to reach a Spanish settlement through a virtually trackless, hostile waste.[5]

After this, Molina was put in a detention camp a mile from Jamestown, a treatment which he reported to the Spanish ambassador in London in a letter he wrote on June 4, "with great labor . . . with a root from the fields." He added that Dale had promised him that he could leave with Argall when he sailed for England, but had broken his word. "From this," he philosophized, "may be seen the want of truth in these men." But as things turned out, Dale took him to England with himself—though not until nearly two years later.

On or just after June 18, 1614, Argall at last got away. After a quick crossing, he reached England in July. Once in London, he reported to Sir Thomas Smythe and the Virginia Company without delay on:

> the present estate of their colony; and [said] that the English were now become laborious and industrious, and were plenteously stored with food of their own, and well furnished with good houses in sundry places for their habitation.

Whereas another chronicler recorded: "In former time the English were extreme slothful and would rather perish in idleness than prosper by labor." [6]

Argall undoubtedly reported what he had been told to report, regardless of his own knowledge, impressions, or opinion. A far different picture was given, however, in the "Brief Declaration" which was drawn up ten years later and signed by twenty-nine of the surviving ancient planters. Of Dale's administration, they wrote, beginning with the building of Henrico,

> he oppressed his whole company with such extraordinary labors by day and watching by night as may seem incredible to the ears of any who had not the experimental trial thereof. Want of houses . . . and pinching hunger . . . made those imposed labors most insufferable, and the best fruits thereof to be no better than the slaughter of His Majesty's subjects by starving, hanging, burning, breaking upon the wheel and shooting to death: some (more than half famished) running to the Indians to get relief [and] being

> returned were burned to death. . . . Under this tyrannous government the colony continued for the space of five years [1611–16], in which time many whose necessities forced the breach of those laws, by the strictness and severity thereof suffered death and other punishments . . .[7]

What the truth of the matter was is difficult to know. There are few contemporary records of what went on in Jamestown and the rest of the colony. Ralph Hamor had sailed with Argall, and John Rolfe was apparently too busy with tobacco to keep a diary or write letters. Thus while it is certain that peace still reigned with the Indians, the peace that reigned within the colony may have been the peace of a detention camp.

In England, meanwhile, an investigation of Argall's behavior in New England and Acadia was under way. In October, 1613, when Admiral Henri de Montmorency wrote to the King about the raid on what France considered a legitimate settlement, the Privy Council had been noncommittal. Three weeks elapsed. Prodded into action, apparently, the same Council went on record that no word had been received from Jamestown since June, 1613, which was before the "raid" and that an inquiry would be instituted as soon as Argall himself returned to England. This was announced for the spring of 1614.[8]

Upon his arrival, therefore, Argall was faced with charges that he had encroached on French rights in Canada to the damage of the honor of the King of France and of the exchequer of the Marquise de Guercheville. The specific date when he was examined is not known. The records of the Privy Council, however, indicate that the matter had not yet been settled when King James' ambassador to France left for Paris late in July.[9] In addition, a partly destroyed manuscript bears witness to Argall's defense when the case was eventually heard, and both he and his lieutenant William Turner were evidently exonerated.[10]

Meanwhile, Captain John Smith had returned from a five-month expedition to New England, during which he mapped the coast from Maine to Cape Cod. Although he heard that there were French ships forty leagues to the west, Smith saw no trace of Frenchmen for the simple reason that Argall had removed all signs of their occupancy.

By an odd quirk of fate, it was Smith who suffered for Argall's "misdeeds," while Argall himself went free. For in 1615 Smith ran afoul of a French privateer who took him prisoner without due cause and who excused himself by accusing Smith of "responsibility for Samuel Argall's raid on the French settlement in Maine in 1613." Smith was able to escape when a storm wrecked the privateer but seems never to have recouped what he lost when he was captured.[11]

In London, Argall appears to have taken no small umbrage at the very questioning of his actions. He was obeying orders, he maintained, and nothing more, and he had kept his word to the Frenchmen in the face of the Governor's harshness of temper.

In obvious disgust, Argall apparently even thought of severing connections with the Virginia enterprise — though not with his cousin, Sir Thomas Smythe. A terse entry in the Court Minutes of the East India Company, of which Sir Thomas was Governor, reads:

> November 8, 1614. Captain Newport to be spoken with, Captain Argall having become a suitor for employment.[12]

Newport obviously was "to be spoken with" as a man who might have something pertinent to say about Argall's character or ability. He in fact had left the Virginia Company himself after taking Sir Thomas Dale to Virginia in 1611, only to be publicly insulted by the irascible Dale on their arrival at Jamestown. Within three weeks or so of his return to England, the East India Company gave him the command of the ship *Expedition* in their twelfth "voyage to India," surely on the recommendation of Sir Thomas Smythe.

He had arrived back in the Downs on July 10, about the same time as Argall.[13]

While it is impossible to know precisely what changed Argall's mind with regard to the East India Company, it is clear that news of some change of policy in the Virginia Company must have reached his ears. From the outset, the company had set its collective mind on making a profit on its investment. As the years rolled by and disappointment turned into something not far short of despair, it became evident that the colonial scheme would have to be given over unless substantial additional capital were forthcoming. With additional capital and increased investment in men as well as matériel, the Jamestown colony might still be turned into a profitable enterprise. (John Rolfe was struggling with the problem from another point of view when he introduced West Indian tobacco into the necessitous James River economy.) And lo, the idea of a public lottery came up.

Queen Elizabeth had sponsored a lottery in 1567 to raise money "for the reparation of havens and the strength of the realm." Though it was not entirely a success, the idea was not abandoned, and a few smaller lotteries were drawn after King James came to the throne.

Then, at the time of the Third Virginia Charter, in 1612, the government had authorized the company to augment its financial resources through lotteries. To be sure, the "First Great Standing Lottery" held that same year had disappointing results, and an attempt was made to remedy the deficiency through a flurry of smaller lotteries. But in 1614 plans for a second lottery were afoot. These included, in addition to whatever funds might come in from the lottery proper, an appeal to the towns, cities, and counties of England for support for the company. All of this activity may well have been an important factor in Argall's decision to continue with the Virginia Company.

Finally in February, 1615, the Privy Council, after much hesitation, consented to a widespread appeal, and a broadside, or public announcement, of the lottery was printed.[14] That month or the next, Samuel Argall again boarded the ship *Treasurer* for the Virginia Company. He evidently had something more than mere navigation in mind.

From the time of Argall's Virginia trading voyages of 1612, it had begun to be patent that he was not only a skilful mariner but also a trader of no small gifts. True, he had inherited some capital, and more than one modest annuity, which taken together could have made possible his purchase of a share in the *Treasurer*. But that, most clearly, was only a beginning.

On his return from the "raid" on Acadia, Argall dropped a hint as to how he proposed to augment his personal resources — if he was not already engaged in doing it. In 1615, Ralph Hamor wrote:

> I have heard it credibly reported, even from the mouth of Captain Argall, that in one small ship, and in one voyage, the French have cleared eight thousand pounds by trade with the Indians for furs, which benefit will be as easily by us procured.

By that token, the fur trade would have been a logical reason for Argall's addiction to a northerly route from England to Virginia by way of the New England coast and New York and Delaware Bays.[15]

Whatever the truth of the matter, Argall, noted for his discovery of a quick route to Virginia in the "height" [latitude] of thirty degrees, occupied himself from late February, or very early March, until the summer of 1615 in reaching Virginia from England by a more northerly and shorter route.[16] No-one really knows what he did for so long a time on the way.

In fact, it is difficult to know just what Argall did *after* he got to

Virginia. The best informed people in England seemed not to know about either his activities or those of anyone else in Virginia. George, Lord Carew of Clopton, for example, wrote to His Majesty's ambassador to the Great Mogul in India, in January, 1616, that "the plantation at Virginia and Bermuda sleeps." [17] Did Argall find that literally true?

There had indeed been years, not too long before, when the bulk of the colony spent the hours daydreaming, if not sleeping, each imagining himself a Roman proconsul and subordinate to no-one on the scene. But with the arrival of Gates and De La Warr, some measure of work had been stimulated. Next came Dale, a year later, with a will to convert the slovenly colony into a beehive, with overtones of an army camp.

Gates' return to England (and thence to his post in Holland) had left Dale a free hand to put the colony on its feet. Gates also left George Yeardley, a former captain in his company in the Netherlands, as deputy to his own deputy. (Captain Argall was a navigator, able commander, and trader, but not an "executive.") Yeardley was of the same mental make-up as Dale. He was heir to the military tradition most succinctly expressed by Shakespeare, "It fits thee not to ask the reason why." [18] So he could hardly be expected to contribute any great originality to Dale's undertakings.

Up to, and for a while after, Argall's return, Yeardley spent most of his time at Bermuda Nether Hundred, where he managed the largest and busiest of the James River settlements. Bermuda Nether Hundred then had a population of one hundred and nineteen, more or less, including a few farmers and an undisclosed number of men who toiled at such manufactures as pitch and tar, potash, and charcoal. Dr. Alexander Whitaker graced the establishment with his presence and his religious inspiration.[19]

It was here that Samuel Argall found the most evidence of activity on his return in 1615. A "chief city" was being constructed just then across the Appomattox from Bermuda Hundred and fifteen miles by water below Henrico. And because it prospered, other "towns" or plantations were soon started in the neighborhood. All these settlements, each actually numbering but few souls by any standard, formed part of Dale's plan for dispossessing the Indians of enough of their lands to "protect" the English who had squatted there.

In fact, Dale hoped to cut off the whole peninsula, as has been said. With an eye to this, and surely prematurely, a decision was reached to make available to those who invested in the Virginia Company, or went in person to settle, all the land from Henrico on the west to Smith's Island off Cape Charles on the east.

According to a "Brief Declaration" of the Virginia Council dated 1616, this stretch of land was in the "actual possession" of the English "by the Natives' liking and consent." [20] But that the Indians consented or that the area included all the peninsula between the James and the York is highly doubtful. The English had murdered or driven away all the Indians who did not submit to their rule, but the territory they effectively held cannot have extended more than a very few miles inland from the river. Not even Kiskiack, which Dale had originally chosen as his "second" plantation, is mentioned as occupied by the English at this time.

Thus Dale and Yeardley were planting an extensive colony in the wilderness. Single-mindedly, they struggled to make the home of the Indians safe for the colonists. With the Gospel sometimes in one hand, but a musket always in the other, they had brought about their kind of peace with Pocahontas' people.

Within the English pale, another kind of peace prevailed. The Gospel was in hand daily, but so (almost daily) were the knout, the gallows, and the firing squad. It had been commanded that order reign, and at last it did. Even Argall seems to have thought it wise to "lie low."

CHAPTER 12

Leaving the Forest Behind

AFTER RALPH HAMOR left for England in 1614 with that tireless ferryman of colonists and supplies, Captain Samuel Argall, John Rolfe was made Secretary and Recorder of the colony. Then, surely, he and the Princess Pocahontas moved to live in Jamestown, at least for the winter. Summer possibly saw them closer to the fields where Rolfe's experiments with tobacco prospered.

Rolfe served in his new post for a year and ten months. Yet the only known record he left of the colony's activities was the "True Relation" which he wrote in London in (1616–1617). It contains statistics, encouragement, and propaganda, but little history.

Perhaps there was no history. Perhaps the three hundred and fifty-one colonists scattered along the James River with their twelve dozen head of cattle, six horses and mares, two hundred and sixteen goats and unnumbered hogs did nothing beyond laboring in the forests and fields and tinkering with their petty manufactures. Perhaps in reality the colony, in a sense, still slept.

This could not have been to Dale's liking. He had asked Lord Salisbury in his letter of August 17, 1611, to which reference has been made before, for two thousand men to "render the whole country unto His Majesty." Care was taken not to supply him with those men. He had to do what he could without them. Conceivably he was disappointed.[1]

Then, he had been granted permission to absent himself from service with his company in the Netherlands as of January 10/20, 1611, for only three years, and without pay, during which time his command would be held open for him. A short time after, he had married Elizabeth Throckmorton, in England, but she does not seem to have accompanied him to Virginia.[2]

Whether it was his long absence from his wife, or concern about his command in the Netherlands, or a sense of failure in Virginia, Dale had decided as early as 1614 to leave Jamestown. It is small wonder, then, that by the spring of 1616, with Argall's ship the *Treasurer* tied to the trees at Jamestown, or moored off Old Point Comfort, Dale made ready to relinquish his post to Captain George Yeardley and go.

By April, everything was in order, and before the month was out the *Treasurer* sailed. In May, Dale would have completed five years of service as Marshal of Virginia. About half of that time he had also been Deputy Governor. In both capacities he became one of the most controversial figures in American colonial history. Even those who had supported his regime in his own time, and not always merely mildly, delayed but a few years in reversing themselves.

Not only did these colonists berate him for his cruelty, but they also heaped scorn on him for his works. He intended to build a church, they said,

> but not so much as the foundation thereof ever finished, but we [were] contenting ourselves with a church of wood . . . Many other works of like nature were by him done at Henrico and the precincts thereof, but so slightly as before his departure hence, he himself saw the ruin and desolation of most of them . . .[3]

Even the "peace with the Indians" which was attributed in London to Dale's "singular industry and policy" [4] seems, by the same account, to have been far from complete:

> Most part of the time that Sir Thomas Gates and Sir Thomas Dale governed we were at war with the natives, so that by them divers times were many of our people slain, whose blood Sir Thomas Dale neglected not to revenge, by divers and sundry executions, in killing many, cutting down and taking away their corn, burning their houses, spoiling their weirs, et cetera.

It is impossible to know how true these accusations were, but they must be reported.

In any event, before leaving, Sir Thomas Dale made a raid on the Kiskiacks, on the other side of the peninsula, and on the Warraskoyacks, on the other side of the James — to what extent these were "provoked" is far from certain. Next, he left instructions with the Deputy Governor, Captain George Yeardley, to construct certain palisades to protect "some necks of land." [5]

The lading of his ship was another concern of the departing Governor. Dale had a variety of products stowed aboard: some of Rolfe's experimental tobacco; a quantity of sassafras; the usual "samples" of pitch and potash from what was virtually the colony's sole industry; clapboard; and of course sturgeon and caviar.

Then the distinguished Spanish prisoner, Don Diego de Molina, was invited at last to join Dale for his long-promised return to Europe. With him went the renegade English pilot whose fate has already been related. Don Diego's lieutenant was already dead.

But the most important passengers, even including Dale himself, were Pocahontas, the daughter of Powhatan, John Rolfe, her husband, and their little son Thomas. As that indefatigable letter-writer, John Chamberlain, before long wrote, Sir Thomas Dale

> brought with him some ten or twelve old and young of that country [Virginia], among whom the most remarkable person is Pocahuntas (daughter of Powatan a king or cacique of that country) married to one Rolfe, an English man . . .[6]

Dale himself reported his arrival at Plymouth in a letter to his friend and benefactor Sir Ralph Winwood, King James' First Secretary of State since the death of Lord Salisbury. On June 3, from Plymouth, he wrote in part:

> I shall with the greatest speed the wind will suffer me present myself unto you and give you full satisfaction of those parts . . . I shall give Your Honor great encouragements that this Virginia affords (at my arrival) to spur us forwards to inhabit there, if His Majesty wishes to possess one of the goodliest and richest kingdoms of the world, and indeed so fit for no state as ours, if it shall please you honorable fathers of our state to think seriously on it, and His Majesty thoroughly to undertake it . . .[7]

Curiously, there was no mention of Pocahontas.

Captain John Smith, however, soon heard of her arrival. In those very days, his newest book, *A Description of New England,* was being put through the press, and printing was completed on June 18, two days before George Lord Carew jotted down for the benefit of King James' ambassador in India that "Sir Thomas Dale returned from Virginia." In fact, Lord Carew also passed on word that "one Rolfe, who married a daughter of Pohetan called Pocahontas, hath brought his wife with him into England." [8] It is amusing to speculate that in this way the Great Mogul of India may have heard of the Indian Princess from Virginia.

Despite his book just emerging from the press, John Smith hastily put quill to paper again, this time to produce "a little book" addressed to the "most high and virtuous Princess, Queen Anne of

Great Britain." Its subject was Pocahontas, daughter to Powhatan, now known by her Christian baptismal name of the Lady Rebecca.

Eight years later, Smith published in his *Generall Historie* an "abstract" of this epistle, which at least serves to show what he thought of Pocahontas in June, 1616:[9]

MOST ADMIRED QUEEN:
The love I bear my God, my King, and Country, hath so oft emboldened me in the worst of extreme dangers, that now honesty doth constrain me [to] presume thus far beyond myself, to present Your Majesty this short discourse. If ingratitude be a deadly poison to all honest virtues, I must be guilty of that crime if I should omit any means to be thankful.

So it is that some ten years ago, being in Virginia and taken prisoner by the power of Powhatan their chief King, I received from this great Savage exceeding great courtesy, especially from his son Nantaquaus, the most manliest, comeliest, boldest spirit I ever saw in a savage, and his sister Pocahontas, the King's most dear and well-beloved daughter, being but a child of twelve or thirteen years of age, whose compassionate pitiful heart, of my desperate estate, gave me much cause to respect her: I being the first Christian this proud King and his grim attendants ever saw: and thus enthralled in their barbarous power, I cannot say I felt the least occasion of want that was in the power of those my mortal foes to prevent, notwithstanding all their threats.

After some six weeks fatting amongst those savage courtiers, at the minute of my execution, she hazarded the beating out of her own brains to save mine; and not only that, but so prevailed with her father, that I was safely conducted to Jamestown: where I found about eight and thirtie miserable poor and sick creatures, to keep possession of all those large territories of Virginia; such was the weakness of this poor Commonwealth, as had the savages not fed us, we directly had starved. And this relief, most gracious Queen, was commonly brought us by this Lady Pocahontas.

Notwithstanding all these passages, when inconstant Fortune turned our peace to war, this tender Virgin would still not spare to dare to visit us, and by her our jars [brawls, with the Indians?] have been oft appeased, and our wants still supplied; were it the policy of her father thus to employ her, or the ordinance of God thus to make her His instrument, or her extraordinary affection to our Nation, I know not: but of this I am sure; when her father with the utmost of his policy and power sought to surprise me, having but eighteen with me, the dark night could not affright her from coming through the irksome woods, and with watered eyes gave me intelligence, with her best advice to escape his fury; which had he known, he had surely slain her.

Jamestown with her wild train she as freely frequented as her father's habitation; and during the time of two or three years, she next under God, was still the instrument to preserve this colony from death, famine and utter confusion; which if in those times [it] had once been dissolved, Virginia might have line [lain] as it was at our first arrival to this day.

Since then, this business having been turned and varied by many accidents from that I left it at; it is most certain, after a long and troublesome war after my departure, betwixt her father and our colony; all which time she was not heard of.

About two years after, she herself was taken prisoner, being so detained near two years longer, the Colony by that means was relieved, peace concluded; and at last rejecting her barbarous condition, was married to an English gentleman, with whom at this present she is in England; the first Christian ever of that Nation, the first Virginian ever spake English, or had a child in marriage by an Englishman: a matter surely, if my meaning be truly considered and well understood, worthy a Prince's understanding.

Thus, most gracious Lady, I have related to Your Majesty, what at your best leisure our approved histories will account you at large, and done in the time of Your Majesty's life; and however this might be presented you from a more worthy pen, it cannot from a more honest heart. As yet I never begged anything from the state, or any [person]; and it is my want of ability and her exceeding desert, your birth, means and authority, her birth, virtue, want and simplicity, doth make me thus bold, humbly to beseech Your Majesty to take this knowledge of her, though it be from one so unworthy to be the reporter as myself, her husband's estate not being able to make her fit to attend Your Majesty.

The most and least I can do is to tell you this, because none so oft hath tried it as myself, and the rather being of so great a spirit, how ever her stature, she should not be well received, seeing this Kingdom may rightly have a kingdom by her means; her present love to us and Christianity might turn to such scorn and fury, as to divert all this good to the worst of evil. Where finding so great a Queen should do her some honor more than she can imagine, for being so kind to your servants an[d] subjects, would so ravish her with content, as endear her dearest blood to effect that [which] Your Majesty and all the King's honest subjects most earnestly desire.

And so I humbly kiss your gracious hands.

Undoubtedly the original letter was in Smith's own handwriting and signed with his modest, clear, Italian-hand signature — not with the illegible Gothic scrawls so often seen in letters of the time.

It has often been suggested, even stated, that John Smith personally presented Pocahontas to the Queen. In the absence of any reference to such an act in surviving documents, it can only be said that this seems highly unlikely. Smith had one or two friends in court circles, but they were not intimates. King James' court was not easy of access to any but the prominent, the handsome, and the rich. And access through the Virginia Company was virtually out of the question. Smith had in effect severed all relations with the company in general, and had turned his eye toward the group which was backing a colony in New England.

This does not mean, however, that he could not, or did not, appeal to the Queen by letter; or that the abstract he printed differed in substance from the original — indeed the abstract may have been longer than the handwritten letter. Queen Anne was kindly, if frivolous, and would surely have been attracted by such an appeal. But it is too much to say, as has been done, that it was because of Smith that Pocahontas was invited to the court masque on Twelfth Night, 1617. There were others, of far greater importance, who were just as interested in Pocahontas as John Smith.

On her arrival, the Virginia Company allotted a small stipend of £4 a week for her maintenance and that of her son.[10] (John Rolfe was allowed to shift for himself.) At first the family was apparently lodged in the Belle Sauvage Inn, a few yards off Fleet Street just outside Ludgate.[11] Though the hostelry had been in existence for a century and a half by then, its name gave rise to the popular legend that it was named for Pocahontas, and for a while a painting of her served as the inn's sign. The fact is that it was named for the Savage family and was called Savage's Inn. The "Bell" derives from either an old sign of a bell or the fact that it stood close to the "bail," or boundary, of the district.

In any event, the Belle Sauvage was already famous. It was here that a Scottish showman named Banks exhibited his silver-shod horse, which not too long before Pocahontas' day had climbed to the top of old St. Paul's tower, just up the hill — to the delight, wrote Thomas Dekker, "of a number of asses who brayed below."

Here, too, plays were now and then performed by strolling players. Indeed, about the same time, according to that great Puritan William Prynne, at Belle Sauvage Inn there was a "visible apparition of the devil on the stage . . . to the great amazement both of the actors and spectators, while they were profanely playing the *History of Faustus* [by Christopher Marlowe] — the truth of which I have heard from many now alive, who remember it — there being some distracted with that fearful sight." But earlier, a less puritanical playwright had commented on "two prose books played at the Bell Savage, where you shall find never a word without wit, never a line without pith, never a letter placed in vain."

Small wonder it is, then, that "Rare" Ben Jonson should have found Pocahontas at the Belle Sauvage, and in later years introduced her in his comedy *The Staple of News.*[12] In that, a rich uncle, his self-promoting nephew, and his vagabond brother are discussing where to take the nephew's "princess," the wealthy Pecunia, to eat — she being as eager for the nephew as he for her.

The nephew suggests eating at lawyer Picklock's lodging. The uncle agrees. But the boy's vagabond father, Pennyboy Canter, objects:

> *Pen. C.:* Let your meat rather follow you to a tavern.
> *Picklock:* A tavern's as unfit too for a princess.
> *Pen. C.:* No, I have known a princess, and a great one,
> Come forth of a tavern.
> *Picklock:* Not go in, sir, though.
> *Pen. C.:* She must go in, if she came forth: the blessed
> Pokahontas, as the historian calls her,
> And great king's daughter of Virginia,
> Hath been in womb of tavern; — and besides,
> Your nasty uncle will spoil all your mirth,
> And be as noisome.

Not content with this brief mention, Jonson brought up the subject of Pocahontas again in the "Intermean," or "Chorus," where *Tattle* says he would censure the author of the play,

> if he saw cause, for the other princess' sake — Pokahontas, surnamed the Blessed — whom he has abused indeed, and I do censure him, and will censure him: — To say she came forth of a tavern, was said like a paltry poet.

Aside from Ben Jonson's evident amusement at the thought of a princess living in a tavern (or perhaps, of the Indian girl being a princess at all), other heads that were more sophisticated found her presence there understandable, even convenient. The Virginia Company had no intention of squandering its limited resources on Pocahontas' entertainment. But John Rolfe had one resource which could improve the couple's comfort, or social condition.

If he was in truth the man from Heacham in Norfolk, there was a home in Heacham of no mean sort. And in that home was John's mother Dorothy, then aged about fifty-one, who had married Dr. Robert Redmayne, Chancellor of Norwich, some fourteen weeks after the death of John Rolfe, Sr. There was also a brother Henry in London, who was a merchant and perhaps later, a member of the Virginia Company. But he is a shadowy figure about whom nothing else is known. He could possibly have been a year or two older than John, Jr.

An ancient and so far indestructible tradition, perhaps derived from these facts, persists that John Rolfe took his wife the Princess Pocahontas and their child Thomas to Heacham to visit the family — at least, the homestead. An old mulberry-tree in the gardens at Heacham Hall is said to have been planted at the time of this hypothetical visit, and it was known as "Pocahontas' mulberry-tree." But outside the existence of the tree, of which there is a drawing, the only proof of the story which is offered is that in 1605 King James "ordered the planting of mulberry-trees to encourage the silk industry by the cultivation of silk-worms." [13]

In short, no really tangible evidence of a visit to Heacham exists. Yet where tradition is so strong, it would be futile to deny that it could have taken place. There are points that in a negative way lend support to the idea.

The Rolfes were far from a prominent family. Few of their records survive until a later date. Then, if all the family was as Calvinistic as John himself, the others may have been concerned about a marriage with a heathen. It is therefore possible that a visit by so exotic a figure as Pocahontas was kept quiet. Even Henry Rolfe appears on the scene only after her death, when John was looking for someone to take care of little Thomas. What should have been a matter of great family interest, even pride, was ignored, or deliberately forgotten. Or, possibly, John and Henry Rolfe were not of the Rolfes of Heacham.

Putting this mystery aside, it must be mentioned that another tradition, apparently started in 1705 in Robert Beverley's *History,* says that King James was on the verge of throwing John Rolfe in the Tower for marrying a royal princess without first obtaining his permission. This also persists, even though there can be little likelihood that James bothered his royal head about the Indian maid, brought over by the Virginia Company almost as an advertising "gimmick." The King had his own sense of humor.

Be all this as it may, it was not long before Pocahontas was received and entertained by John King, Bishop of London. Whether this was at the instigation of the Virginia Company or of the Rev. Samuel Purchas, that indefatigable collector of information about Virginia and many other places, is not known. In any event, Purchas met John Rolfe, and perhaps also Pocahontas, and borrowed a copy of Rolfe's "Relation of the State of Virginia," which had been prepared for King James. At that time, Purchas was at work on the third edition of his *Pilgrimage,* which is not to be confused with his later and much larger work called the *Pilgrimes.*[14] Thanks to Rolfe's cooperation, he was able to condense the whole to about one-third its original size. This contact, as well as an encounter of Purchas with Sir Thomas Dale, may have brought about the Bishop's dinner party.

Purchas seems to have had his *Pilgrimes* in mind already, for he omitted the account of the Bishop's dinner from the *Pilgrimage.* Then a few years later, when the time came, he related, on page 1774 of volume IV of the mighty *Pilgrimes,* that Rolfe's

> wife did not only accustom herself to civility, but still carried herself as the daughter of a King, and was accordingly respected not only by the Company, which allowed provision for herself and her son, but by divers particular persons of honor, in their hopeful zeal by

> her to advance Christianity. I was present when my honorable and reverend patron, the Lord Bishop of London, Doctor King, entertained her with festival state and pomp beyond what I have seen in his great hospitality to other ladies.[15]

Samuel Purchas was an exceedingly pious — perhaps a somewhat smug and unctuous — divine. At the sight of Pocahontas, done up in the incongruous court dress of the times, his big, round, almost babylike eyes must have opened wider in amazement. Here was personal contact with an apparition from the "vast Unknown" about which he had copied so many other people's reports.

It is likely that Pocahontas and her family were again, or still, at the Belle Sauvage at the time of the Bishop's grand gala. It would have been convenient. Purchas' church was St. Martin Ludgate, a very short walk up Ludgate Hill from the inn, and just inside the old city walls. Not far beyond the church was the Bishop of London's palace, described by a contemporary as "a large thing for receipt [receptions], wherein divers Kings have been lodged, and great house-hold hath been kept." [16]

Despite these amenities, Pocahontas appears to have been taken sick before long. Although the great gate of the inn shut out "the roar and turmoil of Ludgate Hill," the air of London was far from fresh or clean,[17] and a girl accustomed to the unsullied breezes of the virginal forest could not have found the atmosphere breathable.

The city was absurdly overcrowded, with a quarter of a million people, or so, in one- or two-story houses in an area of perhaps a little over two square miles. Above all, the Fleet Valley, only a few yards from the entrance to the Belle Sauvage, had been famous for its "stinking lanes," even in 1560[18] with far fewer people. There is nothing to indicate that the pollution had been abated in the meanwhile.

Pocahontas' state of health was soon noticed, and a better place was found for her to take up residence. This was in Brentford, to the west of London and Westminster, across the river Brent from Syon House, one of the Earl of Northumberland's estates.[19] The Earl's brother George Percy, of Jamestown fame, may possibly have been living there at the time, but there is no record that he and Pocahontas met.

At Brentford the Indian Princess seems to have found rest and health. Nearby there were still traces of ancient forests in the tidy parks across the Thames — a small river by comparison with the James and the York of Pocahontas' homeland. Autumn would soon turn into winter, with the cold and damp of the north and long, long nights. Yet there was peace. And love, within the bounds of John Rolfe's excessive piety.

CHAPTER 13

Pocahontas (and John Smith) in London

ALL THIS WHILE, Captain John Smith was in London. That he should not sooner have tried to visit Pocahontas is hard to understand. Yet there are imaginable causes.

John Smith was anything but an important man in the city, and Pocahontas was being entertained by distinguished members of society. He may have hesitated on account of her "rank." Then there is the matter of John Rolfe, who had arrived in Virginia months after Smith's departure. There is no indication that he and Smith met just then, although Rolfe saw Purchas, at whose house Smith evidently was always a welcome guest.

Furthermore, if Lord De La Warr in any way put himself out for Pocahontas, *there* was another reason for Smith to keep out of the way. We know that Edward Maria Wingfield had despised John Smith. George Percy undoubtedly felt the same way, although he did not say so until some years later. But De La Warr had a family connection with Wingfield through the same ties as he had with Percy. Thus, all three of them would surely have regarded the former President of the Council in Virginia as far from "a fit companion."

But at last Captain John made up his mind to pay at least a

courtesy call on the young lady who had saved his life — so he was convinced — nearly ten years before. Despite recent contrarieties, his colonial plans seemed possible of furtherance once again, and he had to go to Plymouth and the West Country to push them. London clearly had lost interest in Captain Smith.

So it was that sometime in the autumn of 1616, "being about this time preparing to sail for New England," John Smith decided that he could no longer postpone paying his respects to the daughter of Great Powhatan.[1] "Hearing she was at Branford [Brentford]," he wrote,

> with divers of my friends, I went to see her. After a modest salutation, without any word, she turned about, [and] obscured her face, as not seeming well contented. And in that humor, her husband [and I], with divers others, we all left her two or three hours, [while I was] repenting myself to have writ [that] she could speak English.

Smith, for whom Pocahontas was still only the little girl he had enjoyed playing with, and whose intercession when he was captured in December, 1607, had paled into a half-forgotten nightmare, was evidently confused by her silence. He was certain that she had known how to speak English, probably far better than he had known her language. Yet now she said nothing.

Pocahontas, on her side, was evidently deeply affected by the sight of the man for whom she had conceived an unfathomable attraction when she was a thoughtless girl of eleven. To this axiomatic assumption, the further surmise may be added that she had mourned him for dead, and when she had learned that he was alive, had suffered because he made no move to visit her. And now he had come with a typically English busybody's bluster of concern about her health, welfare, and Christian education. She needed a few minutes to decide how to talk to him.

It may even be surmised that she stopped to recall that she had, in one way or for one reason or another, saved him, when he was at the mercy of her father's people. For a year or more, they had seen each other frequently. He had been kind, oh so kind; and she had seen in him a personality who could throw light into the dark mystery of Indian ignorance — though she may well not have thought of the matter in just such terms. Then John Smith had suddenly vanished. Dead, or fled. No-one could or would tell her the truth.

After that, there were the wiles of Argall, himself not unlike Smith but totally disinterested in her personally. And more lies. And more chicanery. And then the man who married her. These thoughts, we may assume, must have crossed her mind.

Rolfe was kind, in his strange way, and passionate and frigid at the same time. An incomprehensible man, who talked of the God of Love and practiced the art of taking advantage of other people and making money — he was the father of her child.

No, it was better to think of John Rolfe's careful kindness and of his growing importance in a world she did not understand. He was important because he *grew tobacco.* What was remarkable about that? Her father, her father's father, and countless others had been growing tobacco for centuries, right in her own country. But then, the whitemen had their peculiar notions. It was up to her to go along with them. In time she would comprehend. Such may have been the reflections that held her back from speaking.

Later, when Smith had returned, Pocahontas at length addressed him. Quietly she reminded him of the days when they knew one another in Virginia, when John Smith visited them in Werowocomoco and talked with her father. And John Smith, years later, had published what he had written down then. Tenderness had stolen into his heart, too. "You did promise Powhatan," she said, that

> what was yours should be his, and he the like to you; you called him father, being in his land a stranger. And by the same reason, so must I do you.

But Smith could not permit this, not in England, not at the court of King James I, where Pocahontas was a King's daughter. John Smith was a captain, but in the social scale he was barely a gentleman, the lowest possible "rank" — any one under that had no rank at all. He tried to explain.

But Pocahontas broke in:

> Were you not afraid to come into my father's Country? Did you not cause fear in him, and all his people (but me)? And fear you here I should call you father? I tell you then, I will, and you shall call me child, and so I will be for ever and ever your countryman. They did tell us always [that] you were dead, and I knew no other till I came to Plymouth. Yet Powhatan did command Uttamatómakkin to seek you, and know the truth, because your countrymen will lie much.

Undoubtedly, John Smith was too well aware of the justness of that charge to protest. He let the matter stand and before long excused himself. He had to make final preparations for his trip to Plymouth, Bristol, and other cities in the west, he evidently explained. He needed financing for yet another voyage of exploration to New England, this time to attempt a permanent settlement there, too.

Although there is no record of his leave-taking, anyone who reads Smith's account of his visit will sense that he was disturbed, possibly deeply embarrassed. Pocahontas was a married woman with a son. She had been married by a minister of the Christian Church. Yet in her behavior, even in her words, there was evidence that her husband was not her true love. Whatever Smith's inner being whispered, his outer self refused to recognize this fact.

Meanwhile, Uttamatómakkin, husband of Powhatan's daughter Matachanna and one of the "ten or twelve old and young" who had come with Pocahontas, had captured the attention of the Rev.

JOHN SMITH'S ADVENTURES IN DECEMBER, 1607

INDIANS DANCING BEFORE MARTIN PRING

Iapassus and His Wife Persuade Pocahontas to Visit Captain Argall's Ship

POCAHONTAS MEETS TWO OF HER BROTHERS AT MATCHCOT

Captain Samuel Argall Harangues the Chickahominies

LO
S. PAULES CHURCH
Bow Church
The Eel Schipes
The Gally fuste
THAMESIS
The Bear Gardne
The Globe

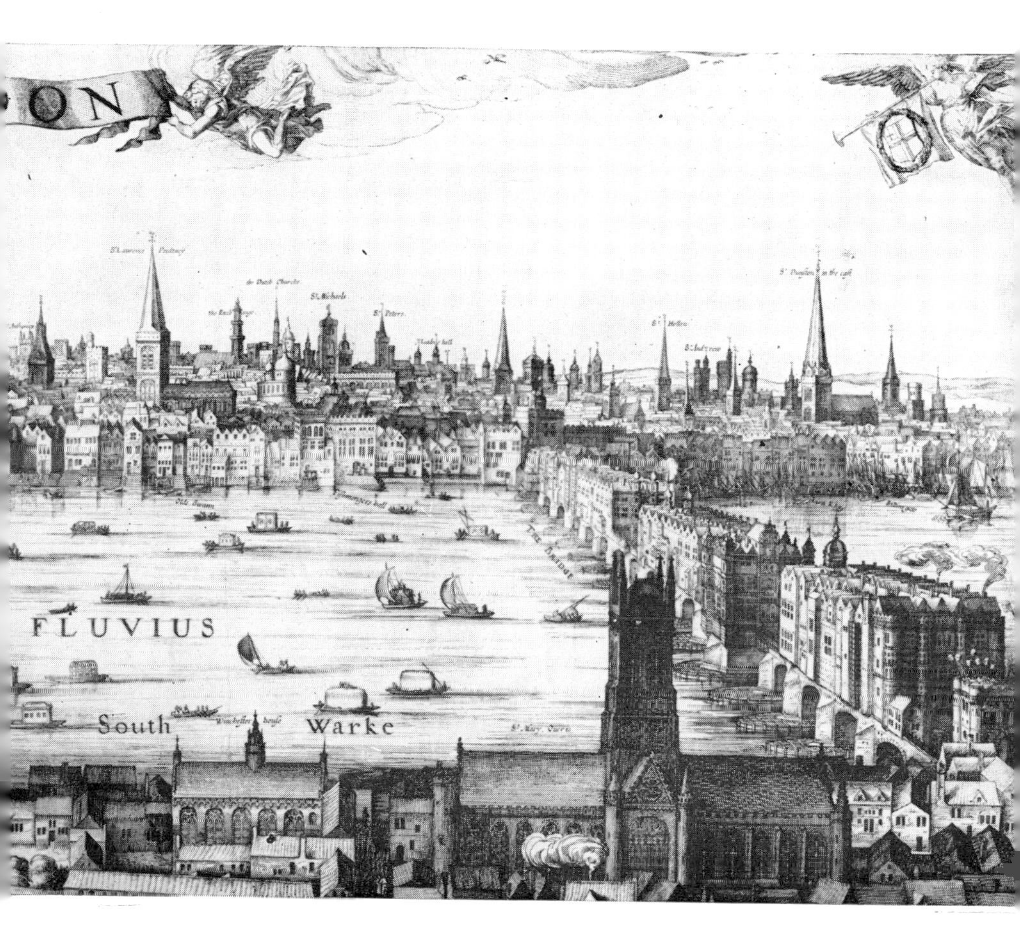

LONDON AT THE TIME OF POCAHONTAS' ARRIVAL

Heacham Hall, Residence of the Rolfe Family

HEACHAM CHURCH (ST. MARY'S)

THE PORTRAICTUER OF CAPTAYNE IOHN SMITH ADMIRALL OF NEW ENGLAND
These are the Lines that ſhew thy Face; but thoſe
That ſhew thy Grace and Glory, brighter bee:
Thy Faire-Diſcoueries and Fowle-Overthrowes
Of Salvages, much Civilliz'd by thee
Beſt ſhew thy Spirit; and to it Glory Wyn;
So, thou art Braſſe without, but Golde within.

Captain John Smith in His Thirty-seventh Year

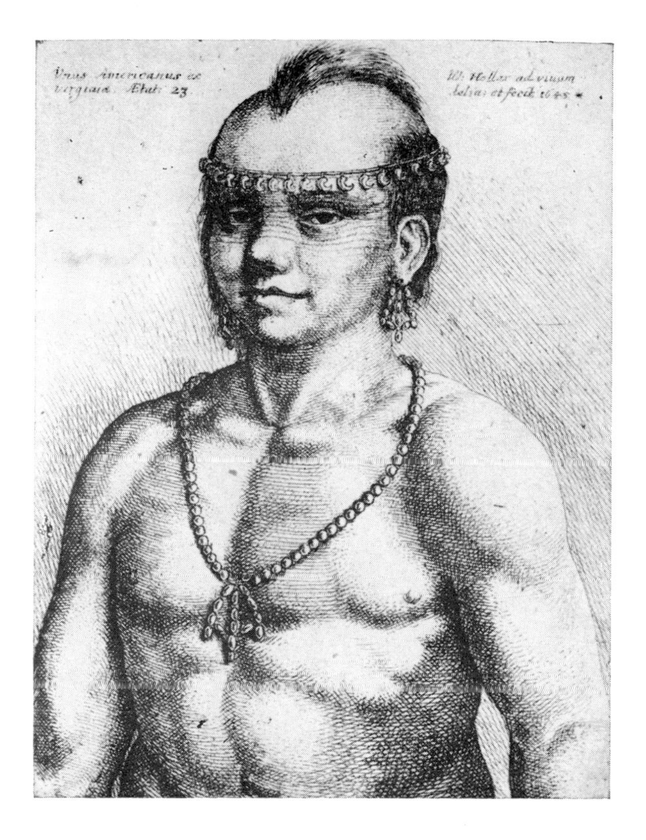

AN UNIDENTIFIED VIRGINIA INDIAN OF 1645

The Pocahontas of Legend

Samuel Purchas.[2] In fact, it is partly through their association that we know that the whole party disembarked at Plymouth.

Purchas was much intrigued by Tomocomo, as everybody in England called him, and spent considerable time in his company. Purchas himself wrote,

> With this Savage I have often conversed at my good friend's, Master Doctor [Theodore] Gulstone,[3] where he was a frequent guest, and where I have seen him sing and dance his diabolical measures, and heard him discourse of his country and religion.

Purchas had already learned a good deal about the Indians from Henry Spelman, five years before. Now he had a live Indian to talk to, through an interpreter whom he identified only as "Sir Thomas Dale's man." From conversations with him, Purchas was able to write,

> But of their opinions and ceremonies in religion, who fitter to be heard than a Virginian, an experienced man and counsellor to Opechancanough, their king and governor in Powhatan's absence? Such is Tomocomo, at this present in London, sent hither to observe and bring news of our King and country to his nation.

Other Indians who had been to London, such as Powhatan's son Namontack, who had seen nothing but the city of London, had reported back to Virginia that they found a lot of houses and men, but little by way of "corn" (cereal plants) or trees. Between these reports and the visible need of the colonists in Virginia, Powhatan and all his subjects got the impression that the English settled there "for supply of these defects." Tomocomo, however, told Purchas that,

> being landed in the West Parts [Plymouth], [he] found cause of admiration at our plenty in these kinds, and (as some have reported)

> began to tell [count] both men and trees, till his arithmetic failed. For their numbering beyond a hundred is imperfect, and somewhat confused.

It seems to have been after one of these conversations that John Smith decided to see Tomocomo. According to his own statement, it was "by chance" that they met, but it may be taken for granted that in some way Samuel Purchas supplied that chance.

Tomocomo, far from being seduced from his own religion by Purchas' pious wiles, was deeply disillusioned by his visit to London. Powhatan had told him to find John Smith and ask Smith to show him God, the King, the Queen, and the Prince (Henry) that Smith "so much had told them of." Purchas had not been of much help in those matters — or perhaps Tomocomo had not asked him. But with Smith before him, Tomocomo was ready.

Had John Smith but been a Roman Catholic in Rome, the answer to that problem would have been simple, so far as God was concerned. A brief visit to the Sistine Chapel would not only have shown Tomocomo God, but heaven, hell, and the angels to boot. It might even have converted Tomocomo to the Christian faith. As it was, the abstract, invisible, and puritanical God of Smith and his fellow Englishmen failed to impress a simpler mind.

Nevertheless, Smith explained things "the best" he could and went quickly on to say that Tomocomo had already seen the King and that he could see the Queen and Prince Henry "when he would." But Tomocomo denied roundly that he had ever laid eyes on the King.

Smith reminded him of the circumstances of the audience, whenever it was, and Powhatan's counsellor was at last convinced. Then he protested:

> You gave Powhatan a white dog, which Powhatan fed as himself. But your King gave me nothing, and I am better than your white dog.

John Smith seems then to have abandoned his efforts to impress Tomocomo, either as to the King of England or the English God. He went to work again on his preparations for Plymouth.

Samuel Purchas, however, was not so easily discouraged. The next time he saw Tomocomo, he returned to the subject uppermost in his mind. Once more utilizing Sir Thomas Dale's interpreter, he inquired further into the beliefs of Powhatan's people.

According to Purchas, Tomocomo explained that their God, Okee or Okeus,[4]

> doth often appear to them in his house or temple, the manner of which apparition is thus: First, four of their priests, or sacred persons (of which he said he was one) go into the house, and by certain words of a strange language ([of] which . . . the interpreter understood not a word, nor do the common people) call or conjure this Okeus, who appeareth to them out of the air. Thence coming into the house, and walking up and down with strange words and gestures, [he] causeth eight more of the principal persons to be called in. All which twelve standing round about him, he prescribes to them what he would have done.

Tomocomo then told how the Indians depend on Okeus in everything. And Okeus holds them by a mixture of fear and confidence in his support. On hunting expeditions, for instance, his presence is revealed by winds "or other awful tokens." But when he takes on human shape,

> his apparition is in form of a personable [handsome, well-built] Virginian, with a long black lock on the left side, hanging down near to the foot. This is the cause why the Virginians wear these sinister locks.

At that point, Purchas, taken aback, blurted out that some of Ralegh's Roanoke colony, back in the 1580's, had borrowed the idea from the Indians in the neighborhood. A clearly unlovely offspring of the lovelock, he said: Christians imitating savages, and they, the devil.

Whether or not the interpreter bothered to translate this comment, it was evident that Tomocomo admired this hair-do immensely. In fact, he found it a great shortcoming of the Christian God that He had not taught the English to wear their hair that way. Then he went on to say that after Okeus stayed with his twelve priests and laymen as long as he saw fit, he departed "up into the air whence he came," adding that Okeus

> was he which made heaven and earth, had taught them to plant so many kinds of corn, had prophesied to them before of our men's coming, knew all our country, [and] whom he made acquainted with his coming hither, and told him that within so many months he would return [to Virginia].

But the Devil or Okeus, as Purchas put it, also told him that on his return he must not go into that house (his temple) until Okeus called him.

To Purchas' endeavors at conversion, Tomocomo turned a deaf ear. Purchas noted that

> he is very zealous in his superstition, and will hear no persuasions to the truth, bidding us teach the boys and girls which were brought over from thence, he being too old now to learn.

When Purchas asked him what became of the souls of people who died, Tomocomo answered by pointing up to the sky. But he quickly added that the souls of wicked men hung between heaven and earth.

Although Tomocomo could have found a far less understanding interlocutor, Purchas all too evidently saw only a vast gulf between the simple religion of the Indians and the social, political, and religious complex which he regarded as the True Faith. With the blindness of most devout believers, he wrote that "the vulgar are held in great awe [of Okeus] by their ignorance," because they attributed the capture of a "good deer" to the benevolence of Okeus. But he saw nothing similar in his most educated friends attributing storms to an angry Christian Deity. With even greater petulance he added, as if it were contrary to morals or decency, that in the event of capturing such a deer, the people brought it to the house of their God before they prepared it for their dinner!

On the other hand, Purchas could not but show admiration for the personal courage and endurance of the Indians. "They hold it a disgrace," he wrote,

> to fear death. And therefore when they must die, they do it resolutely — as happened to one which had robbed the English, and by Powhatan (upon complaint made to him) was fetched six score miles from the place where he lurked, and by this Tomocomo executed in the presence of the English, his brains being knocked out, [yet] showing no sign of fear or dismayedness.

With this, Purchas' notes on the religion and character of the Indians cease. That did not mean, however, the end of his interest. For Purchas seems, at least, to have been one of those who began to stir up real interest in London in educating and improving the lot of the Indians. For several years already and especially since the publication of Robert Johnson's *New Life of Virginia,* in 1612, the Virginia Company had talked of helping the Indians, particularly the children, through education and Christian training.

Now, in 1616, either because of Pocahontas' presence or because of appeals from Alexander Whitaker from Virginia, and from Purchas (and possibly the Bishop of London) on the spot, King James himself got interested. And within a year he issued a letter to the Archbishops of Canterbury and York in which he stated that the Virginia Company was planning the foundation in Virginia of churches and a school for the purpose of educating the children of the "barbarians." [5] He desired the cooperation of the bishops and ministers of the Gospel in moving the people of the realm to contribute to so godly a plan. What was soon to be named the "university and college of Henrico [Virginia]" was already in the bud.

Looking back from the second half of the twentieth century to the first half of the seventeenth, the mere suggestion of a college, not to mention a university, in a colony of three hundred and fifty-one souls strung out in plantations along a hundred and twenty miles of untamed river seems harebrained. Yet rapid growth was at length hoped for and expected in the colony, and the children of the Indians were numerous. No-one seemed to doubt that they would attend. With goodwill and the help of the clergy, the visionary undertaking might well materialize.

Perhaps about the time of Smith's visit to Pocahontas, toward the end of November, 1616, the Virginia Company held a quarter court in London at which Samuel Argall was elected Deputy Governor of Virginia, under Lord De La Warr, in addition to which he seems to have been informally named "Admiral of Virginia." [6] In the latter capacity, he had Ralph Hamor for his Vice Admiral. Other nominations or confirmations or appointments included that of Captain John Martin, the indestructible original colonist, as Master of the Ordnance, and the official recognition of John Rolfe as Secretary. His services to the colony — witness Pocahontas and tobacco — had been distinguished indeed.

About the same time, on November 23, Richard Hakluyt, in one sense the father of Virginia, died in London, and was buried in Westminster Abbey. A scholar to the end, it is perhaps fitting that "his grave is unknown, his works are his sole monument." [7] It was with the death of this great geographer that Samuel Purchas, a far lesser man, took up his work and began the *Pilgrimes* in earnest.

Then, too, or not long after, the return of Argall to Virginia was decided upon, and with him was to go John Rolfe. They would leave as soon as certain details were worked out at subsequent meetings of the Virginia Company courts. Whether Pocahontas was told of this decision at the time is uncertain. It would seem that she was not. Other matters were on foot which her husband did not want to endanger or embarrass.

Queen Anne, King James' royal consort, had already become famous as a patron of "magnificent masques and ballets." [8] The most elaborate of these were often, if not habitually, staged on Twelfth Night, at the end of the Christmas season. In the winter of 1616–1617 there was to be no exception, especially since King James personally was about to put into action a plan which he had been cuddling for a long time: his first trip back to Scotland since his accession to the throne of England, nearly fourteen years before. The 24th of July, 1617, would be the fiftieth anniversary of his proclamation as King of Scots, at the age of one year, one month, and five days.

Ben Jonson was chosen, not by any means for the first time, to create the proper poetry and spectacle for the masque. Plans were already afoot before Hakluyt's death, nearly two months in advance. As early, in fact, as November 18, 1616, Edward Sherburne, financial agent in England for the King's ambassador to the Netherlands, Sir Dudley Carleton, wrote to his master that the masque was in preparation, and that "His Highness means to be [there] in person. This will increase His Majesty's debt by two thousand pounds, as ye report goes." [9]

A fortnight before, on November 3, Prince Charles had been created Prince of Wales, in the Banqueting Hall of Whitehall Palace, where half a dozen of Shakespeare's most famous plays had been staged. King James, who had a weakness for some kinds of ostentation, had had the Hall rebuilt in 1607. But because he still was not happy with its appearance in 1616, he squandered further sums on it "for painting and gilding with part gold and silver a bar for the barriers in the Banqueting House with pyramids and balls at the top, likewise gilded, against the creation of the Prince."

The Prince was not the real cause for the exceptional fastuousness, however. King James kept *that* concealed within the royal breast. Indeed, it was not until the day before the masque that the truth came out, although John Chamberlain, writing to the same Sir Dudley Carleton, said that he heard rumors about the first of the month.

King James' latest, and handsomest to date, favorite, George Villiers, who had been presented to His Majesty in 1614 and had promptly been made cupbearer, had progressed from gentleman of the bedchamber in 1615 to knight and master of the horse in the course of the year. And in 1616 he had been dubbed Knight of the Garter and created Viscount Villiers. Then, on Sunday, January 5, 1617, this same young man of twenty-four was created Earl of Buckingham, the first of non-royal blood to bear the title in more than four centuries.

It was small wonder then that the masque performed on Monday, January 6, "The Vision of Delight," was something exceptional. John Chamberlain, in a later letter to Carleton, wrote that

> the new-made Earl and the Earl of Montgomery danced with the Queen. I have heard no great speech nor commendations of the Masque, neither before nor since, but . . . The Virginian woman Pocahuntas, with her father's Counsellor hath been with the King, and graciously used. And both she and her assistant well placed at the Masque.

Not a word of John Rolfe, nor of the princely rank of Pocahontas. On the other hand, it had already become known that Pocahontas had heard that she was to go back to Virginia, and did not want to. "She is on her return," Chamberlain added, "though sore against her will, if the wind would come about to send them away."

What Pocahontas can have thought of this seventeenth-century "spectacular" is impossible to know. Beyond the enormous cost of such a presentation, which she certainly neither knew nor could have understood, and the touch-and-go altercation between the French and Spanish ambassadors as to "rights" to attend, which would have been incomprehensible to almost anyone, the theatrical realism and pyrotechnics of such an extravaganza must have seemed the product of inconceivable sorcery.

A street scene by daylight. A she-monster delivered of six puppets that dance. Then the moon rising over a night-scene, which turns into a cloud, from which a voice speaks and sings. Then come "Phantasmes," and one of the hours descends, as the scene changes to the bower of Zephyrus, from which Peace sings of many "pleasures." And in the end, a bower opens "to a loud music," and the maskers are discovered as the glories of the spring. Revels follow, until Aurora appears, as the moon and the night descend, singing "I am urged by the Day, against my will, to bid you come away."

How sophisticated a version of the dance of the thirty young women who "came naked out of the woods" to entertain Captain Smith in the late autumn of the year of grace, 1608!

But this was civilized England. The lords and ladies of the English court made up the audience. And near where Pocahontas sat, corsetted in rigid court dress, attended by her unimpressionable Indian guard in "exotic" Indian attire, His Majesty relaxed in gracious dignity, while Phantasy declaimed:

> Behold a King
> Whose presence maketh this perpetual *Spring,*
> The glories of which Spring grow in that Bower,
> And are the marks and beauties of his power.[10]

CHAPTER 14

Peace Draws to a Close

THE CHILL, DAMP AIR of winter settled over London. Fog mixed with smoke slipped in and fought with a pale, low-hanging sun. Pocahontas, Tomocomo, and the other Indians suffered from the unaccustomed nuisance. But in the case of Pocahontas that did not mean that she longed to escape.

Quite the contrary. Something about England had caught her inner being. Not even the common cold or grippe that may be assumed to have assailed her seemed to discourage her. She wanted to stay. Yet nothing she could do or say bore any weight with John Rolfe, newly appointed Secretary of the Virginia Colony. Piously accepting as the will of God the contrary winds that kept him a prisoner in London, John Rolfe merely went on with his preparations for departure.

Sometime during the winter a young Dutch engraver (he was just Pocahontas' age) sought her out. He had completed an engraved portrait of Captain John Smith. As a newcomer in England, he wanted to exercise his talents. Would Pocahontas permit him to engrave a portrait of her as well?

Hardly knowing what an engraved portrait was, Pocahontas agreed. And thus from the hand of Simon van de Passe we have the only likeness of her that unquestionably was made during her life.[1] Copies of the engraving were, of course, available. John Chamberlain, who kept his friend Sir Dudley Carleton informed about everything that happened in London, had already written him more than once about the Indian Princess. In February, he got a copy of the engraving and sent it with his letter of the 22nd:

> Here is a fine picture of no fair Lady and yet with her tricking up and high style and titles you might think her and her worshipful husband to be somebody, if you did not know that the poor Virginia Company out of their poverty are fain to allow her four pound a week for her maintenance.[2]

If Chamberlain was anything but flattering in these comments, we must remember that Indian things, and people, had little which appealed to the English. By their standards, Pocahontas was not beautiful. She may not have been beautiful even by Indian standards. It was her personality, her character, that had beauty. Two famous beauties of Pocahontas' day in London, cousins both named Frances Howard, lacked her inner grace. One, the Duchess of Richmond and Lennox, was foolish, vain, and eccentric. The other, the Countess of Somerset, was a murderess. "Beauty is truth," the poet wrote.[3] Pocahontas was true.

The last weeks of winter slipped by. Before too long the boisterous North Sea must settle down. And since John Rolfe refused to listen, Pocahontas had to shut her grief at leaving within herself.

John Smith was still in the West Country, and she had not seen him again. Tomocomo was useless to talk to, for he only wanted to leave the despised place as soon as he could. As for her other Indian companions, at least three of them already had died in that unfriendly climate, and it is far from certain that she saw anything of the rest. They, too, were prone to sickness, which, since it was costly, displeased the Virginia Company. In whom could she confide?

Captain Argall, now proudly wearing his new title of Admiral, was unquestionably always correct. He bore honors with relative equanimity, much as he bore contrary winds at sea. But so essentially practical and self-centered a man is not apt to endear himself to others. If Pocahontas saw him, she certainly could expect no support for her desire to remain in England.

The councillors of the Virginia Company were even more aloof. They treated her as a Princess — with artificial respect — but even Argall did not regard her as a "sister" of the Princess Elizabeth, now consort of the Prince Elector Palatine in far-off Heidelberg. He knew that she was the daughter of an Indian chief, noble of spirit, but not born of what to the English was the "blood royal."

Between mental and physical pains, by March Pocahontas was ill indeed. Yet even that did not deter Rolfe from his plans. It was only a distemper, he suggested, which the sea voyage might well cure. John Rolfe, unaware that something deeper than superficial illness was gnawing at Pocahontas' health, unaware that she was desperately unhappy, bundled all their many things together and with his wife and little Thomas boarded the ship *George,* Admiral Samuel Argall commanding.[4]

The precise date of their sailing is not known. Argall and a group of associates obtained a grant of land in Virginia on March 20, but Argall himself need not have waited.[5] He undoubtedly knew that the grant was forthcoming. The fact of the matter merely was that the weather made the *George* as loath to leave her moorings as Pocahontas was to start back to Virginia.

Nevertheless, at last the winds permitted the helmsman to guide the ship slowly downstream — down Bugsby's Reach, and Woolwich Reach where Henry VIII's great arsenal already desecrated the generally bucolic shores of the Thames with industrial and military plants.

Here the river swept toward the north, as the *George* passed through Gallions Reach and Barking Reach. The shores there were low and marshy, and signs of human habitations were few. Then another bend in the river, this time to the south, brought the village of Erith into sight, with its church standing at the edge of a long, dreary marsh, half buried in ivy — depressing, funereal.

Near Erith the Thames grew conspicuously wider. On the Essex side the ground rose higher, with chalk cliffs by the river and oak, fir, and ash trees above, crowning the modest eminence now known as Beacon Hill. Not far beyond lay the great bend at the junction of Long Reach and Fiddler's Reach, with Swanscombe Marsh just beyond. A mile back from the river, to the south, the village of Swanscombe was virtually hidden, but for the squat tower of the church of St. Peter and St. Paul.

There, twenty-five miles from the London wharf, the huddled houses and tall church and inn of Gravesend became visible, two miles beyond.[6] Here was the hithe, or landing-place, where so many illustrious visitors had first set foot on English soil. And here, in painful simplicity, as spring came to England, Princess Pocahontas begged to be taken ashore. She was deathly ill.

For her there was no state at all, that day. The *George* dropped anchor, and Pocahontas was carried onto the little wharf. A hundred yards or so away, the three-story inn rose massively before them. Pocahontas was hurried to a room, and a doctor was summoned — that much, at least, may be surmised, for there is no record.

It was too late. Climate, that had killed many an Englishman in Virginia, took the life of Pocahontas in England. Climate, and a broken heart. There is no need to postulate some epidemic, some disease. As Samuel Purchas wrote:

> At her return towards Virginia she came at Gravesend to her end and grave, having given great demonstration of her Christian sincerity, as the first fruits of Virginian conversion, leaving here a

> goodly memory, and the hopes of her resurrection, her soul aspiring to see and enjoy presently in heaven, what here she had joyed to hear and believe of her beloved Savior.[7]

Even before then, John Chamberlain had written in one of his frequent letters to Carleton, on March 29, 1617:

> The Virginian woman (whose picture I sent you) died this last week at Gravesend as she was returning homeward.[8]

Chamberlain was both less kind and less pious than Samuel Purchas. To him she was only a "savage" — not an English lady of quality.

To Purchas she was a savage in another sense. She was one whose soul should be saved for the greater glory of God and His Church. But in any event, had Pocahontas died of some malignant disease, either Purchas or Chamberlain, or both, would surely have mentioned the fact. Lacking respect for humanity in a broad sense, both of them paid more than due homage to reporting facts, as they saw them.

In the obscurely tragic life of Pocahontas there is possibly no more fitting scene than her release. In a busy hostelry near the waterside, where London ends and the encircling sea begins, Pocahontas sank to her death in ever-strange arms. No-one, perhaps least of all her husband, saw life or death as she saw it, and no-one could offer her comprehensible solace. She left the world with incomparable dignity and with her personality unsullied. We may be sure that, true to her people, she sought only to better them, not to betray or delude them. And to accomplish that, she sensed, rather than knew, that London must be her home. For London, not Werowocomoco, was now the capital of Powhatan's empire.

Pocahontas obviously trusted John Smith to the end. Her demeanor on the occasion of their last interview bears this out. She was unhappy that he had not helped, that he had not communicated. But she knew that he was true-blue. The others — well, they "will lie much." She, too, was true-blue. And the other Indians — well, they also "will lie much."

Powhatan, when Pocahontas died, surely was over seventy. He had been aggressive, cruel, and ambitious. He had made a State out of warring, petty tribes. What he demanded from his people in return was puny by comparison. Then, too, for forty years or more he had fought off the relentless tide of white invaders. At last, he had sought peace.

Pocahontas was his living emblem of that desire. Now their joint hope, that redman and whiteman could live together, was about to be put to the test. Pocahontas' son, scarce two years old, might take the lead in time. Meanwhile?

In the parish church of St. George, Gravesend, it was recorded, with pathetic indifference to accuracy:

> 1616 [1617] [March] 21 Rebecca Wrothe wyffe of Thomas Wroth gent. A Virginia Lady borne, was buried in the chauncell.[9]

The pious, proper obsequies performed, perhaps even in haste, Admiral Argall, Secretary Rolfe, and other mourners including Tomocomo, boarded the *George.* The wind was — God be praised! — propitious. The murky Thames and insalubrious London were soon left far behind.

Little Thomas, however, had not been well all along. John Rolfe began to doubt the wisdom of venturing across the Atlantic with him. The voyage around the Isle of Thanet and through the English Channel had been brief, to be sure, and the water smooth. Still, as Rolfe later wrote to Sir Edwin Sandys, that distinguished member of the Virginia Council, those "who looked to him had need of nurses themselves," and were incapable of attending to him.[10]

Samuel Argall thought it wise to interfere. Getting the backing of other passengers — how characteristic of him! — he advised Rolfe to land Thomas at Plymouth and to write to Henry Rolfe, John's brother, to come down from London and take charge of him.

When they reached Plymouth, it happened that Sir Lewis Stukely, Vice Admiral of Devon, was only too glad to act as foster-father to Thomas until Henry Rolfe arrived. Thus the matter was solved. Thomas was left with Sir Lewis, eventually picked up by his uncle Henry, and raised and educated in England. He did not see his native land again until he was a grown man of twenty.

All of this had taken time. Eager as Argall was to assume his post in Virginia, the *George* did not sail from Plymouth until Thursday, April 10, 1617. The next day they lost sight of the tip of Cornwall, and four weeks later, on Friday, May 9, the *George* was off Cape Cod.

Since most of the voyage had been foggy, such speed was a tribute to Argall's nautical skill. At least comparable was his success in getting the ship safely to Old Point Comfort six days later, still through fog. Five weeks from Plymouth was good time.

Argall had been away from Virginia for almost thirteen months. During that time, the colony had had relief from Dale's tyranny — as they called it — under Yeardley, the Deputy Governor. Shrewd and practical though he was, he was so easy-going that, as Nathaniel Powell and three other early colonists later wrote, he

> had a Savage or two so well trained up to their pieces [guns], they were as expert as any of the English, and one he kept purposely to kill him fowl. There were divers others had Savages in like manner for their men. Thus we lived together, as if we had been one people, all the time Captain Yeardley stayed with us . . .[11]

Captain Smith had disapproved of giving European arms to the Indians. In 1612 he had cited Newport's trading swords for turkeys with Powhatan as "an ill example." Not long after, he said to Powhatan personally, "As for swords and guns, I told you long ago I had none to spare." [12]

In contrast, Yeardley, already beginning to evince a certain liking for pomp, had received the "new Governor" at Jamestown with "his company in a martial order, whose right hand file was led by an Indian." And before long, Argall observed that the Indians were

> as frequent in their [the colonists'] houses as themselves, whereby they were become expert in our arms, and had a great many in their custody and possession.

Argall categorically did not like "those proceedings," and "altered them agreeable to his own mind." [13] And as if in confirmation of the wisdom of a more cautious policy, no sooner had Argall sent Tomocomo to tell Opechancanough of his arrival and to invite him to Jamestown, than Tomocomo began to rail against England, the English people, and "particularly his best friend Thomas Dale." Argall promptly "disproved" all Tomocomo's reports "before Opechancanough and his Great Men [counsellors], whereupon (to the great satisfaction of ye Great Men) Tomakin [Tomocomo] is disgraced." [14]

It was on this occasion that the Governor learned that Powhatan had gone to stay with the King of Moyomps on the Potomac, leaving the government of his people to Opechancanough and Opitchapan.[15] At the same time, Opechancanough and his counsellors learned of the death of Pocahontas.

On June 8, 1617, John Rolfe wrote to Sir Edwin Sandys about all this. After a description of their voyage, he briefly stated that the colony was "in good estate and enjoying a firmer Peace and plenty," although for lack of boats it was "much ruined and in great want." Then, after mentioning the Indians as "very loving," he got down to the main subject of his letter:[16]

> My wife's death is much lamented; my child much desired, when it is of better strength to endure so hard a passage, whose life greatly extinguisheth the sorrow of her loss, saying all must die. But 'tis enough that her child liveth.

There is even a hint that the subject of the "college" for Indian children was brought up at the time, for in the same letter, Rolfe wrote, laconically, "The Indians very loving, and willing to part with their children."

But with all Rolfe's general meekness, it is evident that, between his marriage to Pocahontas and his appointment as Secretary of the colony, he was a little set up. Three quarters of the way through, he gets around to the point:

> Now my last request at this time is to yourself, whom I have found a father to me, my wife and child . . . that you would be pleased, as you have begun and been one of the principal instruments herein, to continue your noble favor and furtherance even for my child's sake, being the living ashes of his deceased mother, and that you will still be the means . . . in obtaining so liberal a stipend, [that it] may not die with my wife, but continue for her child's advancement, which will the better enable myself and him hereafter to undertake and execute what may be commanded and required from us.

Not content with this, Rolfe added a postscript which reflects, in its clumsy phrasing, the concern that seems to prey on his mind:

> May you please you, Sir, as occasion shall be offered, to remember me for some place of command and some estate of land, to be confirmed to me and my child, wherein I have formerly found your love and readiness, for which I shall rest much bound unto you.

Between the date of this letter and some extracts of documents issued by Argall under date of June 7 and 9, it may be surmised that the *George* was about to sail back to England. In his letter of

June 9, Argall hastily sent word that there was a lack of ministers, "Master [Alexander] Whitaker being drowned," and that he "desires another Governor be sent — in ye meantime [he] will use his best endeavors, on which he prays they'll put ye best construction."

Again, Argall the practical, tidy, and disciplinarian commander! The anarchic colony was not to his liking. But he was not another Dale.

However, the religious problem was real. He reverted to that again, before closing the letter. He desired "Sir Dudley Digges may solicit a Bishop to give Master Wickham power to administer [the] sacrament, here being no other person."

With these and other letters signed and delivered to the Master of the *George* and other pressing matters attended to, Argall was able to turn to a project initiated by the Council for Virginia nearly a year before he had sailed for Virginia — possibly the real reason for his being nominated deputy to Lord De La Warr in the first place. For Argall had evidently gained the respect of the Council for his matter-of-fact, unemotional manner of carrying out orders.

As has been mentioned, it was decided in 1616 to divide the "lands in Virginia, as well to every man's person that went himself to the Plantation, as to every particular man that had adventured [invested] his money." This division was to affect only the lands on both sides of the James, "and all about the new towns erected." [17]

Although most of the records are missing, it seems that Argall first set the bounds for four "Incorporations and Parishes," namely: James City, Bermuda City, Henrico, and Kecoughtan. In addition, it is evident that he would do the same for the twenty-four hundred acres he personally had been assigned by the grant dated March 20 — whether he had it in hand before he left or not.

This grant included the area he called Argall's Gift or Argall's Town, better known at the time as Paspahegh.[18] Argall saw that this was well surveyed and well run, for that was part of his nature.

Other settlements then planted were at Martin Brandon, Smith's (later, Southampton) Hundred, Weyanoke, Flowerdieu Hundred, Martins Hundred, and Maycock Hundred. Furthermore, Argall went to work to mitigate at least the *application* of the *Laws Divine Moral and Martial,* instituted largely by Gates and Dale, and published in London by William Strachey.

He pardoned at least three men, of whom two would have otherwise suffered the death penalty. He issued a number of commissions to able men. He drew up recommendations regarding "ye most convenient times and seasons of ye year for ye magazine ship to set forth from England towards Virginia." There was a good deal about the handling of tobacco in this document, officially signed by John Rolfe, hinting that the Governor and the Secretary-Recorder were working very close together.

Before his first year in office drew to a close, Argall made a few additional appointments, and on March 10, 1618, penned a letter to the Virginia Company, only an abstract of which remains. This reads in part:

> The Governor tells ye Company in what a ruinous condition he found ye Colony by ye carelessness of ye people and lawless living and how he has improved almost every thing . . . Indians so poor [they] can't pay their debts and tribute. Powhatan goes from place to place visiting his Country, taking his pleasure in good friendship with us. [He] laments his daughter's death but [is] glad her child is living, so doth Opechancanough. Both want to see him, but desire that he may be stronger before he returns . . .

Argall concluded this letter with a personal note:

> [The Governor] desires another Governor to be sent. All desire the Lord De La Warr (who is our Lord Governor) to return to his government, where he'll find all things in good order and prosperity.[19]

A month later, Great Powhatan died, somewhere in the forest. John Rolfe, his son-in-law, reported the event in a "relation" dated June 15:

> Powhatan died this last April, yet the Indians continue in peace. Itopatin his second brother succeeds him, and both he and Opechancanough have confirmed our former league.[20]

Itopatin was another name for Opitchapan. Although he inherited the overlordship, he was a much weaker man and ruler than Powhatan. It was Opechancanough who held the "empire" together, until he assumed the power himself.

Meanwhile (the date is completely uncertain) Captain Yeardley, apparently disappointed that Argall had been sent to Virginia as Deputy Governor (a post he undoubtedly craved for himself), had taken ship and returned to England. Not, however, before he had acquired a thousand acres twenty-odd miles up the James from Jamestown, in addition to twenty-two hundred acres he already owned across the river near modern Weyanoke Point. He had also acquired a wife, Temperance Flowerdieu. His exodus from all that acreage was obviously to make sure of his holdings before the Council in London, and perhaps also, with his new wife's assistance, to promote himself in their eyes. After all, both Yeardley and the former Miss Flowerdieu were ancient planters, with eight or more years of residence in the colony.

After, but certainly not because of, Yeardley's departure, Indian problems seem to have once again come to the fore. That these problems were of the colonists' own making is hardly to be questioned, and the tenor of Argall's "Proclamations or Edicts" of May 18 points to this:

> Against private trucking [bartering] with savages and pulling down palisades.
>
> Against teaching Indians to shoot with guns on pain of death to

> learner and teacher, and how to hunt deer or hogs, without Governor's leave . . .
> No man to shoot but in defense of himself against enemies till a new supply of ammunition comes, on pain of a year's slavery . . .
> No trade with ye perfidious savages nor familiarity, lest they discover our weakness.[21]

Argall evidently believed, as did John Smith, that a strong, well-armed colony was the best guarantee of peace with the Indians. But that did not mean that overfriendliness and overconfidence were not dangerous. The great bulk of the Indians, if not specifically all of them, still wanted to rid themselves of the importunate foreigners.

Word had long since reached London, however, that Governor Argall was dictatorial, grasping, and only interested in lining his own pockets. Lord De La Warr, who was Lord Governor for life, had sailed for Virginia early in April, 1618, and it was decided to speed the Council's recommendations regarding Argall by special ship, as will shortly be seen. De La Warr, unfortunately, died en route — the accounts are conflicting as to when, where, and why — but his widow landed safely at Jamestown the end of July or the beginning of August. This unhappy event not only forced Argall to remain as Governor but even resulted in the gravest crisis of his rule.

One Captain Edward Brewster had come to Virginia in 1610, apparently on Lord De La Warr's own ship, which was under the command of Samuel Argall. Immediately upon their arrival, after a voyage of two months, Brewster was given a commission of some importance, and it is evident that he considered himself under the Lord Governor's protection.

On these slim grounds, Brewster took it upon himself to defy the authority of "Samuel Argall, Esq., Admiral and for the time present principal Governor of Virginia," as he styled himself. Obscure though the matter remains, Argall seems to have issued certain orders personally to a servant of Lady De La Warr. But Brewster countermanded these orders by telling the servant to disobey Argall and to quit the work assigned to him. Under martial law, the punishment for such insubordination was death, but Argall "commuted" this to taking an oath from Brewster,

> That he should not speak ill of Captain Argall's government; nor ever again return into the territories of Virginia; and to protect Captain Argall from being called to an after account for his government . . .[22]

And so on. Brewster protested violently and, sent home to England, went to work to stir up animosity against Argall. That he succeeded is shown by the hailstorm of protests against Argall's "tyranny" which reached England by summer, 1618.

Brewster's prolonged baiting was more important in Argall's career than the merely legal aspects of the case.[23] There can be little doubt that Brewster misbehaved, probably mutinously — but so did hundreds of self-centered gentlemen of his type. Brewster also caused trouble by becoming the spokesman for the ever-present elements in Virginia which were unhappy with whatever government they had or with any government at all. Curiously these anarchists were ultraconservative, and, less curiously, they were essentially unproductive of anything other than trouble.

In London, in the meanwhile, more complaints had reached the Virginia Council, not only about Argall's alleged rapacity, as has been mentioned, but also about general mismanagement, shortage of provisions and housing, insufficient arms and munitions, and means of transportation to boot. The arrival of a saucy letter from Argall by the magazine-ship the *George,* early in August, finally prodded the Council into taking a stand. This took the form of two separate communications to Virginia.[24]

The first was a letter to Argall, dated August 22, 1618, signed by Sir Thomas Smythe, his deputy Alderman Johnson, and four other distinguished members of the Council. It criticized Argall sharply for his attitude to the Council, for many evasions or even violations of instructions, for mishandling of Indian trade, and for a host of other charges evidently presented to them by malcontents. And it closed:

> Either you must think highly of yourself or meanly of us, as that being our substitute you will presume to offer us these wrongs . . . and we have written to the Lord Governor [De La Warr], which we doubt not but his Lordship will impart unto you, and so we rest your very loving friends.

The other communication was a letter to Lord De La Warr. It was dated the next day, and signed by Smythe and Johnson, and only two other members of the Council. It opened:

> We are now enforced to write unto your Lordship of [an] important matter of another nature, which is touching Master Samuel Argall, whom we made Governor in your Lordship's absence . . . We have received from him by the *George* a very strange letter which, together with the informations which we have by sundry witnesses lately come from thence against him, do import more uneasiness and discontent to the adventurers here and more hazard to the plantation than ever did any other thing that befell that action from the beginning.

The letter then went on to enumerate in detail various charges of arrogant conduct, engrossing profits for himself, virtually embezzling the company's stores, and, above all, gathering all trade with the Indians into his own hands. The adventurers were so disturbed, according to the letter, that they had barely been restrained from appealing to King James himself, although James was at the time far away on one of his "progresses." The Council therefore begged

De La Warr to "cause him [Argall] to be shipped home in this ship, the *William and Thomas*" to satisfy both the adventurers and the company by answering the various charges.

But Lord De La Warr had died on his way across the ocean, as we know. News of this did not reach England until October 5, while his ship arrived safely at Jamestown before the end of July. Therefore, when the *William and Thomas* at last turned up early in 1619, Argall not only received the letter addressed to himself, but also that addressed to the Governor General.[25]

Meanwhile, the London Council had appointed another man to the post of Governor General in place of De La Warr, and on January 19, 1619, this distinguished representative sailed from London. It was none other than Captain George Yeardley.

Someone in England who was loyal to Argall, knowing or strongly suspecting that something was wrong, almost at the same time saw to it that a pinnace was made ready at Plymouth and sent post haste to Virginia. All that is known about the business is that the pinnace made better time than Yeardley's ship, and arrived in Virginia "about Easter time."

Argall meanwhile had carried on as before. On Easter Sunday itself, March 28, he officially announced "the bounds and limits of Jamestown," as he had been instructed to define them.[26] Very shortly after, the pinnace arrived. Within four or five days, Argall appointed Captain Nathaniel Powell Acting Governor and left Virginia for the last time.

CHAPTER 15

"Like a Death-web Spun . . ."[1]

GEORGE YEARDLEY had somehow done very well in Virginia. Not only did he have many acres of property, but he had also picked up a good deal of ready cash, or its equivalent. In fact, he is reputed to have spent nearly three thousand pounds sterling "furnishing himself" for a projected early return to Virginia[2] — presumably after Lord De La Warr had sailed to supplant Samuel Argall. In one way or another, the Virginia Company was impressed by George Yeardley. And just about that time, the news of the death of De La Warr reached London.

This was reported on October 5. The news was passed on to Sir Dudley Carleton by John Chamberlain nine days later. Not long after, possibly at the Quarter Court of the Virginia Company, October 21, Yeardley was nominated Governor of Virginia. And on October 25, the traveler-geographer John Pory wrote to his friend Sir Dudley Carleton to convey this information. Pory was a well-known disciple of Richard Hakluyt, gifted but intemperate, and at the time desperately in search of something to do. He wrote in part:

> Capt. Yeardley chosen governor . . . departs immediately thither [to Virginia] with two ships and about 300 men and boys. The greatest difficulties of that plantation overcome.[3]

Yeardley's appointment was made official at the Michaelmas Quarter Court of the Virginia Company on November 18. At this time, he received his instructions as Governor — instructions that came to be known as the "Great Charter." Lord De La Warr may have had the same instructions, but on November 18, 1618, it was all put down in black and white. Yeardley had a commission to establish a Council of Estate and a General Assembly for Virginia which were to give the planters a voice in their own government, for the first time.

Six days later, in token of his approval, King James knighted Captain Yeardley at Newmarket in Suffolk. And on November 28, John Pory again wrote to Carleton. This time he had news of great importance to himself, for he had been without definite occupation since February:

> No longer ago than yesterday the Council of Virginia . . . did, at the instance of Sir George Yeardley, the new elected Governor, choose me for their Secretary in Virginia. This Sir George Yeardley hath married my cousin german [first cousin], and infinitely desires my company.[4]

Pory had requested an "allowance" to equip himself before setting out and a "maintenance" for the duration of his stay, but the Council was unsympathetic. Pory wrote that they were "as dry as pumice-stones." Yeardley was forced to help him out of his own pocket — or perhaps out of the colony's funds, when he got there.

On this same day, John Chamberlain dipped his quill in some uncommonly acid ink and conveyed what *he* thought to his friend Carleton:

> Here be two ships ready for Virginia, and one Captain Yeardley, a mean fellow by way of provision goes as Governor, and to grace him the more the King knighted him this week at Newmarket;

> which hath set him up so high that he flaunts it up and down the streets in extraordinary bravery [ostentation], with fourteen or fifteen fair liveries after him.[5]

Ridiculed by Chamberlain in England, Yeardley was snubbed by Opechancanough in Virginia. For unexpressed reasons, the haughty old Indian refused to visit the colony. "Some" of the colonists, probably those who were still aware that Indians peopled the illimitable forest around them, wondered apprehensively if he intended keeping his "former promises."

But the potential threat from outside was forgotten in the face of the very real relief from abuse of power within the colony which was brought by Governor Yeardley. In pompous legal language that flows inexorably on for more than five thousand words, the Company clearly instructed their representative to govern "with the advice and assistance" of the Council of Estate which it had set up, to ease the tax burden, to begin "to allot and lay out" certain public lands in Virginia, and to effect many further measures, all listed in detail.[6]

In addition, the Company had issued an "ordinance and Constitution" which provided a General Assembly composed of two burgesses chosen by the inhabitants to represent each town, hundred, or plantation, and this Assembly was to be summoned by the Governor once a year.

For the first time in American history, the people were permitted to choose their own representatives. The General Assembly was not as free a body as the Parliament in London, but its authorization was an important step toward self-government.

The Assembly met in the church at Jamestown on July 30, 1619, and continued in session, except for Sunday, August 1, until August 4. The Council of Estate took its place around the Governor in the choir, while the twenty-two burgesses sat in the body of the church. The latter represented the four "cities" (Jamestown,

Charles City, Henrico, and Kecoughtan), Argall's Gift (a suburb of Jamestown), three hundreds, and three plantations.

These chief settlements did not represent all the inhabited sites. Isolated homesteads were scattered pretty well along the James. But what is significant is that Kecoughtan, at Old Point Comfort, was the only place of consequence which was separated from all the others by more than ten miles.

Above the "city" of Henrico there was nothing. Neither were there any settlements away from the river. One large plantation, Martin's Hundred, held a grant of a hundred and twenty-five square miles, from the James to the York just west of Kiskiack, but there was no permanent place of occupation on the York. There the Indians were free to live as they pleased.

As a consequence Richard Frethorne, a later settler in Martin's Hundred, expressed his fears of the Indians: "The nighest help that we have is ten miles of [from] us . . . [Here] we lie even in their teeth." [7]

In fact, sporadic Indian attacks on the whitemen had never come to a full halt. Why should they? Even with Yeardley's arrival, there had been only about a thousand colonists occupying the Indian lands. But by the end of 1619 further "supplies" (of colonists) had added at least another thousand. This meant that more than two thousand white invaders were settled where the same number of Indians had lived when the first three ships arrived in 1607. It would take more than mere sniping now to save their land from a white take-over.

At this juncture and about the time the Great Assembly was called, a Pole who had been in the colony for eight or ten years and whose appellation had been remodeled from "Robert the Pole" to Robert Poole, began stirring up trouble among the Potomac Indians for his personal benefit.

This tribe had long been friendly with the English, partly because of the good treatment they had exchanged with young Henry Spelman and partly because of Samuel Argall. Robert connived with Opechancanough, and by downright perjury was able to have Henry Spelman sentenced to seven years of servitude. This effectively silenced Spelman. Robert was then able to take out his spite on the unfortunate Potomacs. The records are strangely silent as to what actually happened, but it seems that Robert somehow played into the hands of Opechancanough to the damage of the Potomacs. Yet he got no favors in return. Opechancanough loved no whiteman.[8]

There were further troubles at the time, also obscure, but which arose from Robert's services to Governor Yeardley as a trader and interpreter. The renewed use of European weapons as a medium of exchange seems to have profited the Governor (and Robert) while strengthening Opechancanough's position vis-à-vis the English. All these shadowy and shady developments pale in the light of the unexpected arrival at Jamestown of a Dutch man-of-war, followed shortly by the *Treasurer* — that noted ship of Sir Robert Rich and his associate Samuel Argall.[9]

The *Treasurer* had been sent out in April, 1618, while Argall was still in Virginia under a private commission from Charles Emanuel the Great, Duke of Savoy, to plunder in the West Indies. Not long before Argall's departure, the *Treasurer* had appeared at Jamestown and was refitted by Argall. Thereupon her commander, Captain Daniel Elfrith, was authorized to obtain salt and goats for the colony. The ship did touch at Bermuda, where some corn was picked up (but apparently no salt or goats), but then sailed for the West Indies. There, Elfrith met a Dutch captain with his man-of-war, whose pilot was an Englishman. The two captains made friends and "determined to hold consortship" to Virginia.

On their way, they got separated, and the Dutchman arrived alone "about the latter end of August," 1619. According to an undated letter from John Rolfe to Sir Edwin Sandys (January 1619/20),

> he brought not anything but 20 and odd negroes, which the Governor and Cape Merchant [in charge of the stores] bought for victuals (whereof he was in great need as he pretended) at the best and easiest rate they could.

Despite the phrasing, the twenty and odd unfortunates were most likely sold as indentured servants, not slaves in the later meaning of the term. White servants were sold in just the same way. Nevertheless, they proved to be the germ of Negro slavery in the later United States. Servantship to slavery was but a simple step where greed was the rule.

In the same letter, Rolfe took up the cudgel for the deposed Samuel Argall, who had had "many accusations heaped upon" him. Rolfe recounted that Elfrith had warned, just before leaving Virginia, that the colonists' lack of fortification would soon prove their undoing, because they might expect "the Spaniard would be here next spring." Rolfe reminded the Company in London that Argall had also complained about the same defect in their defences.

The rest of the letter was taken up with Indian troubles brought about by Robert the Pole and various deaths in the colony. In his last paragraph, however, Rolfe once again defended Argall with obvious sincerity, while assuring Sir Edwin that he had never before seen "amongst so few . . . so many falsehearted, envious and malicious people," as in the colony.[10]

At the same time, another letter was sent to Sandys by John Pory which was less appreciative. Assuring him that Governor Yeardley had had "more than ordinary affection for Argall," he had been still bound by his commission to reveal his [Argall's] faults. Yeardley, he wrote, "only doth wish that Captain Argall, being rich, a bachelor, and devoid of charge, would not so excessively intend his own thrift." Despite the quaint language, the meaning is clear.[11] Yet Sir George Yeardley himself was no less interested in intending *his* "thrift."

Notwithstanding the flurries with the Indians, the colony seemed to be settling down to slow but steady progress. Then came a new blight, which would have bolstered Indian hopes had any certain word of it reached their ears. Winter brought some sort of pestilence to the colony which took "divers hundreds" of lives, resulting in "almost the utter destruction of some particular plantations." [12]

Several remedies for the colony's plight were suggested in London, but the chief one was the discouragement of so much tobacco-growing. More solid commodities were needed, the Council said, such as iron, cordage, soap-ashes and potash, timber, silk, and even vineyards. It was all easily said. Nevertheless, tobacco continued to reign virtually unchallenged.

So passed the days in Virginia. To quote John Smith's report, the three-year term of Governor Yeardley "being near expired, the Council here [in London] made choice of a worthy young gentleman, Sir Francis Wyatt, to succeed him." And the Company strongly recommended to Wyatt the "suppressing of planting tobacco, and planting corn, not depending continually to be supplied by the Savages." [13] It was impossible not to refer to the Indians as such.

Sir Francis[14] sailed with an imposing fleet and a large body of colonists. It was to be the beginning of a new era. For he was the first (and eventually the only) Governor sent to Virginia by the Company, under any administration other than that of Sir Thomas Smythe. (Later, the King himself did the appointing.)

Meanwhile, a devout soul with all sorts of family connections had arrived in Jamestown. His name was George Thorpe. Through his grandmother, Margaret Throckmorton Thorpe, he was distantly related to Sir Walter Ralegh's widow, and more closely to Sir Thomas Dale, the recent Governor. Furthermore, he had ties by marriage with Lord De La Warr, with the huge and influential Berkeley family, and even with Samuel Argall.[15]

George Thorpe had somehow acquired an Indian boy (the word need not be taken in its literal sense) before he left England and had taught him to read and write. Since the Berkeleys were interested in colonizing Virginia, Thorpe saw that the conversion of "savages" would help promote this, as well as add the Indians to the anti-Catholic population of the earth and, eventually, to the heavenly hosts available to combat the Devil. In Virginia, he was quickly encouraged. And a few months of being there convinced him that things were not so bad as some said.

In a letter written on December 19, 1620, a year after his arrival, Thorpe seemed to excuse a long silence by explaining that they

> are now in the business of examining witnesses concerning Captain Argall, wherein we sit commonly till midnight . . . [but] notwithstanding, Sir, that you will hear many strange reports both of the death of our own people and of others [Indians?], yet be not discouraged therein, for I thank God I never had my health better in my life . . . and [I] am persuaded that more do die here of the disease of their mind than of their body.

In fact, out of his enthusiasm he boasted that he had found a way to make such a good drink of Indian corn that he had at times preferred it to good strong English beer. This may have been the inspiration for American Bourbon whiskey.

Although there is no mention of the Indians in this letter, there is evidence in other sources that George Thorpe was already their self-appointed friend, protector, and benefactor. His object was evidently "to bind them unto him by his many courtesies." Nothing was too good for them. For example, if they were afraid of the great English mastiffs, Thorpe had the mastiffs killed "to the great displeasure of their owners."

Five months later, Thorpe wrote a stirring defense of the Indians to Sir Edwin Sandys:

> if there be wrong on any side, it is on ours, who are not so charitable to them as Christians ought to be, they being . . . of a peaceable and virtuous disposition . . . They begin more and more to affect English fashions, and will be much allured to affect us by gifts, if the Company would be pleased to send something in matter of apparel and household stuff, to be bestowed upon them. I mean the Kings [werowances] . . .

And to suit action to words, Thorpe built a house for Opechancanough, which was

> a fair house, according to the English fashion, in which he took such joy, especially in his lock and key, which he so admired, as locking and unlocking his door a hundred times a day, He thought no device in all the world was comparable to it.

Nevertheless, the Chickahominies were restive, and there was other trouble. As far back as October, 1619, an Indian named Nemattanon, called Jack of the Feathers by the English, as already mentioned, "because he commonly was most strangely adorned with them," turned up at Charles City, saying that Opechancanough wanted the help of eight or ten Englishmen with their arms. A tribe called the Massituppamohtnock which lived about one day's march above the "Falls" (at modern Richmond) had murdered "certain women of his, contrary to ye law of nations." [16]

Opechancanough offered to equip the English with moccasins and said his men would carry the English weapons until they should be needed in battle. He would share the booty of male and female children, he said, as well as corn and other things, and he would divide the conquered land with the English, half-and-half.

Yeardley and the Council had found this raid "lawful and well-grounded." Despite reports to the contrary, Opechancanough had not hitherto been cooperative, and this would be one way to oblige and please him. Not only that, it might also produce some captive Indian children, "as well for private uses of particular persons [as servants] as to furnish ye intended College."

This, they claimed, would advance a blessed work, "seeing those Indians are in no sort willing to sell or by fair means to part with their children." Then, too, their cooperation in this manoeuvre might win amity and confidence from Itopatin, the Great King, as well as Opechancanough, and from their subjects the Roanoke, Powhatan, and Pamunkey river tribes. Such ill-balanced thinking was not uncommon in the colony.

But nothing happened. At least, there seems to be no record of any such "cooperation" actually put into effect. Instead, the colonists continued to die like flies. The foundation of the college dawdled. And the months dragged by. Not even the silkworms really prospered.

On June 27, 1621, Thorpe wrote to Sir Edwin Sandys that within the next ten days he would visit Opechancanough, "who hath divers times sent for me." Opechancanough was to have further information about an unnamed something which Thorpe had offered him at a previous meeting. Thorpe hoped for success. But again there is no record of what happened, if anything.

A certain reward for Thorpe's efforts, however, came from London. The Council wrote that it approved of "taking in of Indian families" as a great means of civilizing and christianizing "that Nation." At the same time they sent a veiled warning for the Governor and Council in Virginia not to be thereby "entrapped, nor that the Savage have by this access means to surprise you." [17]

This advice was brought, along with other letters and communications, by the newly appointed Governor Wyatt. It reached Virginia sometime before November 18, the Sunday on which date Yeardley's commission expired and on which Wyatt was sworn in. It is to be assumed that the information was passed out at the General Assembly which was soon called.

Meanwhile, and not long before, John Pory, the Secretary, Ensign Thomas Savage, and others had made a trip up Chesapeake Bay and the Potomac River, where they found a "China Box" at one of the villages where they stopped. The "King" of the village told them that it was sent from another King, who dwelt ten days' journey to the west, over the hills. This western King, he said, lived near a great sea and got the box from a people who came in great ships and wore clothes and swords something like those of the English. These people, he added, "were called Acanack-China" — a notable example of a wish being father to mishearing.[18]

The explorers hurried back to inform Wyatt, who had been installed while they were away, that they doubted

> not but to find a safe, easy, and good passage [there] to the South Sea [Pacific Ocean], part by water, and part by land, esteeming it not above an hundred and fifty miles from the head of the Falls, where we are now planted.

Again, nothing happened. But the arrival of several ships from England took up much of the local Council's time and the colonists' energy. Most of them brought stories, of course. In fact, one of them, the *Tiger,* had been blown so far off course that she was taken by Turkish pirates somewhere, but released.

In February, 1622, John Pory went exploring once more — this time to the south, to the Chowan River in modern North Carolina. This was the region that had been explored by Ralph Lane thirty-six years before. Pory found quantities of the silk-grass which was so eagerly sought and located a pine forest over twenty miles long.[19] The forest was important for potash and soap-ashes, since the trees available for such things in Virginia were relatively scattered.

Then, on or shortly after Ash Wednesday, March 6, Jack of the Feathers appeared before the house of a colonist named Morgan. Morgan had commodities which he wanted, and he came to persuade him to go to the Pamunkey country, twenty or twenty-five miles to the north, to trade. Morgan agreed to make the trip.

Two or three days later, Jack reappeared at Morgan's house, alone. Two young servants, boys in training, saw him and asked where their master was. Jack answered that he was dead. The boys, seeing that Jack was wearing a cap of Morgan's and suspecting him of murder, tried to get him to go to George Thorpe's house with them. Jack put them off with what he thought was a plausible story, but the boys were insistent. Somehow they got hold of a gun and brought the Indian down with a shot.

Hauling Jack into a boat, the two then started to row him to where they knew the Governor was, not over seven or eight miles away. Jack, however, knowing that the shot was fatal, asked the boys to do him two favors. One was not to tell anyone that he was killed by a bullet; "the other, to bury him amongst the English." He had been so famous among the Indians that they thought that he could not be killed by any Englishman.

Opechancanough, as soon as he heard of this affair, sent dire threats of revenge to Governor Wyatt. But Wyatt only answered in still stronger terms. Opechancanough then feigned to yield and forego any revenge. He told the messenger to tell Wyatt "that he held the peace concluded [between them] so firm, as the sky should sooner fall than it dissolve."[20]

This was about March 15. On Wednesday, March 20, a handful of Englishmen who were lost were guided courteously and safely back to their plantation. That same day, a servant of Ralph

Hamor's named Browne, who had been living among the Warraskoyacks to learn their language, was sent back affably to Jamestown.

These attentions and other small favors served to increase the confidence of the English that Opechancanough's storm had blown over. That day and the next, a number of Indians pleasantly borrowed English boats to cross the James. The peace indeed seemed firm.

Friday morning, March 22, the usual Indians came unarmed to the English houses with deer, turkeys, fish, furs, or whatnot to truck and sell for the usual glass beads and other trifles. Some, upon invitation, sat down to share the colonists' breakfast. Others were out in the fields, where the men were planting corn or tobacco, gardening, making bricks, sawing wood, or at work on houses. All was as on other days before.

Then suddenly, as if at a preconcerted signal, the Indians turned on the whitemen. Seizing their weapons, their tools, and any arms they could find, they attacked the helpless colonists. As the official report read:

> And by this means that fatal Friday morning, there fell under the barbarous hands of that perfidious and inhuman people . . . three hundred forty seven men, women, and children, most by their own weapons. And not being content with taking away life alone, they fell after again upon the dead . . . defacing, dragging, and mangling the dead carcasses into many pieces, and carrying some parts away, with base and brutish triumph.

It was five years and one day since the body of Pocahontas had been peacefully laid to rest in St. George's Church in Gravesend. Would the peace she sought for Virginia be the peace of the grave, too? If so, for redman? Or for white?

CHAPTER 16

The Aftermath

FROM THE SCRIPTURES, as rendered into English by authority of King James, and published in 1611:

> Dearly beloved, avenge not yourselves, but *rather* give place unto wrath: for it is written, Vengeance *is* mine; I will repay, saith the Lord. (ROMANS, 12, 19)

> Love ye your enemies, and do good, and lend, hoping for nothing again; and your reward shall be great, and ye shall be the children of the Highest: for he is kind unto the unthankful and *to* the evil. (LUKE, 6, 35)

After the calamity, a month or more of beserk activity slipped by before Governor Wyatt was able to pen a letter to London.[1] Two ships had arrived in the interim, the *Bona Nova* with fifty new colonists, and the *Discovery* with twenty more. The *Bona Nova,* arriving on Sunday, April 7, in fact reached Jamestown before the Governor had gotten around to appointing local commanders to take charge of the hardest hit centers, or to transport those in the more exposed plantations to places of greater safety.

By that time the Governor and Council in Virginia, according to their letter of the last week in April, had decided

> to quit many of our plantations, and to unite more nearly together in fewer places the better for to strengthen and defend ourselve[s] against them [the Indians]. We have thought most fit to hol[d] these few places: James City with Paspahegh and certain plantations on the oth[er] side of the river over against [opposite] the city, and Kecoughtan and Newport News, Southampton Hundred, Flowerdieu Hundred, Shirley Hundred, and a plantation of Master Samuel Jordan's.

While Wyatt admitted that the colony should not have been permitted to spread itself out so haphazardly, he did what he could to repair the damage. It was not a simple matter, just at the planting time, to concentrate people, cattle, household goods, provisions, and all, in a handful of places.

He therefore begged London for help of all kinds, not the least of which was the Council's cooperation in authorizing only the Governor and Council *in* Virginia to allocate property to future colonists. It was pointed out that the Council *for* Virginia had mistakenly set aside properties for various colonists without consideration of local needs and expedience.

With this letter went the details of the massacre, which have already been mentioned. It needs to be noted here only that, if the pre-massacre population of twelve hundred and forty is more or less correct, more than one-fourth had been killed, leaving about nine hundred survivors. John Smith, combined with his printer, managed to praise Almighty God for sparing "eleven parts of twelve," which is glaringly false — perhaps the eleven should have read seven.[2]

This letter, along with an unknown number of other communications, must have reached London some time before July 3, 1622, for on that date the Quarter Court for Virginia "entreated" Sir Edward Sackville, brother (and heir) of the third Earl of Dorset,

> to acquaint the Lords of His Majesty's Council with the massacre of the English Colony in Virginia by the Indians there, and with the

> present [immediate] necessity of arms and people to make a reparation.

Two weeks later, Sir Edward reported to the next court that His Majesty had "apprehended . . . with great indignation" the cause of the massacre as being,

> that the planters in Virginia attended more [to] their present profit, rather than their safety, and pleasing their humors and fancies by living so scatteringly and dispersedly.

Nevertheless, His Majesty was "sensible" of the loss of so many of his subjects and the resultant state of the colony, and "was graciously pleased" to promise assistance to the company and the colony.[3]

Two weeks and one day passed, and on August 1, the Treasurer, Henry Earl of Southampton, and the Council for Virginia addressed a formal communication to Sir Francis Wyatt, Governor and Captain General of Virginia, and to the rest of the Council of Estate there.[4] Since communications of those days tended to be far from laconic, this letter ran to thirty-five hundred and more words. It criticized the colonists for putting on airs, with excess of fancy clothing and drinking, and blamed almost anybody for the disaster but the Council for Virginia. This was to be expected.

But what was not precisely to be expected, perhaps, was the vicious tenor of the Council's comments on the Indians. Because these comments, one fifth of the entire letter, have direct bearing on the future of the people on whose land the English had settled, the concluding part of the letter is here given in full. It is hardly consistent with the precepts of the Christian Church which the Council pretended to foster:

> These [foregoing paragraphs] are part of the remedies that are to be applied for the repairing of this late disaster. As for the Actors thereof, we cannot but with much grief proceed to the condemna-

tion of their bodies, the saving of whose souls we have so zealously affected. But since the innocent blood of so many Christians doth in justice cry out for revenge, and your future security in wisdom require, we must advise you to root out from being any longer a people, so cursed a nation, ungrateful to all benefits, and uncapable of all goodness: at least, to the removal of them so far from you as you may not only be out of danger, but out of fear of them, of whose faith and good meaning you can never be secure.

Wherefore, as they have merited, let them have a perpetual war, without peace or truce; and although they have deserved it without mercy too. Yet, remembering who we are, rather than what they have been, we cannot but advise not only the sparing, but the preservation, of the younger people of both sexes, whose bodies may by labor and service become profitable, and their minds not overgrown with evil customs, be reduced to civility, and afterwards to Christianity.

And because there is a necessity not only in the thing itself, but in the speediness of effecting it, we think it fit that, besides that certain way of famishing (whereunto we doubt not but you have ere this given a good beginning by the burning of their corn, or the reaping it to your own benefit), you add and put in execution all other ways and means of their destruction, not omitting so much as to provoke their neighboring enemies (by reward of beads and copper upon the bringing in of their heads) to the fierce pursuing of them: and that at such times especially as yourselves may issue out upon them likewise, which we think should be often done from all parts of the colony together.

But for a full securing of yourselves, and a certain destroying of them, we conceive no means so proper, nor expedient, as to maintain continually certain bands of men of able bodies, and inured to the Country, of stout minds and active hands, that may from time to time (in severed [separate] bodies) pursue and follow them, surprising them in their habitations, intercepting them in their hunting, burning their towns, demolishing their temples, destroying their canoes, plucking up their weirs, carrying away their corn, and depriving them of whatsoever may yield them succor or relief: by which means in a very short while both your just revenge and your perpetual security might be certainly effected.

As for the maintenance of those men with victuals and munition, we conceive it just and equal that it should be by a general levy throughout the whole Colony; in regard whereof, the one moiety [half] of the prise [things seized], as well of the persons of men for slaves as goods, should be unto the Colony for fortification and other public uses; and the other moiety divided amongst the soldiers themselves; in further satisfaction of whose travails and hazards we do purpose a liberal recompense, out of the labors of those young people which by His Majesty's gracious favor we hope to obtain out of the several counties of this realm, which, as it shall be bountiful to all, so it shall be redoubled to them into whose hands the principals either in execution or contrivement of this treachery shall fall.

But if any can take Opechancanough himself, he shall have a great and singular reward from us. As for those Indians whom God used as instruments of revealing and preventing the total ruin of you all, we think a good respect and recompense due unto them, which be [by] a good and careful education of them may best be expressed and satisfied; whereby they may be made capable of further benefits and favors.

We send you a copy, etc.,

Your very loving friends,
THE TREASURER AND COUNCIL FOR VIRGINIA.

Wyatt and his colonists went to work with a will. Armed with all the power that advanced technical means could supply, stinted only by a purse watching Council, the whitemen set out to incapacitate, subject, enslave, or destroy the redmen.

Powhatan's people had neither Christian voices nor arms nor manpower to save them. Not even their fellow redmen came to their help — for Indian solidarity was as nonexistent as English understanding.

In a savage burst of revenge, the pious subjects of King James I began the historic march of progress across the land that left the survivors of the original inhabitants herded into reservations. There, in poverty and denial, they were allowed to eke out a livelihood from some of the most inhospitable soil in all America.

Pocahontas had long lain in her unmarked spot by the Thames in England. The peace she sought, and for a few years gave to the colony, was gone. It would not come again until the last vestige of Indian independence was surrendered to the white invaders from across the seas.

CHAPTER 17

What Happened to the Three Englishmen in Pocahontas' Life

John Rolfe

ON MARCH 10, 1622, John Rolfe, "of James City in Virginia, Esquire, being sick in body, but of perfect mind and memory," dictated his last will and testament. The surviving probate copy does not state whether he himself wrote or even signed the original, but there were five signatures which declared it to be genuine: Rev. Richard Buck, Temperance Lady Yeardley, John Cartwright, Robert Davis, and John Milward.[1]

John Rolfe almost certainly died of natural causes before the fateful Friday of the massacre. Sometime after his return to Virginia in 1617 he had married again. The last Mrs. Rolfe was Jane, daughter of William and Joan Pierce who curiously seem to have crossed the Atlantic on separate ships in 1609–1610 — he, on the *Sea Adventure* (with Rolfe), arriving in 1610, and she, on the *Blessing* (with Gabriel Archer), reaching Jamestown safely in 1609. There seems to be no record of whether Jane accompanied her mother or her father, but in any case she was in Virginia by the summer of 1610.

There was one child of this marriage, Elizabeth Rolfe, who was born in 1620. To his wife and Elizabeth, John Rolfe left a parcel of some 1700 acres near Mulberry Island, fifteen miles downstream from Jamestown. Nothing further seems to be known about Elizabeth, beyond the fact that she was living in 1625. Her mother, Jane Rolfe, had remarried — a Captain Roger Smith — and the little girl was living with the Smiths after the massacre. So was one of the Negroes brought to Jamestown in 1619.[2]

The bulk of John Rolfe's property, however, went to Thomas, his son by Pocahontas. The property near Smith's Fort, across the river from Jamestown, went to Thomas as well as a tract near to, or adjoining, this plantation which had been given to him by Opechancanough.

It would seem that Thomas Rolfe returned to Virginia by 1635 when he was about twenty. Nothing further is known until 1641, when Thomas requested the permission of the Governor to visit his aunt "Cleopatra and his kinsman Opechancanough" — what good Algonkian name lurks behind that absurd importation from Egypt? And shortly thereafter, Thomas was appointed Captain of Fort James, this honor requiring his virtual denial of his Indian ancestry. Opechancanough ordered a second massacre of the English in 1644, far less damaging than the first, and in it as well as in the war that followed, Thomas had to aid the whitemen against his mother's people. At this time and just before he was murdered, Opechancanough reached an agreement with Governor Berkeley that gave the English full rights to the peninsula between the James and the York, from the fall-line to Chesapeake Bay.

About then, Thomas Rolfe married Jane Poythress, daughter of Captain Francis Poythress, a not inconsiderable landholder near Henrico. The couple had a daughter, another Jane, who married Colonel Robert Bolling in 1675. Whether Thomas and his wife were still alive at the time is not known. Thomas is mentioned in a land patent dated September 16, 1658, but history is silent about both of them thereafter.[3]

Jane Rolfe and Colonel Bolling had one child, a son named John, born in 1676. Jane died in childbirth or very shortly thereafter. John Bolling, also named Colonel later in life, was thus the sole living descendant of Pocahontas as the seventeenth century closed.

With the birth of John Bolling the younger, however, the line was perpetuated. Not only did John (born in 1700) marry Elizabeth Blair and beget four sons and three daughters, but his five sisters, all younger than himself, also married and added twenty-six known branches of the family. A few of these survived into the 1800's, of whom the most famous was surely Pocahontas' granddaughter's granddaughter's grandson, John Randolph, the noted member of Congress who served from the end of Washington's administration almost continually till that of Andrew Jackson. By the time Randolph died, there were literally hundreds of Pocahontas' posterity, scattered far and wide.

One of these hundreds has written a "Resumé" of the Pocahontas stock which seems worthy of reproduction:

> they were more prudent than enterprising, more wasteful than liberal, more amiable than censorious, more respected than distinguished, more honest than able, more patriotic than indifferent, more conservative than radical, more pious than bigoted, and while a few fell to the depths of worthlessness, but none to crime, a few also rose to the height of genius and virtue.[4]

Samuel Argall

John Rolfe had married Pocahontas for a variety of reasons which must forever remain obscure to the modern mind. He who made such a marriage possible patently had a less-complicated mental make-up. Captain Samuel Argall evidently was a man of disciplined mind, who preferred stratagems to force and pressure to bloodshed. He heard that Pocahontas was visiting the Potomac werowance and immediately set about abducting her *solely* for the "ransoming of so many Englishmen as were prisoners with Powhatan; as also to get such arms and tools as he, and other Indians, had got by murder and stealing from others of our nation." [5]

Such nuances of feeling as religious conversion or an Anglo-Algonkian détente to be wrought through her can hardly have occurred to him. Thanks to this detached point of view and to his insistence on the maintenance of a policy of "what is right is right" (witness the treatment of the Frenchmen he captured), Argall's act unbelievably brought peace. That the peace was short-lived was the fault of the Three Gray Sisters who spin the web of human destiny, not Argall's.

Thus, when he returned to England in apparently indecent haste to defend himself against a host of accusations the justice of which has still remained far from attested, it can hardly come as a surprise that within three months of his arrival the East India Company included him among four captains to "be conferred with" regarding possible employment.[6]

Although nothing came of this immediately, the proposal indicated that Argall was not without friends. But he was also not without bitter enemies. As a result, it is impossible to judge, on the basis of surviving documents, to what extent Argall may have been guilty of what were then called depredations. That he had his own pocketbook at heart cannot be denied, nor that his feet customarily rested on the solid ground of orders issued to him by the Virginia Company. There seems to be no way today to separate the motive of personal gain in some of Argall's administrative actions from his care to see that Company instructions were obeyed.

In any case, a long, drawn-out inquiry was instituted in London, which Argall apparently faced with equanimity. Only once does he seem to have lost patience, and then it was over a matter of four oxen of which a widow in Virginia claimed she had been despoiled. The widow carried the matter to the highest court — the King himself. When King James referred the matter back to the Virginia Company and the widow retracted her complaint, saying she had been incited to it, Argall, perhaps not without reason, "with some extraordinary vehemency" declared that he suspected some of the Virginia Council itself of doing the inciting.

Pinned down as to whom he accused, Argall baldly stated that he suspected Sir Edwin Sandys. Sir Edwin was shocked by this charge, but there is no evidence that Argall's outburst damaged his case. Indeed, all that resulted was that Sir Edwin complained that Argall was never brought to a "full and final trial" because of his "great friends" and that Argall's answers did not satisfy him, personally.[7] It seems hard to believe that Sir Edwin, the "great parliamentarian," should have been stymied by Robert Rich, second Earl of Warwick (after the death of his father in March, 1619) or even by the financial and mercantile power of Sir Thomas Smythe. On the other hand, it could well be that Samuel Argall's own surefooted self-defence did the trick.

It may also be that Captain Brewster's personal attack on Argall, which was by far the most virulent and the most persistent, aided rather than weakened Argall's case. Argall, by attending almost every meeting of the Virginia Company from June 9 to December 15, 1619, brought it about that the matter was in substance turned over to four commissioners to study, two for him, and two against. With that, all sense of urgency subsided. In fact Brewster, after repeatedly insisting on a hearing from May 12, 1619, to May 17, 1620, only got one the following May 23, and then with relatively little satisfaction.[8] Some five years later, Brewster was still complaining.

In the interim, Argall was out of London for a while early in 1620, on unexplained matters, but was involved in another legal inquiry in July. This was a suit by his friend Captain John Bargrave against Sir Thomas Smythe and others of the Virginia Company. Argall was called only as a witness, but again the courts moved very slowly indeed. This inquiry is of importance here only in that, in a sense, it heralded the storm that was to bring about the end of the Virginia Company in 1624.[9]

Also in 1620, Argall joined with seven other early personal adventurers in petitioning the lords of the Council for Virginia "to have some man of quality" sent as Governor of Virginia. They were disappointed in Governor Yeardley. Argall was evidently at loggerheads with Yeardley already, although Yeardley had given his eldest son the name Argall. But the signatures on the petition of Sir Thomas Gates, Captain Francis West, Captain Daniel Tucker (ex-Governor of Bermuda), and other responsible members of the Company bear witness to something more than casual spite or personal animosity.[10]

In June, the Council issued the "Declaration," already mentioned, which painted a glowing picture of progress and hope for the future. Whether this was published before the petition or deliberately ignored it, Samuel Argall was already turning his attention to what appeared to be an important new employment.

Pirates had long been a nuisance and often a danger to all seagoing nations. Algiers was their so far inexpugnable nest, from which vindictive ships, singly or in groups, sailed out to terrorize peaceful merchantmen. England had not had a navy of any consequence since Queen Elizabeth's day, but by 1617 the Earl of Southampton was urging King James to assemble one to rid the Mediterranean and the Atlantic of these pests, and before the end of August an expedition was ready. It was composed of royal ships and armed merchantmen. Samuel Argall was given the command of one of the largest of the latter, for his old friend Sir Robert Mansell had been appointed Admiral of the fleet of eighteen ships. Sir Robert had been Vice Admiral of the Narrow Seas ever since Argall had known him. At the same time, Sir Richard Hawkins, son of the great Elizabethan navigator Sir John Hawkins, was named Vice Admiral for the 1620 expedition.[11]

The expedition was perhaps mistaken in conception, was probably mismanaged despite Hawkins, the Vice-Admiral, and Argall, and was certainly unfortunate in its timing. It set sail October 12, turned into the roadstead of Gibraltar nineteen days later, and shortly after received a setback off Algiers. Mansell might have recouped his losses, but the twelve-year truce between the Dutch and the Spaniards had lapsed in April and war was being resumed. The English navy was needed at home. Consequently, before the end of July, 1621, Mansell was recalled, to be kept "under hatches" as John Chamberlain picturesquely put it, until the end of 1623.[12]

Hawkins was excessively depressed by what was for him an ignominious end to a career. In the spring of 1622 he was in ill health. On April 16, he signed his will, and on the next day, during discussions of the Algerian expedition in the Privy Council, he "died of vexation." [13]

Samuel Argall came out of the inglorious exploit with no damage to his reputation. Hearing that "certain Hollanders were upon the coast of New England trading with the Indians between Cape Cod and Bay de la Warre," he quickly took it into his head to establish an English colony on the "Manahata" (now Hudson) River, where he had encountered the Dutch eight years before.[14]

Since that encounter, however, the clique in Plymouth which had been making efforts to found a "North Virginia" colony in the region named New England by Captain John Smith had come to life again. Sir Ferdinando Gorges had long been the moving spirit of this design, and on November 3, 1620, he obtained a charter for a Council for New England.

There were questions of rights to be solved between the new

New England Council and the old Virginia Council, but the Privy Council orders of June 18, 1621, settled all such matters. In other words, just before Samuel Argall returned from Algiers, Gorges was in a position to go ahead with his plans for colonizing New England.

Gorges seems unfortunately never to have made plans without finding stumbling blocks. Late in 1620, the group of English religious dissenters from Leyden, Holland, who have since become famous as the "Pilgrims," settled at Plymouth, Massachusetts. The Plymouth group was granted a patent, and the Dutch were ignored (for the time being). But Gorges' proposed colony still remained to be activated. He went to London to see what could be accomplished.

It was then, apparently, that Gorges met Samuel Argall — if their paths had not crossed before.[15] Because of this encounter, Argall switched his interest in ousting the Dutch from Manhattan to backing the proposed New England colony, and before May, 1622, he was added to the reborn Council, which now totaled forty members. His presence was noted at the first recorded meeting of the Council, on "Saturday the last of May, 1622" — though May 31 fell on a Friday.

Quickly becoming one of the most active councillors, Argall was named Admiral for New England. (In 1617, the New England promoters had promised John Smith that title.)[16] And on June 26 he was knighted by King James at Rochester. By then his residence had been changed to the manor in Walthamstow of which his grandfather Thomas had been lord more than half a century before. It is evident that Sir Samuel was a man of means by 1622. As to his professional abilities, there had never been any doubt.

Argall seems to have been busy with the affairs of the New England Council through 1622 and 1623, and after. At that time Ludovic Stuart, Duke of Lennox and second cousin of the King, was President. Created Duke of Richmond as well in 1623, Ludovic suddenly died on February 16, 1624. George Villiers, created Duke of Buckingham at the same ceremony as the Duke of Richmond, succeeded to the presidency of the Council.[17] A meeting between Buckingham and Argall was then inevitable, but to understand its importance for Argall we must glance at Buckingham's career.

Buckingham was more interested in England and Europe than in the colonization of New England. King James was failing in health. Buckingham all but ruled England in his name, and the Thirty Years War on the Continent, involving the King's daughter and her husband, was infinitely more important to both the Duke and his master than the uncomfortable toehold on the primeval wilderness of America. Just then, at the zenith of Buckingham's career, James I died. It was March 27, 1625.

James I was succeeded by Charles I. Buckingham persuaded Charles to develop an anti-Spanish policy and to that end to build up the British navy. In testimony of Buckingham's success, the new King's first public appearance was when he went to inspect the new Royal Navy and other shipping at Blackwall.[18]

That was in April, 1625. During the summer, a plan for the harassment of Spanish ports was worked out, and Sir Edward Cecil, nephew of King James' late Secretary of State, was made Lord Marshal and General of the Sea and Land Forces and was created Viscount Wimbledon.

Shortly thereafter, Cecil received word from Buckingham that there were "about eighteen sail of Dunkirk ships [privateers] gone towards the west, keeping the French coast towards Spain," and that he should call a council of war to take steps to "meet with them."

A not unexpected outcome of this was that on September 8, 1625, Argall, noted for his ability as a navigator, was appointed

Admiral of a fleet of twenty-four English and four Dutch ships to intercept the Dunkirkers.[19] Buckingham surely had something to do with the appointment.

The next day, Cecil signed his instructions for Argall, and Argall issued his commands for his Vice Admiral and Rear Admiral, with twenty-two supplementary details for the ship-captains. (The old sea-dog in him breathes in every line of these.) Argall was a professional. Whether it was Buckingham personally, Cecil, or someone else who noticed this does not matter.

Sir Samuel did not capture any of the ships he was sent to capture. But not to return empty-handed, he collected a long queue of Dutch and French prizes. These, he intimated, were carrying on traffic with the Spanish Netherlands.

Some months passed before it was determined that this was not entirely true. By that time, however, Sir Samuel had already been chosen captain of the *Swiftsure,* the Earl of Essex's ship in the Spanish expedition. Then, Buckingham arrived at Plymouth on October 1, inspected the fleet, and on October 3, commanded that the *Swiftsure* forthwith sail for Falmouth, there to await the rest of the fleet before sailing for Spain. (Dutch ships, of course, formed part of this fleet, too.)[20]

At last, on Saturday, October 22, the expedition sighted their chief goal, Cadiz. Cecil determined to land his own men inside the bay, at Puerto Santa María, while Essex was instructed to anchor the ships bearing the ground forces as near the shore as possible and also near the same port. A battle ensued which lasted until midnight, with little damage to the English ships.

Meanwhile, Argall, in the absence of Essex, was commanded on October 25 to sail his squadron up the bay, to the right, to Puerto Real, "there to charge, take, sink or burn all the ships and vessels that were there, of the subjects of the King of Spain, or other enemy."

That night, Argall sent boats to explore the river, and to sound, and after much exchanging of messengers and the like, the Admiral, Cecil, Lord Wimbledon, approved Argall's decision to retreat. The project was unsound. This was accomplished safely on October 27, although not without skirmishes in which some men were killed.

Two days later, Cecil decided to abandon the Cadiz expedition. The return voyage was uneventful, and on Monday morning, December 5, the fleet sighted the coast of England again and "stood in for Falmouth."

Seven weeks later, Sir Samuel Argall was dead. On January 28, 1626, John Pennington, a veteran navigator who was one of Buckingham's trusties, wrote to the Duke from Plymouth apologizing for his delay in "the business committed to my care" and mentioning that the *Swiftsure,* Argall's ship, was to come from Falmouth, among other details.

On page three of this letter, a new paragraph reads as follows, without further introduction:

> The master of the *Swiftsure* hath been very backward in bringing about of his ship, and very cross to his Captain, Sir Samuel Argall, as the report goes, which broke his heart, and four days since [i.e., January 24, 1626] he departed this life.[21]

Such was the end of Captain Sir Samuel Argall. He had deep pride in efficiency, and that pride was dealt too great a blow. Just as had Sir Richard Hawkins four years before, Argall died of vexation —"a broken heart" Pennington called it. As had, perhaps, Pocahontas.

Argall's will, probated on March 21, 1626, is long and detailed and appears to have been written in his own hand.[22] The bequests show that Sir Samuel was possessed of considerable property yet was not a truly wealthy man. But the most revealing detail in the will is a bequest of a hundred pounds sterling and "all my lands, tenements [holdings], goods and chattels lying and being in Virginia" to Annie Percivall, the wife of Samuel Percivall of London, chandler, "to have and to hold unto her forever." There seems to be no further mention of Annie Percivall in Sir Samuel's surviving papers.

By way of postscript to this provision of Sir Samuel's will, there is a statement in the 1633 Visitation (census) of London, signed by Alexander Bolling of London, scrivener, to the effect that he is the husband of Anne, daughter of Sir Samuel Argall.

Samuel Argall mentioned no wife in his will; there is no known record of his marriage, and Anne is not mentioned as his daughter. The conclusions to be drawn are clear. Anne's mother remains anonymous, for the moment. But it is well worth noting that Anne's husband, Alexander Bolling, must have been a cousin of John Bolling of Yorkshire whose son Robert married Jane Rolfe, daughter of Thomas Rolfe and granddaughter of Pocahontas.

Captain John Smith[23]

After his visit to Pocahontas outside London, in 1616, John Smith went to the West Country — Bristol, Plymouth, and so on — trying to get backing for the New England colony *he* had in mind. (It differed from some of the other proposals.) At the same time, he toyed with a project for whale-fishing under the ægis of the King of Denmark. Denmark produced nothing, and from the West Country he got only wild promises which, when the time came to act, dwindled to a petty exploring voyage. And even that went wrong. When his three ships were ready, contrary gales held them prisoners in Plymouth harbor. Before the gales subsided, three months later, the expedition had been called off.

With this bit of misfortune added to previous failures, Smith abandoned all active participation in colonial ventures to dedicate himself to writing about them. His first book on New England appeared while Pocahontas was in England. In 1620 he put out another on the same subject. These two little books, supplemented by the map of New England which graced the first work in 1616, were of notable consequence in the 1620 voyage of the Pilgrims to Cape Cod and Plymouth, Massachusetts. In fact, Smith offered his services to the Pilgrims, but, probably suspicious of his domineering personality and his religious leanings, they said, in Smith's words, "my books and maps were much better cheap to teach them than myself."

By then, John Smith had appealed to the Virginia Company for financial aid, but there is no record that he ever got it. At about the same time, the steward, or major-domo, of the Berkeley estate, John Smyth by name, was proposing before the same Virginia Company that a history of the Virginia colony be written. Captain John Smith seems to have heard of this and taken up the idea. And in 1624, after boundless effort and in great haste, Smith's chef-d'oeuvre was published: *The Generall Historie of Virginia, New-England, and the Summer Isles* [*Bermuda*].

To produce this work, John Smith begged for, and received, financial assistance from the widow of Ludovic Stuart, first president of the New England Council. It brought him fame and satisfaction. People of importance got interested in him, apparently for the first time.

In short order thereafter, Smith produced an odd handbook for sailors in 1626 and, a year later, a *Sea Grammar* which, though it was deeply indebted to the work of Sir Henry Mainwaring, was for years the only manual for seamen in English.[24] Three years later,

Smith published a curious hodge-podge of autobiography and hearsay Virginia history called the *True Travels* — to abbreviate the twenty-two-word title. And in 1631 his summary of "how to erect a plantation" came out. This wistful work was composed while he was a guest of Sir Humphrey Mildmay at the Mildmay manor near Danbury, Essex.

The *Advertisements for the unexperienced Planters of New-England, or any where: Or The Pathway to experience to erect a Plantation* had hardly appeared on the market when John Smith was taken sick. Back in London, where he had a room or small apartment in the mansion of Sir Samuel Saltonstall, he called for a scrivener and dictated his last will and testament. Given a goose-quill for his signature, he was unable to hold it firmly. The quill stuck on the paper, and spattered. At last, he gave up. The scrivener wrote "the mark of the said John Smith" around the spatter, and the witnesses signed their names in attestation.[25]

Before the day was out, that 21st day of June, 1631, John Smith died. For twenty-three years his pen had been employed in the service of English colonization, as had his wits, his arms, and his determination. If only because he was the first major writer in the history of American literature, the last paragraph he "writ . . . with his own hand" is worth quoting. It has pertinence even today:

> Lastly, remember as faction, pride, and security, produces nothing but confusion, misery, and dissolution; so the contraries well practised will in short time make you happy, and the most admired people of all our plantations for your time in the world.

Such was the humble farmer from Lincolnshire whose life was somehow saved by Pocahontas. Small wonder it is that his name, above all others, is still associated with hers. The poetry of legend is truer than the bald fact of history.

L'envoi

In the woods of Powhattan,
  Still 'tis told by Indian fires,
  How a daughter of their sires,
Saved the captive Englishman.

WILLIAM MAKEPEACE THACKERAY
"Pocahontas" [26]

Appendixes

APPENDIX I

Notes on So-called Relics of Powhatan and Pocahontas

It is far from the author's inclination to "debunk" anything or anybody. Nevertheless, it would seem desirable to cast an inquiring eye over those relics of the past which have been associated with Powhatan and Pocahontas. Although at least one of these is undoubtedly genuine, doubts can soundly be raised regarding at least one of the rest. The status of inquiry at the time of writing is as follows.

Powhatan's Mantle

This object is in the Ashmolean Museum, Oxford. It measures roughly 233 x 150 cm. (7′ 8″ x 4′ 11″) and is made of four pieces of tanned buckskin bearing a design in shell beads depicting a standing human figure flanked by two quadrupeds and a series of large rosettes. It is customarily identified with an entry in the catalogue of John Tradescant the Younger, published in London in 1656:

> *Pohatan,* King of Virginia's habit all embroidered with shells, or Roanoke.

Dr. William C. Sturtevant, of the Smithsonian Institution, and Mr. Christian F. Feest, of the Museum für Völkerkunde, Vienna, have been studying the matter, and (although there is "more work to be done") are of the opinion now that the mantle "is Virginia Indian and from the early 17th century," but they "doubt that it is a mantle or habit, and the association with Powhatan seems not to be firmly documented" (personal letter to me, dated October 2, 1968).

While subscribing to this judgment, I myself make so bold as to suggest that Powhatan's mantle was more likely made of raccoon skins (see Arber, *Smith, Works,* 19; Barbour, *Jamestown Voyages,* 185). Just such an item is listed in the Tradescant catalogue directly below the Powhatan "habit," a "Matchcoat of Virginia made of raccoon-skins" — apparently now lost.

In addition, Mr. Feest notes that although John Tradescant the Elder was a friend and beneficiary of John Smith, the latter "does not seem to have contributed to Tradescant's collection of curiosities," which, judging from the catalogue, did not include his library (Feest, *Miscellany II,* 10). Smith did, however, bequeath half his books to the elder Tradescant, whose library in turn joined that of Elias Ashmole, the whole of which was donated to the Bodleian Library, Oxford, before the end of the seventeenth century. There, in 1966, I personally examined all former Tradescant volumes which might conceivably have belonged to Smith, but did not find a single book inscribed by him.

Pocahontas' Mulberry-tree

Tradition has it that an old mulberry-tree in the gardens at Heacham Hall "was planted at the time of a visit of John Rolfe and his wife." The sole support for this assertion seems to be the fact that "in 1605 King James I ordered the planting of mulberry-trees to encourage the silk industry by the cultivation of silk-worms" (see *Rolfe Family Records,* II, 14, with a drawing of the tree).

Simon van de Passe's Engraving of Pocahontas

This noted engraving is signed by the artist, and there is no occasion to doubt its authenticity. The date when prints of it were available is attested by John Chamberlain, "Here is a fine picture of no fair Lady . . ." (letter to Carleton, already mentioned, dated February 22, 1616/17; *Letters,* II, 57).

Oil Portrait of Pocahontas, Now in the National Portrait Gallery, Washington, D.C.

This portrait has been called the "Rolfe," the "Gorleston," and the "Booton Hall" portrait. Its history is unfortunately confused, but a tradition that it was long owned by the Elwin family seems to be uncontested (see Appendix II for the connection between the Elwins and the Rolfes). It was acquired from the Elwin heir by Francis Burton Harrison, a descendant of Pocahontas who was Governor of the Philippines, 1913–1921. Twelve years later it "entered the Mellon Collection" and from there passed to the National Gallery of Art and the Smithsonian Institution's National Portrait Gallery (information sheet sent me early in 1964).

There are accounts of the portrait in Arber, *Smith, Works,* cxxxvi, and *Rolfe Family Records,* II, 20–21, but since the accuracy of both of these have been contested or contradicted, it seems best to omit the details. Let us consider it as of now.

While I am neither an ethnographer nor an art historian, a careful inspection of the painting has led me to doubt that it was painted from life. In fact, as will be suggested below, it seems to have been a copy of the van de Passe engraving, done in oil. There is not even any evidence that the painting dates back to the early seventeenth century, although it is known to have been in existence in Norfolk at least since the 1760's or 1770's. Only a chemical test could establish its true age, and this is most likely out of the question, since it would cause serious damage to the painting. The National Portrait Gallery can therefore go no further than to say, in their latest information sheet, that the "ultimate origin" of the portrait "has not yet been determined."

Nevertheless, thanks to the cooperation of Dr. Sturtevant and the National Portrait Gallery, I believe that the following details present strong evidence to support the hypothesis suggested above. A European portrait-painter of 1616–1617 would surely have noticed that Pocahontas was "brown" or "tawny," like the rest of her people. But the color of her skin in the portrait is clearly European, and her hair is a European brown, not an Indian black. Relying only on the engraving, a painter-copyist would not have recognized his own error.

Then, as Dr. Sturtevant has observed, compared with the engraving, the features have been smoothed out, losing some individuality and appearing less Indian. Furthermore, the ornamentation of the clothing is simpler in the painting, and such particulars of the engraving as the following are missing in the painting: the plume on the hat, the bead or loop edging of the hatband, the damask-like watering of the cloth of the coat and its turned-back left edge, and the bracelet on the right wrist. In addition, the lace on the ruff and cuffs and the design on the handle of the fan have been simplified. These differences are much more consistent with a derivation of the painting from the engraving, Dr. Sturtevant says, "than with the reverse filiation."

Again, the portrait gives Rolfe's Christian name as "Tho:," for Thomas, not as "Joh:," for John. It is hard to believe that a painter doing a portrait from life of the spouse of Master John Rolfe would have put down "Thomas." On the other hand, a painter who was copying van de Passe's engraving could readily have made such a slip, particularly if he got to work on it after Pocahontas was dead and John Rolfe had sailed for Virginia, leaving Thomas, their son, in England. In fact, there is the puzzling recording of John Rolfe as Thomas in Book 5 of the Parish Register at Gravesend, already mentioned. *That* error was made when Thomas was barely two years old.

Another "minor slip," pointed out by Dr. Sturtevant, is "Rebecka" on the framing inscription, for the "Rebecca" of the engraving, and perhaps also the small size of the æ of "Virginiæ" is also significant: "the painter saw that the badly planned spacing had required squeezing in the ligature, and corrected for it in his copying" (personal letter).

Finally, the National Portrait Gallery suggests that the painting "may have been done from the drawing which was used to engrave the plate from which the engraving was printed" (information sheet of May, 1969). I agree with Dr. Sturtevant that there is no reason "to posit a lost sketch for the engraving as the model for the painting."

The Sedgeford Portrait of Pocahontas with her son Thomas Rolfe

This portrait was purchased by Eustace Neville Rolfe (1845–1908) of Heacham Hall "from Mrs. Charlton, who stated that 'her husband had bought it in America years ago'" (*Rolfe Family Records,* II, 22). It now hangs in the home of Mr. and Mrs. Alexander J. Stevenson, in West Calder, Midlothian. (Mrs. Stevenson is a grandniece of Eustace Neville Rolfe.) Thanks to their courtesy, I was able to inspect the painting, and to convince myself that it has nothing to do with Pocahontas. Dr. Sturtevant believes that it may represent "an 18th-century Iroquois woman and child" (personal letter).

The So-called Turkey Island Portrait

This again has nothing to do with Pocahontas. The original, which was presented to Ryland Randolph (a descendant who died in 1784), has been lost or destroyed. A copy of it made by Thomas Sully was reproduced in McKenny and Hall, *Indian Tribes,* in 1844.

The Gravesend Portrait

This also has no connection with Pocahontas. It hangs in St. George's Church, Gravesend, and "is a reproduction of a painting formerly in the possession of Mr. Plews Howdon, who was a lay reader at Northfleet Church [a couple of miles from Gravesend] . . . The style of dress would appear to be much later than that in the authentic painting at Washington . . . more like Queen Anne or Georgian" (letter from Mr. Robert Heath Hiscock, author of *A History of the Parish Churches of Gravesend,* dated October 28, 1968). While I was unable to view the painting myself (it was temporarily in storage when I was there), the reproduction of it in Mr. Hiscock's book shows that he is quite right.

The Pocahontas Vase

This is another heirloom of the Elwin family. Its present owner, Mrs. Elwin Stock, was kind enough to show this to me personally and to point out the initials *M* and *R* which are crudely scratched on the (tarnished) silver rim and which are considered some sort of proof of Pocahontas' ownership. To my untrained eye, these proved nothing. The family tradition, over certainly very many years, is more convincing.

This small earthenware vase, only a span high, could be described as "pale mushroom" in color, and is decorated by the application of stamps or reliefs. There seem to be traces of salt glaze, although I had no magnifying glass handy. After comparison with similar pottery in the Victoria and Albert Museum and consultation with the Keeper of the Ceramics Department, Mr. Charleston, I can say that it is typical of the vases produced in the Rhine valley from the end of the sixteenth century to the disruptions caused by the Thirty Years War. That it *could* have belonged to Pocahontas there can be little doubt. That it in fact did remains to be proven.

The Pocahontas Earrings

These, "of a peculiar white shell, set in silver," belonged to John Girdlestone Rolfe, who died about 1874. They are described in *Rolfe Family Records,* II, 21–22 and 324, as being "identical with the earrings represented in the Sedgeford portrait." Since I had no photograph of the Pocahontas earrings with me when I inspected the portrait, I can only say that there is a strong resemblance. The important point is that the Pocahontas of the van de Passe engraving wears pearl-drop earrings of a type quite common in the days of Queen Anne (of Denmark), and very different from the well-known "relic."

Marguerite Stuart Quarles, in her *Pocahontas* (p. 24), goes into considerable detail regarding the preservation of these earrings in the family of Henry Rolfe (of Narford?), and their origin and setting (p. 47). But the account in *Rolfe Family Records,* II, 323–24, claims that they belonged to John Girdlestone (also "Gurdleston") Rolfe, a grandson of Girdlestone Rolfe of Lambeth, believed to have descended from the family of John Rolfe of Heacham (see Appendix II). They are now owned by the Association for the Preservation of Virginia Antiquities, and are on exhibit in the National Park Service Visitors' Center at Jamestown, Virginia.

Pocahontas' Skeleton

In 1895 one Charles Ap Thomas published a little book in Gravesend called *Ye true Narrative of ye Princess Pocahontas* in which he wrote that "tradition . . . gives the place of her death as at a hostelry or cottage" on the London Road, and "her burial on the site, or in the close vicinity, of the then disused old parish church of Saint Marie's . . ." (p. 34). A leaflet placed in the copy of this book belonging to the Gravesend Central Library, however, points to the absurdity of this tradition, adding the "opinion . . . that by consent of the Rector [of St. George's Church] (the Rev. N. Frankwell) the remains of the Princess were placed in the Rector's vault . . ." To this Mr. Hiscock, in his book referred to above, adds that there were other burials under the chancel in St. George's in the seventeenth century.

In any event, St. George's was renovated in 1892, and a new chancel was built. Two vaults were found, both of which were empty, along with two coffins below the east window, which were not inspected. Five years later, when the north aisle was built, "a large number of charred bones and skulls were found." These were buried outside, in the grave of the Curd family.

In 1907, the London *Daily Mail* of July 22 (p. 5, col. 7) published an item, as follows:

> A skeleton has been unearthed at Gravesend, which is thought to be that of Pocahontas, the famous Indian princess, who, tradition says, saved the life of Captain John Smith . . .

Alas, the skull turned out to be that of a Negro who had been killed by a blow on the back of the head.

The quest for Pocahontas' remains was nevertheless not abandoned.

In 1923 a group was organized by the Virginia art critic J. Page Gaston and permission was obtained to open the Curd family grave and inspect the "coffin" which they hoped to find. Their efforts were worse than fruitless, for after digging up a quantity of cans and rubbish, "including the bones of a pig, sheep, ox, dog, cat and rabbit," an assortment was found of remains of "at least 130 individuals" which could by no stretch of the imagination be connected with Pocahontas.

Long before all this, however, a gruesome story had been circulated which would account for the absence of any material evidence of the burial of Pocahontas in Gravesend. According to this, "the coffin of the Princess was stolen by body snatchers and taken up the river to London where their attempts to sell it were foiled." The body in question was reinterred, and by 1851 all trace of it was lost. The origin of this tale was probably the burial of an Indian squaw in St. John the Evangelist, Waterloo Road, in 1835.

The First Continental Reference to Pocahontas' Death

While it is in no sense a matter of a relic, it is worth noting here that a German translation of Ralph Hamor's *True Discourse* was published by Levinus Hulsius in Hanau in 1617. In this, the news of Pocahontas' death was inserted, along with some additional and wholly imaginary details: she "was baptized in the *Infantinstrasse* [!] in London, attended by many knights and ordinary folk . . ." and so on (see Heilbronner, "Earliest Printed Account," p. 274 and note 4).

A "Portrait" of Powhatan

John Smith's 1612 map of Virginia contains a "portrait" by William Hole, with the caption, "Powhatan Held this state & fashion when Capt*ayn* Smith was deliuered to him prisoner." Christian F. Feest has demonstrated in his "Virginia Indian in Pictures" (pp. 6 and 21) that Hole composed this from elements in various depictions of Carolina Algonkian Indians in Theodor de Bry's *America,* Part I, with the exception of Powhatan's feather crown. This is either a realistic element or an engraver's addition taken from some unidentified picture of South American Indians.

(Note: I am indebted for this reference to Dr. Sturtevant, who has also contributed many suggestions to the whole of Appendix I. I take this opportunity to express my sincere thanks.)

APPENDIX II

Notes on the Rolfe Family

The family name of Rolfe dates back to the Domesday Book in Nottinghamshire and Norfolk. By the seventeenth century it appears in the records of at least twelve other counties as well as the city of London. Under such circumstances, it is hardly surprising that a Rolfe by the name of John should have proven, and continue to prove, difficult to identify, despite his marriage to Pocahontas. The chief obstacle is that there seems to be no contemporary evidence of the place, or even the county, from which he hailed.

To be sure, Pocahontas' husband stated in a letter of 1617 that he had a brother named Henry who then lived in London and who is recorded elsewhere as the guardian of Pocahontas' son Thomas. Brother Henry is presumably the one who had been an investor in the Virginia Company since 1618 or 1619. But this bit of evidence is of no real help with either John or Henry. No known document links a John or a Henry Rolfe of any specific locality with the Indian princess.

Nevertheless, the investigations of various descendants of the Rolfes of Norfolk have produced evidence of a traditional or circumstantial nature which seems to connect both John and Henry with the Norfolk branch of the family. For at least two centuries, a portrait of Pocahontas has been in the possession of the Elwin family of Booton Hall, near Norwich, along with a vase said to have belonged to her, and the Elwins are descended from a Rolfe named Anne who was born in

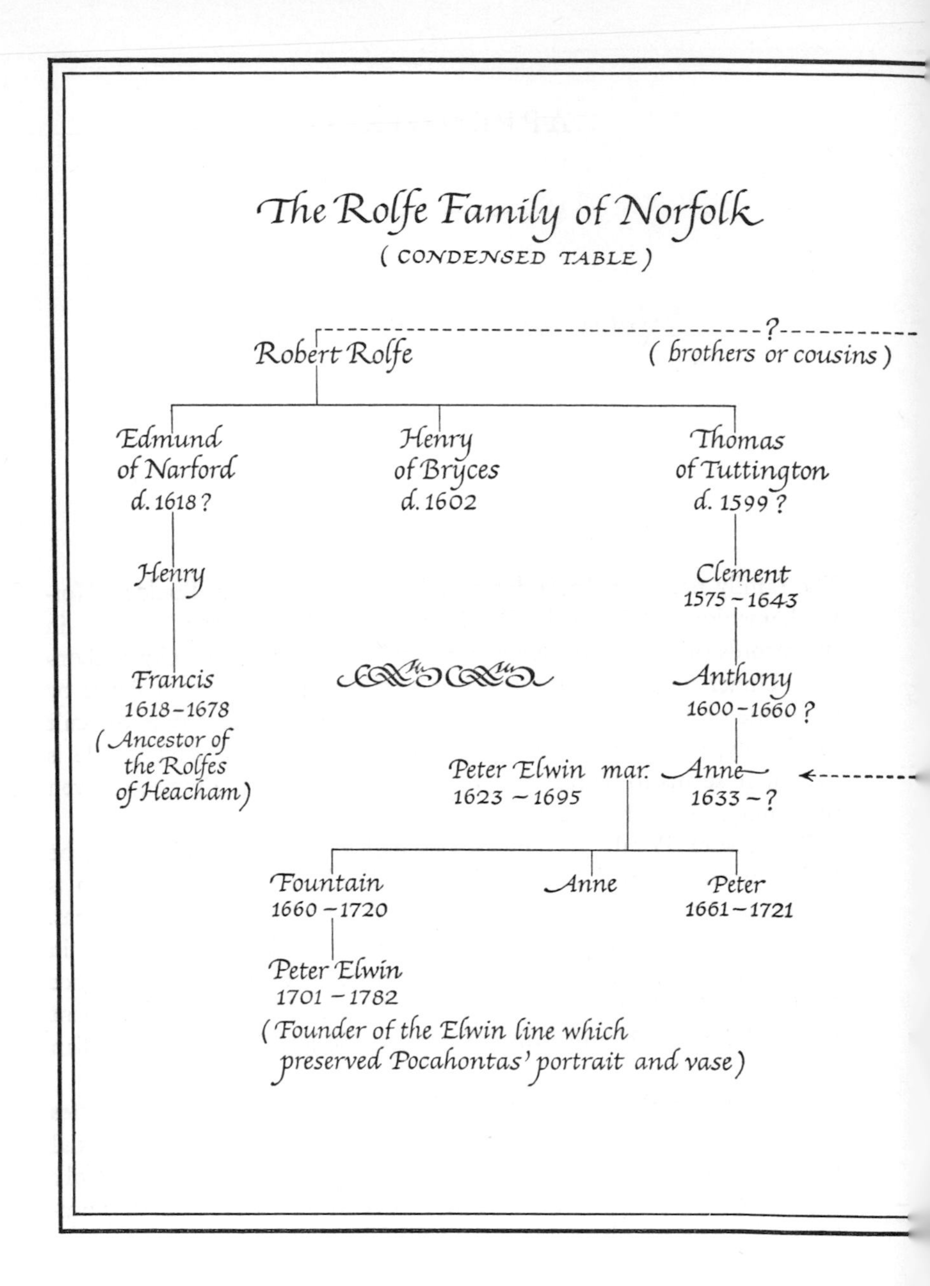
The Rolfe Family of Norfolk
(CONDENSED TABLE)
?
Robert Rolfe
(brothers or cousins)
Edmund
of Narford
d. 1618?
Henry
of Bryces
d. 1602
Thomas
of Tuttington
d. 1599?
Henry
Clement
1575 – 1643
Francis
1618–1678
(Ancestor of
the Rolfes
of Heacham)
Anthony
1600–1660?
Peter Elwin mar. Anne
1623 – 1695
1633 – ?
Fountain
1660 – 1720
Anne
Peter
1661–1721
Peter Elwin
1701 – 1782
(Founder of the Elwin line which
preserved Pocahontas' portrait and vase)

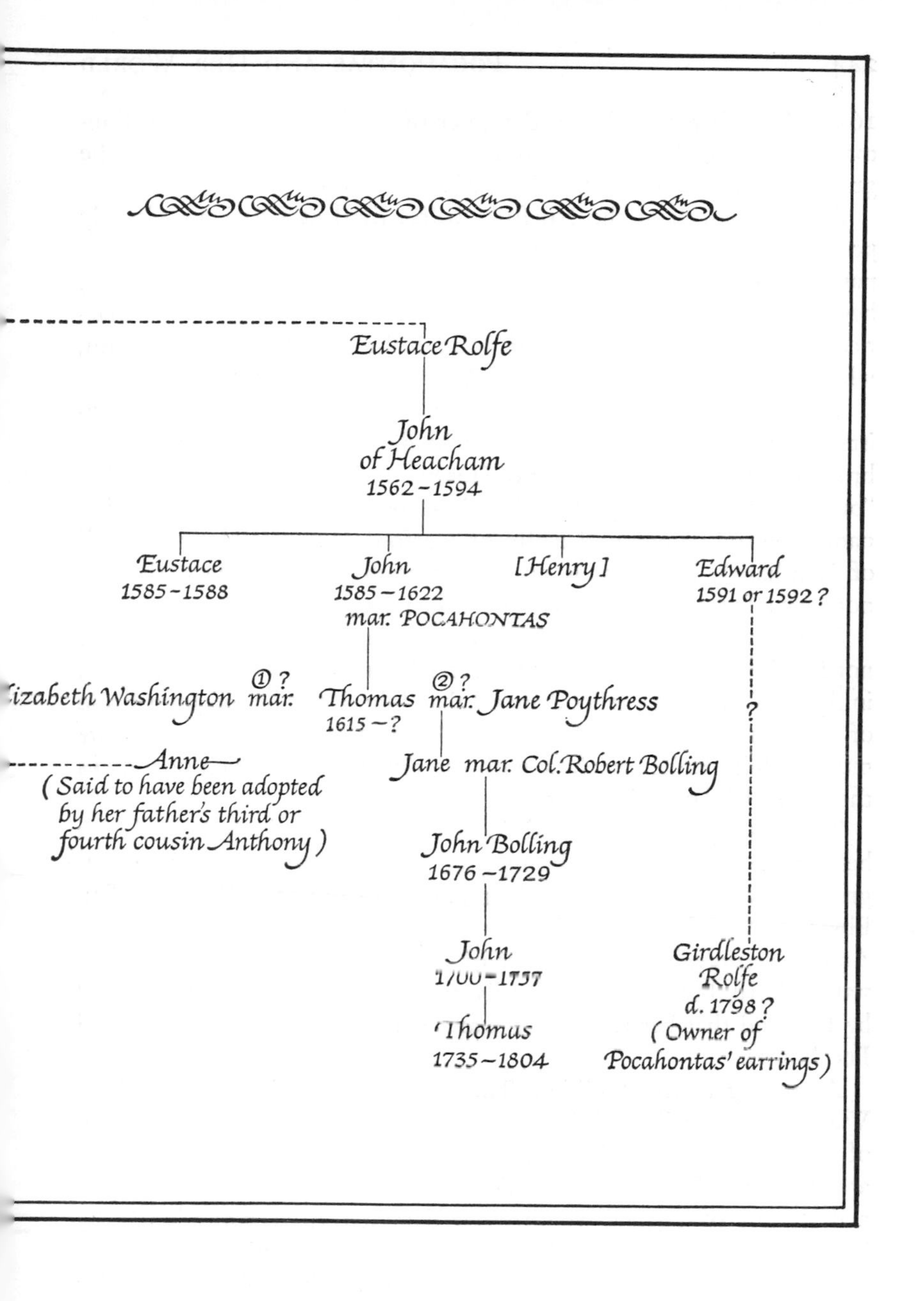

Eustace Rolfe
John
of Heacham
1562 – 1594
Eustace
1585 – 1588
John
1585 – 1622
mar. POCAHONTAS
[Henry]
Edward
1591 or 1592 ?
izabeth Washington
① ?
mar.
Thomas
1615 – ?
② ?
mar. Jane Poythress
?
Anne
(Said to have been adopted
by her father's third or
fourth cousin Anthony)
Jane mar. Col. Robert Bolling
John Bolling
1676 – 1729
John
Thomas
1735 – 1804
Girdleston
Rolfe
d. 1798 ?
(Owner of
Pocahontas' earrings)

1633. Anne is recorded as a daughter of Anthony Rolfe of Tuttington, seven or eight miles from Booton Hall, and Anthony was the grandson of a Thomas Rolfe who died about 1599.

Another branch of the Norfolk Rolfes lived at Heacham (locally pronounced Hitcham), on The Wash, fifty miles to the west. Between parish records and family tradition, it has now been established almost beyond question that the John Rolfe who went to Virginia and married Pocahontas was the son of John Rolfe the Elder of Heacham, who was a first or second cousin of Thomas Rolfe of Tuttington.

The difficulty has remained, however, that the Heacham Parish Register records a twin brother of John who died in infancy and a younger brother named Edward, but no Henry. It has been suggested that "brother" Henry was in fact John's second or third cousin of that name, the son of Edmund Rolfe of Narford (fifteen-odd miles south of Heacham), but there is no documentary proof. In fact, there is not even a family tradition to support the hypothesis.

The matter could well remain a genealogical conundrum were it not for the physical existence of several Pocahontas relics, as described in Appendix I. These relics demand that John Rolfe be the John Rolfe of Heacham. Indeed, in the case of the vase and the oil portrait, we must tie John Rolfe somehow with the Elwin family which now owns the one and did own the other.

The most reliable Elwin tradition seems to be that both these objects belonged to Anne Rolfe, who married Peter Elwin and was the great-grandmother of the Peter Elwin reported (erroneously?) as the first Elwin owner of the portrait (see Arber, *Smith, Works,* p. cxxxvi). Anne is *recorded* as the daughter of Anthony Rolfe of Tuttington, as stated above, but the Elwin family tradition is that she was *adopted* by him and that her real father was Thomas, son of John Rolfe and Pocahontas.

According to this tradition, Thomas Rolfe married one Elizabeth Washington "by license" in St. James Church, Clerkenwell, borough of Finsbury (London), in 1632. (Thomas would have been seventeen at the most.) Elizabeth either died in childbirth or shortly thereafter, and because of Thomas' youth, their daughter Anne was adopted by Thomas' third or fourth cousin Anthony, fifteen years his senior. When he left for Virginia, perhaps two years later, Thomas then gave his mother's portrait and her vase to Anthony to keep for Anne. In this way they came into the Elwin family, presumably in the 1650's.

The Pocahontas earrings, on the other hand, are said to have been inherited through Edward, the youngest brother of John Rolfe of Heacham, "traditional" ancestor of Girdlestone Rolfe of Lambeth, who died in or before 1798 (Elwin family tradition). The *Rolfe Family Records* (II, 22), however, states that Girdlestone was descended from Henry Rolfe of Bryces (Kelvedon, Essex), brother of Edmund of Narford and uncle of the Henry who has been thought to be identical with John Rolfe's brother Henry. Since Henry of Bryces had no sons, it is not clear how Girdlestone Rolfe would have inherited the Rolfe family name.

Because the Rolfe picture is puzzling and confusing, a genealogical table is appended. To avoid further complications, only the most pertinent names are shown. At the same time, my debt to Mrs. Florence Carson for genealogical assistance should be repeated here. Her *Elwin Family Tree* is a masterpiece of research.

(Note: The Henry Rolfe who migrated to New England about 1638 was from Wiltshire and unrelated to the Rolfes of Norfolk.)

APPENDIX III

Copy of John Rolfe's Letter to Sir Thomas Dale Regarding His Marriage to Pocahontas

(Literatim, except for silent expansion of contractions, after the copy in the Bodleian Library, MS Ashmole, 830, folios 118–119v)

When your leisure shall best serve you to pervse theise lynes,[1] I trust in God the begynninge will not strike you into a greater admiracion, then the ende will gyve you good content. It is a matter of noe small moment, concerninge myne owne particular, which heare I impart vnto you, and which toucheth me soe nearely as the tendernes of my Salvacion. Howebeit I freely subiect my selfe to your grave & mature Iudgement, deliberacion, approbacion and determynacion: assuringe my selfe of your zealous admonicions & godly Comfortes; either perswadinge me to desist, or encouraginge me to persist herein with a religious feare, & godly care: For which (from the very instant that this beganne to roote it selfe within the secrett bosome of my hart) my dailye & earnest prayers have byn, still are, and ever shalbe powred foorth with a sincere & godly zeale to be directed, ayded and governed in all my thoughtes, woordes, and deedes to the glory of God, and for my eternall consolacion: to persever wherein I never had more neede, nor (till nowe) coulde ever[2] ymagyne to have byn moved with the lyke occasion: But (my Case standinge as it doth) what better worldly refuge can I heere seeke, then to shelter my selfe vnder the safety of your favourable proteccion? and didd not my Cause proceede from an vnspotted & vndefiled Conscience)[,] I shoulde not dare to offer to your viewe & approved Iudgement these passions of my troubled Soule, soe full of feare and tremblinge is hipocrisie & dissimulacion. But knoweinge myne owne innocency, & godly fervour in the whole prosecucion hereof, I doubt not of your beninge acceptance and Clement construction. As for malitious depravours & turbulent Spiritts, to whome nothinge is tastefull, but what pleaseth there vnsavoury palate, I passe not for them: beinge well assured (by the often tryall and provinge my selfe in my holiest meditacions and prayers) that I ame called herevnto by the spiritt of God: and it shalbe sufficient for me to be protected by your selfe in all vertuous & pious endeavours. And for my more happy proceedinge herein my daily oblacions shalbe ever addressed to bringe to passe soe good effectes, that your selfe and all the worlde maye truely saye, this is ye woorke of God and merveilous in our eyes./

But to avoide teadious preambles, and to come more neare the matter, First suffer me with your patience to sweepe & make cleane the waye wherein I walke from all suspicions and doubtes which maye lye covered therein, and faithfully to reveale vnto you what shoulde move me herevnto.

Lett therefore this my well advised protestacion, which here I make betweene God and my owne Conscience be a sufficient wyttnes, at the dreadfull day of Iudgement (when the secretts of all mens hartes shalbe opened) to condemne me herein yf my chiefe intent & purpose be not to stryve with all my power of boddy and mynde in the vndertakinge of soe waighty a matter (noe waye leade[s?] soe farr foorth as mans weaknes may permytt, with the vnbridled desire of Carnall affection) for the good of the Plantacion, the honour of our Countrye, for the glorye of God, for myne owne salvacion, and for the Convertinge to the true knowledge of God and Iesus Christ an vnbeleivinge Creature, namely Pohahuntas: To whome my hart and best thoughtes are and have byn a longe tyme soe intangled & inthralled in soe intricate a Laborinth, that I was even awearied to vnwynde my selfe thereout. But Almighty God whoe never faileth his that truely invocate his holy name, hathe opened[3] the Gate and ledd me by the hande, that I might playnely see and discerne the safest pathes wherein to treade./

To you therefore (most noble Sir) the Patron and Father of vs in this Countrye, doe I vtter the effects of my longe Contynued affection (which have[4] made a mighty warre in my medytacions) and here I do truely relate to what issue this dangerous Combatt is come vnto: wherein I have not onely examyned, but throughly tryed & pared my thoughtes even to the quicke, before I coulde fynde and fitt wholesome and apt applicacions to cure soe dangerous an vlcer. I never failed to offer my dailye and faithfull prayers to God for his sacred and holye assistance, I forgatt not to sett before myne eyes the frailtie of mankynde, his pronenes to ill, his indulgency of wicked thoughtes, with many other imperfections, wherein man is daylie insnared, and often tymes overthrowen, and them Compared with my present estate.

Nor am I ignorant of the heavy displeasure which Almighty God Conceyved against the Sonnes of Leuie and Israell for marrienge of straunge wyves, nor of the inconvenyences which maye thereby arrise, with other the lyke good mocions: which made me looke aboute warely and with circumspection, into the groundes and principall agitacions which thus shoulde provoke me to be in love with one, whose education hath byn rude, her manners barbarous, her generacion Cursed, and soe discrepant in all nutriture from my selfe, that often tymes with feare and tremblinge I haue ended my pryvate Controversie with this, Surely theise are wicked instigations hatched by him whoe seeketh and delighteth in mans distruction, And soe with fervent prayers to be ever preserved from such diabolicall assaultes I have taken some rest. Thus when I haue thought, I have obteyned my peace and quyetnes: beholde, an other but more gratious temptacion hath made breaches into my holiest and strongest meditacions; with which I have byn putt to a newe tryall, in the stricter manner then the former. For (besides the many passions and sufferinges which I have daylie, howerly, yea in my sleepe endured even awakeinge me to astonishment, taxinge me with remissnes and Carelessnes refusinge and neglectinge to performe, the duety of a good Christian, pullinge me by the eare, and cryenge why doest not thowe endeavour to make her a Christian; and these haue happened to my greater wonder, even when shee hath byn farthest seperated from me, which in Common reason (were it not an vndoubted woorke of god) might breede a forgettfullnes of a farre more woorthy Creature) besides this I saye, the holy Spiritt of God hath often demaunded of me, why I was Created? if not for transitory pleasures and worldly vanyties, but to labour in the

Lordes vyneyard there to sowe and plant, to nourishe and encrease the Fruytes thereof, daylie addinge with the good husband of the Gospell somewhat to the Tallent: that in the ende the Fruytes may be reaped to the Comfort of [the] Labourer in this lyfe, and [his salvation] in the worlde to comme, And yf this [be], as vndoubtedly This is [,] the service Iesus Christ requyreth of his best servantes:[5] And woe to him that hath theise Instrumentes of pietye offered and putt into his handes, and willfully dispise to woorke with them. Lykewyse addinge heerevnto her greate apparance of love to me, her desyre to be taught and instructed in the knowledge of God: her Capablenes of vnderstanding[,] her aptnes and willingnes to receyve any good impression, and also the spirituall besides her owne incytementes stirringe me vpp herevnto. What shoulde I doe? shall I be of soe an vntoward a disposicion to refuse to leade the blynde into the right waye? shall I be soe vnnaturall not to gyve breade to the hungry, or soe vncharitable not to Cover the naked? shall I dispise to actuate theise pious duetyes of a Christian? shall the base feare of displeasinge the worlde overpower and withholde me from revealinge to man theise spirituall woorkes of the Lorde, which in my medytacions and my prayers I have daylie made knowne vnto him. God forbidd: I assuredly trust he hath thus dealt with me for my eternall felicitye, [and] for his glory, and I hope soe to be guyded by his heavenly grace, That in the ende by my faithfull paynes and Christianlyke labour I shall attayne to that blessed promise pronounced by the holye Prophett Daniell to the righteous, that bringe many to the true knowledge of God, namely, that they shall shine lyke the Starres for ever and ever. A sweeter comfort cannott be to a true Christian nor a greater encouragement for him to labour all the dayes of his lyfe in the performance thereof, nor a greater gayne of Consolacion to be desired at the hower of death, and at the daye of Iudgement. Agayne for the lawfullnes of marriage. I hope I doe not farre erre from the meaninge of the holy Apostle, That the vnbeleivinge husband is sanctified by the beleivinge wyefe, and the vnbeleivinge wiefe by the beleivinge husband &c. vppon which place Master Calvin in his Institucions lib. 4. Cap: 16: Sect. 6: sayeth, Even as the Children of the Iewes were called a holy seede, becawse beinge made heires of the same Covenant which the Lorde made with Abraham, they were different from the Children of the vngodly: For the same reason even yett also the Children of Christians are accompted holye, yea although they be the yssue but of one parent faithfull, and (as the Prophett wyttnesseth) they differ frome the vncleane seede of Idolatry. And thus with my readinge and Conference with honest and religious persones have I receaved noe small incouragement, besides serena mea conscientia, [the cleerenesse of my conscience,] pure from the fylth of impuritye quæ est instar muri ahenei [which is vnto me, as a brasen wall].[6] If I shoulde sett downe at lardge the perturbacions and godly motions which have stroue within me in this my godly Conflict, I shoulde but make a tedious and vnnecessary volume, but I doubt not these shalbe sufficient both to Certifie you of my true intentes, in dischardginge my duety to God, and to your selfe. To whose gratious providence I humbly submytt my selfe for his Glorye, your honour, our Countryes good, the benefitt of this Plantacion, and for the Convertinge an irregenerate to regeneracion which I beseech God to graunte for his deare sonne Christ Iesus sake.

Nowe if the vulgar sorte, whoe square all mens actions by the bare rule of theire own filthines, shall taxe or taunt me in this my godly labour. Lett them knowe tis not my hungrye appetite to gorge my selfe with incontinencye, Sure (if I woulde and were soe sensually inclyned) I might satisfie suche desire, though not without a seared Conscience, yet with Christians more pleasinge to the eye and lesse fearefull in the offence vnlawfully Comytted. Nor am I in soe desperate estate that I regarde not what becometh of me, nor am I out of hope but one daye to see my Countrye: nor soe voyde of Freindes, nor meane in Birth but there to obtayne a matche to my greate content: nor have I ignorantly passed over my hoapes there, or regardlessly seeke to loose the love of my Friendes by takinge this Course. I knowe them all & have not rashely overslipped any: But shall it please God thus to dispose of me (which I earnestly desire to fullfill my endes afore sett downe) I will hartely accept it as a godly taxe appointed me. And I will never cease (god assistinge me) vntill I have accomplished and brought to perfection soe holy a woorke, in which I will daylie praye God to blesse me to myne and her eternall happines. And thus desireinge noe longer to lyve to enioye the blessings of God, then this my Resolucion doe tende to suche godly endes as are by me before declared, not doubtinge of your gracious acceptance, I take my leave beseechinge Almighty God to rayne downe vppon you such plenitude of his heavenly graces as your harte can wish and desire. And soe I reste

At your Comaund most willinge
to be desposed./
Io: Rolfe./[7]

[Complete transcription printed by kind permission of the Bodleian Library, Oxford.]

Notes and Comments

Notes and Comments

The notes and comments which follow have been restricted to those plainly essential, and references to sources have been pared to the bone (see the bibliography for details). Further elaboration would be of little use to the non-specialist, while the specialist can surely do with a hint, especially since modern editions of original sources are generally well indexed.

Epigraph. Henry James, *A Little Tour in France* (Boston, 1885), 48.

Chapter 1

1. The chapter heading is taken from John [Daly] Burk's *History of Virginia from its first settlement to the commencement of the revolution* (Petersburg, Va., 1822) I, 234.
2. On the Algonkians and the various tribes in general, see Hodge, *Handbook,* where they are listed alphabetically, and Swanton, *Indians of the SE U.S.,* thoroughly indexed. The latest broad survey is to be found in Peter Farb, *Man's Rise to Civilization* (Part 2 is useful). See also the important article, "The Indians of Northeastern North America," by Jacques Rousseau and George W. Brown, *DCB/DBC,* I, 5–12, followed by an alphabetical list

of tribal names. Feest's introduction to *Indianer Nordamerikas* is also valuable.

The adjective "Algonkian" (often spelled Algonquian) is derived from the name of the Algonkin tribe, so named (probably) from the Micmac meaning "at the place of spearing fish or eels (from the bow of a canoe)." On the distribution of the Algonkians, see Hoffman, "Ancient Tribes Revisited." There is a useful linguistic map in Meillet and Cohen's *Les Langues du Monde.*

3. Strachey, *Historie,* 56. Strachey and John Smith are among the chief sources for Powhatan and the early history of Jamestown (see bibliography). There are frequent references also in Barbour, *John Smith,* and Barbour, *Jamestown Voyages.*
4. See Speck, "Powhatan Tribes," 302, and Flannery, *Analysis,* 115 and 183.
5. There is a convenient summary of all this, with citation of sources, in Lewis and Loomie, *Spanish Jesuit Mission;* consult Index. See also the more elaborate study in Zubillaga, *Misión Jesuítica,* 391–428.
6. On Ralegh's lost colony, see D. B. Quinn, *Raleigh & the British Empire,* revised ed. (New York, 1962), 101–9. The quotation is from Quinn, *Roanoke Voyages,* II, 811.
7. With regard to the prowling ships, at least one is attested in Savannah Bay, in 1605, the *Castor and Pollux* (English, with a French captain — information from Professor David B. Quinn who discussed the matter with me in Liverpool in November, 1967). On the omens in Mexico, see León-Portilla and Garibay, eds., *Visión de los Vencidos,* 1–38.
8. The suggested analyses of Indian names are mine. They are based on (1) apparent linguistic relationship between *Matoaka* and Cree *mātowd'kāo,* "he [she] plays with him [her, it]" and (2) Strachey's *wingan,* "good, satisfactory with regard to beauty," with the common Algonkian feminine ending from which English borrowed the word "squaw." Strachey's "Little-wanton" is probably close to the meaning the name had. Here it clearly means a playful, sportive, and even pampered, pet child.

Chapter 2

1. The narrative through Chapter 5 is based on the writings of John Smith, Gabriel Archer, and George Percy, all to be found in Arber, *Smith, Works,* and Barbour, *Jamestown Voyages.* These three men, along with William Strachey (who arrived three years later), have all reported occasional "Indian accounts" of happenings not attested or confirmed in any strictly European source. In an attempt to present the picture as much as possible from the Indian point of view, I have made use of these stories and in addition have filled in a few gaps by deductive reasoning. Nothing has been postulated, however, which is not demanded by later events.
2. There are two sources for this story: Smith's *True Relation* (see Arber, *op. cit.,* 18, and Barbour, *op. cit.,* 184) and Wingfield's "Discourse" (see Arber, *op. cit.,* lxxxvi, and Barbour, *op. cit.,* 227). Smith's account is first hand; Wingfield's, derived from Smith. Both accounts were written in 1608. Yet Smith attributes the raid on the Rappahannock chief to "the year before," while Wingfield says it was "some two or three years before us."

   Curiously, a personal letter from Professor David B. Quinn, of the University of Liverpool (dated March 10, 1969, and which arrived after this volume went to press), has informed me that a document has come to light among the papers of the Marquess of Salisbury at Hatfield House which bears witness to the presence of two or more American Indians in London early in September, 1603. While Professor Quinn has not yet completed his study of this document, it is worth mentioning that here is proof that such a raid as the one recounted to Smith by the Indians was far from impossible and that here is even a hint that Wingfield may be closer to the truth than Smith as to the date of the raid. In short, was it an *English* ship which stole a handful of Indians from the Rappahannock village?
3. See Strachey's *Historie,* 67–68. Powhatan dispersed the population of Kecoughtan about the time Pocahontas was born. Strachey is the source also for the names of Pochins and other werowances (*op. cit.,* 63–69).

4. See Archer's report in Arber's *Smith, Works,* lv; Barbour, *Jamestown Voyages,* 97–98.
5. This was the implication in Wingfield's account (see Arber, *Smith, Works,* lxxvi; Barbour, *Jamestown Voyages,* 215). From the Indian point of view, it was not exactly near: almost 200 miles off and in the heart of hostile territory.
6. See Strachey, *Historie,* 64–65, as well as Percy's "Observations" (Arber, *Smith, Works,* lxxi; Barbour, *Jamestown Voyages,* 143), and Barbour, *Jamestown Voyages,* 173, note 4. Swanton's "Sun Worship" (see bibliography) curiously has no reference to oaths by the sun, but see Flannery, *Analysis,* 157.
7. For full studies of Captain Smith, see Bradford Smith, *Smith,* and Barbour, *John Smith.*
8. These events, recorded by Smith, point strongly to his having read the account of the Roanoke colony by Thomas Hariot, "A brief and true report" (see Quinn, *Roanoke Voyages,* I, 375–76).
9. There was a permanent Rassawek in Monacan territory, at the junction of the James and Rivanna Rivers, 45–50 miles to the west. I have assumed that Rassawek is a cognate of Nassouac in Maine (see Barbour, *Chickahominy,* 224), with an alteration of initial consonant often found between various Algonkian dialects.
10. It was commonly believed in England at the time that the Pacific Ocean or a great bay thereof lay just to the other side of the Appalachian mountains, and one of the explorers' fondest dreams was to find a way there, by rivers, lakes, and portages.

Chapter 3

1. This is Smith's first account (Arber, *Smith, Works,* 18–19; Barbour, *Jamestown Voyages,* 185). The rest of the narrative is taken from the revised version published in 1624 (Arber, *Smith, Works,* 400).
2. The theory regarding what happened to Smith is partly mine and partly the result of consultation with Indian specialists. For some reference to the custom of adoption and for a number of sources, see Flannery, *Analysis,* 127–28. On the initiation of young men

into the tribe, see Swanton, *Indians of the SE U.S.*, 712 and 815, and Barbour, *Jamestown Voyages*, 147–49, with original documents.

3. There are several points here. First, the "Falls" at Richmond were merely rapids then. Second, the Pocoughtaonacks apparently were a strong nation living in the general direction of the Great Lakes (see Chapter 1, page 7, also Hoffman, "Observations," 195–98). Third, Moyaones appears to be an error for Moyomps (variously spelled), a people who were subject to Powhatan while the Moyaones were enemies (see Ferguson, *Moyaone*, 10–11).
4. The sugar-loaf hat was conical and rounded at the top. Though the shape and material were popular in England, it was curiously unsuited to the climate of Virginia. Werner Müller's *Die Religionen der Waldlandindianer Nordamerikas*, 27, mentions the silly clothing of the Europeans but misses the point of some of the gifts later brought to Powhatan (see Chapter 4, note 5).
5. The Englishmen had settled in Paspahegh hunting-grounds.
6. Flannery's *Analysis*, 118–22, has a good summary on *roanoke* and *wampum*, with references. See also Hodge, *Handbook*, II, 392–93, 539, and 904–9.
7. The sting-ray has been described as poisonous, but its real menace seems to lie in its "long tapering tail . . . armed near the middle with a flattened sharp-pointed bony spine, serrated on both sides, capable of inflicting a severe wound" (*OED*, s.v.). Stingray Point, Va., between the mouths of the Rappahannock and the Piankatank, commemorates the episode.

Chapter 4

1. Arber, *Smith, Works*, 442–45; Barbour, *Jamestown Voyages*, 210–11 and 241–45.
2. Arber, *Smith, Works*, 123–24; Barbour, *op. cit.*, 412–13.
3. For the fullest treatment of Namontack, see Barbour, *op. cit.*, which also contains the documents (consult Index, under Namontack). The account of Namontack's murder is in Arber, *Smith, Works*, 638–39, and the relationship of his murderer, Machumps, to Powhatan is in Strachey, *Historie*, 61–62.

4. Arber, *op. cit.,* 124; Barbour, *op. cit.,* 413–14.
5. For example, the 1632–1633 inventory for probate of the will of Henry Percy, ninth Earl of Northumberland, a wealthy man, lists for "His Lordship's Chamber," "one elbow chair, four high stools, and two low stools," only, and for the dining "parlour," "eleven Turkey work stools, two 'greeche backe' chairs, two leathern stools" (*Batho Papers,* 116–17). See also the generalities in *Shakespeare's England,* II, 119–33.
6. Arber, *op. cit.,* 124–25; Barbour, *op. cit.,* 414.
7. The entire episode which follows, to the end of the chapter, is to be found in Arber, *op. cit.,* 131–38, and Barbour, *op. cit.,* 421–29.

   Smith's approach to Powhatan recalls a passage in Plutarch: "Study your adversary, however dangerous and hard to handle, and see if he does not somehow permit a contact such that you may put him to your own use and gain advantage" (my translation from the Greek text in Loeb Classical Library, Plutarch's *Moralia,* II, 8, last sentence in 86 F).
8. The population of Werowocomoco numbered only between 125 and 150 souls but was at the moment undoubtedly augmented by additional fighting men. How many these were and whether they came accompanied by women and children cannot be known.
9. Arber, *Smith, Works,* 455. The story comes from Smith's *Generall Historie,* which contains so much information about Pocahontas not to be found in his previous works that its truthfulness has sometimes been questioned. I incline to believe that the *Generall Historie* is basically sound, but contains no small amount of elaboration. A well-told story is not fundamentally untrue merely because it has been elaborated.
10. Smith's visit to Werowocomoco ended about February 8, 1609. He and Pocahontas met again late in 1616 (see Chapter 13).

Chapter 5

1. Whether Smith used "intended" in the now obsolete sense of "understood" (what Powhatan had in mind) or in the then-and-now current sense of "planned" is anyone's guess. The basic account of the events narrated in this chapter is Smith's (see Arber,

Smith, Works, 139–74, and Barbour, *Jamestown Voyages,* 430–64), supplemented by George Percy's "Trewe Relacyon," in Tyler's *Quarterly,* III (1922), 259–82.

2. Orapaks can be *guessed* to have been in the neighborhood of Cold Harbor battlefield, nine miles ENE of the State Capitol in Richmond as the crow flies (lat., 37° 25′ N, long., 77° 17′ W).
3. The story of Ratcliffe's expedition is taken from Percy's "Trewe Relacyon," which most likely dates from about 1625. I have not run across any other reference to a "son and daughter" of Powhatan's accompanying Ratcliffe.
4. Percy ("Trewe Relacyon," 266) explained that the men on the pinnace who had not gone ashore were also attacked by Indians but apparently picked up Shortridge and eventually got back to Jamestown with a total of sixteen men out of the full complement of fifty with which Ratcliffe had started out.
5. Arber, *Smith, Works,* 498.
6. Spelman's manuscript was offered for sale in London in 1871. A year later, it was printed there by Henry Stevens, an American bibliophile and bibliographer who spent over forty years in England collecting Americana for himself and various institutions. It was reprinted in Arber, *Smith, Works,* ci–cxiv, but seems to have mysteriously disappeared since.
7. See Neill's *History of the Virginia Company,* 408, and Kingsbury, *Records,* I, 189, no. 628.
8. Percy seems to have been sick all the while. If not, it is an eloquent commentary on his character to state that from mid-October, 1609, until mid-May, 1610, he did not visit the outpost a single time.

Chapter 6

1. Hasted's *Kent,* II, 418; *Harl. Vis.,* XIII–XIV and XLII, under the various surnames involved. Other information from a manuscript family-tree of the Argalls kindly prepared for me by Mr. P. A. Lyons, Assistant, Cathedral Archives and Library, Canterbury. This family-tree has supplied the date of Samuel Argall's baptism, thus solving the long discussed problem of his age in 1609.

2. On the Scotts of Scot's Hall, see Scott, *Memorials.*
3. Will of Richard Argall, Somerset House, P.C.C., 25 Leicester, 1588.
4. H.M.C., *De L'Isle and Dudley MSS,* II, 521 (reprinted in Collins, *Letters,* II, 223–24), and III, 79–80. Although there is a mass of material in Germany on the siege of Rheinberg in 1601, no reference to Lieutenant "Argull" has yet turned up. (In Rheinberg, the Verein der Geschichtsfreunde, and in Cleves, the Stadtarchiv, are the repositories.) It is known from a document in the Public Record Office, London, however, that Samuel Argall's older brother Richard was standard-bearer in Nieuport (Netherlands) to Captain Scott, very likely a younger brother of Sir John Scott and a cousin of the Argalls (list of officers at Nieuport, 4 July 1600, State Papers, Holland, S.P. 84, vol. 60, fo. 207).
5. P.R.O., Chancery Papers, C. 24/473, Part 1, Argall's testimony, signed by him, August 4, 1620.
6. See the documentation and discussion in Barbour, *Jamestown Voyages,* 235 and 249.
7. *True and Sincere Declaration,* 9.
8. Arber, *Smith, Works,* 476. This 1624 version differs slightly from that of 1612 (*ibid.,* 159, and Barbour, *Jamestown Voyages,* 450, with the correct date of Argall's arrival).
9. Arber, *op. cit.,* 159; Barbour, *op. cit.,* 450.
10. It was apparently during Argall's first fishing trip that he was spotted not far from Cape Henry by a Spanish ship under Captain Francisco Fernández de Écija, who had been sent from Florida to spy on the Jamestown colony. Écija fled when Argall sailed toward him. Argall seems to have kept the encounter to himself, perhaps because he had instructions not to "offend" the Spaniards. (I have assumed that the fishing-ship was Argall's, not to raise even more puzzling questions.) On Écija, see Barbour, *Jamestown Voyages,* 307–11.
11. Arber, *Smith, Works,* xciv–xcvii; Barbour, *op. cit.,* 279–83; Purchas, *Pilgrimes,* XIX, 1–4.
12. *True and Sincere Declaration,* 9–10.
13. *Ibid.,* 20.
14. For dates, see Barbour, *op. cit.,* 285–87.

15. The most convenient source for these details is Brown, *Genesis,* 400–17 (various documents).
16. De La Warr's standard-bearer, Anthony Scott, was a younger brother of Sir John Scott and may have been the Captain Scott under whom Samuel Argall's brother served in the Netherlands (see note 4, above). The basic documentation for the narrative from here to the end of the chapter is in Purchas, *Pilgrimes,* XIX, 5–72, and in Percy, "Trewe Relacyon," 268–73.
17. Purchas, *Pilgrimes,* XIX, 50.
18. There are two accounts of the incident, which vary in details: Purchas, *Pilgrimes,* XIX, 66, and Strachey, *Historie,* 65–66.

Chapter 7

1. This and the following quotations are all from William Strachey's "A true reportory of the wracke [wreck], and redemption of Sir Thomas Gates, Knight . . ." in Purchas, *Pilgrimes,* XIX, 13, 67, and 61.
2. From Argall's own account in Purchas, *Pilgrimes,* XIX, 73–84; Somers' last word to Argall, 78.
3. Stow, *Annals,* 1631 ed., 1018b.
4. Strachey, *Historie,* 65–66.
5. Samuel Argall's sister Mary, baptized November 2, 1572, married Reginald Kempe, Esq., whose older half-sister Anne Kempe married Sir Thomas Sherley. The daughter of Anne and Sir Thomas, Cecily Sherley, married Thomas West, who became Lord De La Warr in 1602.
6. Percy, "Trewe Relacyon," 273.
7. *Relation of . . . Lord De La Warr,* 5–6.
8. These and the following details are taken from Percy, *op. cit.,* 273–75.
9. Strachey, *Historie,* 67.
10. *Relation of . . . Lord De La Warr,* 14.
11. The account is based primarily on Spelman's own "Relation," in Arber, *Smith, Works,* ciii–civ.
12. Henry Spelman returned to England on the same ship but was back in Virginia within four years.

13. Percy, *op. cit.*, 275–76.
14. See "A Breife declaration of the Plantation," P.R.O., State Papers, Colonial, C.O. 1/3, folios 78^{r}–86^{v} (the beard incident is on fo. 84^{r}). The rest of this chapter draws heavily on Percy, "Trewe Relacyon," 276–82; the "Answere of the generall Assemblie in Virginia," of February 20, 1623/4, printed in Neill, *Virginia Company,* 407–11; and Prince, "First Criminal Code."
15. A distinguished modern historian has ignored a comma and named Dale "Knight Marshal." This is an absurdity. He was Sir Thomas Dale, Knight, Marshal of Virginia.
16. See the two communications from Dale, printed in Brown, *Genesis,* 488–94 and 501–8.
17. This episode is recounted in Whitaker's letter to Rev. William Crashaw (Brown, *Genesis,* 497–500).
18. Most of the basic material is in Brown, *Genesis,* 507–22, with other documents in *A.H.R.,* XXV (1920), 467–79. The English pilot who was sent to the Spanish ship and was kidnapped was John Clark. He was taken to Spain and finally released in 1616, reaching London about the same time as Don Diego. The renegade English pilot was Francis Lymbry, long in the service of Spain. Dale took him along, too, but had him hanged before they reached England (Arber, *Smith, Works,* 525; and see various references in Brown, *Genesis*).
19. Percy's letter and the £74 account are in Shirley, "George Percy," 239–40. The other sums are in Batho, *Household Papers,* 90.
20. Two pertinent studies of Sir Robert Rich are: Beatty, "The Olde Rebell Warwick," and Whitley, "The Colonizing of America." There are brief biographies in *DNB;* Brown, *Genesis;* and the 11th edition of the Encyclopaedia Britannica. There is an unpublished doctoral dissertation by Professor Wesley Frank Craven, "The life of Robert Rich, second Earl of Warwick, to 1642," but no full life seems to have been written or published.

Chapter 8

1. See Strachey, *Historie,* 62. The efforts which have been made to twist this into a garbled version of Rolfe are useless, since Rolfe did not marry Pocahontas until some months after the approxi-

mate date on which a copy of the *Historie* was presented to Henry, Earl of Northumberland, according to Strachey's biographer (see Culliford, *William Strachey,* 130).

2. The chief source of much that follows is Argall's letter to Master Nicholas Hawes, preserved in Purchas, *Pilgrimes,* XIX, 90–95. As to the "latitude of forty degrees" (over 40 miles north of Atlantic City, N.J.), the entire coast of what is now the United States from Cape Fear, N.C., to Passamaquoddy Bay, Me., was called Virginia until well after the events narrated in this book.
3. Chamberlain, *Letters,* I, 367.
4. Lord De La Warr's "Relation," in Purchas, *Pilgrimes,* XIX, 89.
5. Argall's spelling is used here. Hodge, *Handbook,* II, 208, lists it as Pastanza. Spelman, who lived there but was only semi-literate, called it Pasptanzie, and the Council in Virginia wrote Pascoticons in 1623/4. Although the "correct" form cannot be determined, it should be noted that a Pasquotank tribe existed in North Carolina a century later.
6. There is no mention of buffalo or bison in Hariot, Smith, Strachey, or John Lederer; but Beverley's and Lawson's histories refer to buffaloes in Virginia (154) and North Carolina (119) respectively.
7. Bartolomé Faujas de Saint-Fond, editor of the works of Bernard Palissy (Paris, 1777), wrote humorously: "Terra sigillata is one of those holy remedies thought up by imposture, perpetuated by superstition, consecrated by idolatrous priests, used out of respect and preserved up to our time by custom and ignorance [*l'habitude de l'ignorance*]" (notes, 670–71).
8. Hamor's account of the incident is contained in his *True Discourse,* 4–7. His account has been combined with Argall's throughout the rest of the chapter.

Chapter 9

1. The best summary of what is known about John Rolfe is John Melville Jennings' "Biographical Sketch" in the facsimile edition of Rolfe's "True Relation," 11–20. For many further details, see Robert Theodore and Amy Günther's *Rolfe Family Records,* Vol. II, 1–23. Volumes I and III were published in one volume by

their son Albert Everard Gunther, with several references to Rolfe and Pocahontas (see Index). Further material, as yet unpublished, was supplied to me by Mrs. Florence Carson, of London, and a resumé of this appears in Appendix II, incorporated with the findings of the Gunthers.

2. Strachey's "True Reportory," in Purchas, *Pilgrimes,* XIX, 5–72. See p. 13 on Rolfe. The account of the shipwreck which follows is based on this "letter." Shakespeare's *The Tempest* almost certainly grew out of the incident (see Halliday, *Shakespeare Companion,* 486).
3. *True and sincere declaration,* 12.
4. *Ibid.*
5. Strachey's "True Reportory," see note 2, above; and Cullimore's *William Strachey,* 154.
6. Ravens had known Captain Newport since 1590 and had sailed with him before. See Barbour, *Jamestown Voyages,* 58.
7. See Jennings, "Biographical Sketch," 12–14, with notes; also, Harcourt's *Voyage to Guiana,* 105 and 122, the latter passage hinting that there would be no difficulty about getting seeds.
8. See Hamor's *True Discourse,* 6–7, which has supplied much of the rest of this chapter.
9. See the end of Argall's letter to Hawes, Purchas, *Pilgrimes,* XIX, 94–95.
10. The reconstruction of what happened before and during Argall's two "raids" on the French settlements has been enormously aided by the recent publication of Father Campeau's *Première Mission d'Acadie,* and by various biographies in the *DCB/DBC:* Argall, Biard, Jean de Biencourt and his son Charles, La Saussaye (listed under Le Coq), Brother Du Thet and Father Quentin, S.J., and numerous references to Madame de Guercheville (see Index, under Pons). For manuscript sources consulted, see Bibliography, under Manuscripts.
11. For a sound study of Argall's behavior in Acadia and later in Jamestown, see "The Aspinwall Papers," 41–47 and notes.
12. The most conclusive statement, I believe, is in Stokes, *Iconography,* IV, 38–39. It is true that Adriaen Block was surveying the region during the winter of 1613–1614 and after losing one ship by fire was building another. Argall may well have met him. For

Argall's later interest in Dutch activities, see the brief note in Chapter 17.

13. This bizarre proceeding is narrated in a letter of June 18, 1614, from Dale to the Rev. Dr. Richard Mocket, who had just been elected warden of All Souls' College, Oxford, though Dale of course did not know this. The letter was included as an Appendix in Hamor, *True Discourse,* 51–59.

Chapter 10

1. *Rolfe Family Records,* II, 15. The expression may only have been a paraphrase of a passage in Rolfe's letter to Dale (see note 2).
2. This letter is transcribed in Appendix III.
3. The reference is to the MS in the Bodleian Library, Oxford, which is a copy of the original, apparently lost. The signature is similar to Rolfe's but not quite the same.
4. Jennings, "Biographical Sketch," 14.
5. Hamor's account of the entire proceeding is in his *True Discourse,* 10–16, on which a large part of this chapter is based.
6. See Dale's letter, Hamor, *op. cit.,* 51–59.
7. Also in Hamor, *op. cit.,* 59–61.
8. See Brydon, *Virginia's Mother Church,* 22–23.
9. The description is from my personal observation; the narrative, from Hamor (see note 5).
10. From Rolfe's *True Relation.* See facsimile ed., 21ff for a discussion of the surviving MSS.

Chapter 11

1. According to John Smith, Thomas Savage was thirteen in the summer of 1608 (Arber, *Smith, Works,* 27; Barbour, *Jamestown Voyages,* 194).
2. The basis for the story of this entire episode is in Hamor, *True Discourse,* 37–46.
3. John Smith's extracts from Hamor show "Matchot" instead of "Matchcot." "Matchot" is mentioned twice (Arber, *op. cit.,* 513

and 517) and is shown on Smith's map of Virginia (Barbour, *op. cit.,* facing p. 374) on the south side of the Youghtanund River, not far above West Point. This does not make sense, so far as Hamor's story is concerned. The same map, furthermore, shows another "Matchot" (or Matchutt) on the Mattaponi, which is little more appropriate. But the Zúñiga map of 1608 (Barbour, *op. cit.,* facing p. 239) has a "Maskunt" (possibly for Mashkunt, or Machkunt) far up the Pamunkey, through which Smith was led in December, 1608. This seems to me the best location of the three, despite some confusion even in this case.

4. See Chapter 4, note 3.
5. See Hamor, *op. cit.,* 27, and Molina's letter in Brown, *Genesis,* 743–45. The reference to their execution in Hamor is veiled, but unmistakable.
6. See Stow, *Annals* (1631), 1018b–1019a.
7. P.R.O., Colonial Papers C.O. 1/3, fo. 81^{r-v} (Crown copyright), printed in *Colonial Records,* 74–75.
8. See Brown, *Genesis,* 677–80.
9. *Ibid.,* 733–34.
10. B.M., Cotton MSS, Otho E. VIII (84), folios (new numbering) 252^{r}–253^{v}.
11. Barbour, *John Smith,* 322.
12. *C.S.P., Col., East Indies, 1513–1616,* 333.
13. Purchas, *Pilgrimes,* IV, 213.
14. See Robert C. Johnson, "Lotteries," 259–81.
15. See Hamor, *op. cit.,* 36. For the value of £8000 in 1615, note that the inventory of the goods, chattels, etc., of the ninth Earl of Northumberland after his death in 1632 was "valued and appraised" at a total of only £8713 13*s* (Batho, *Household Papers,* 132), though the Earl was a wealthy man.
16. Brown, *Genesis,* 760, suggests that Argall sailed in February. His will, however, hints that he signed a lease on property in Walthamstow on March 5 (P.C.C., 69 Hele, 1626). I suppose an agent could have signed for him.
17. Brown, *Genesis,* 733. The date was January 24, 1616, but Carew's "news" dated back at least to early December, 1615, if not to word brought over by Argall. There is little surviving information about ships from Virginia to England in this period.

18. *Pericles,* I, i, 157. Nora Miller Turman's biography of Yeardley is unfortunately without footnotes and tends to romanticize. There is no other. Dale also lacks a full biography, though one is in preparation by Mr. David Dewey Scarboro, Jr., who has already written a thesis on the subject (Emory University, 1963) from which he has kindly supplied me with extracts.
19. See Rolfe's "Relation" of 1616–1617, which exists in more than one MS and in three printed forms. Because of this, I suggest that interested readers look for the paragraph beginning "At Bermuda Nether Hundred . . ." which is toward the end of whatever copy of the "Relation" they consult.
20. See Brown, *Genesis,* 775–79.

Chapter 12

1. See Brown, *Genesis,* 503, and Winwood, *Memorials,* III, 309.
2. Elizabeth Throckmorton was related in one way or another to a wide variety of famous people. Her mother was a Berkeley, and through that family she had many connections. Through her aunt Anne Throckmorton, who married Sir John Tracy, she was a first cousin of Lord De La Warr's sister-in-law and of the father-in-law of Captain Nathaniel Powell, of Jamestown fame. Through her grandfather Sir Thomas Throckmorton she was a second cousin of the Captain George Thorpe who was trying to convert Indians in Virginia when he was massacred in 1622, and a more distant cousin of the Kellam (or Kenelm) Throckmorton who died in Jamestown in 1607, and of the Elizabeth Throckmorton who married Sir Walter Ralegh. There were further ties with the Berkeley family and others too numerous to mention. As to Lady Dale's presence in Virginia, I have found no direct statement that she went there with Sir Thomas, and the latter's suit (through Ralph Hamor) for Powhatan's youngest daughter, "whom [he] would gladly make his nearest companion, wife and bedfellow," seems to belie her presence. Mr. Scarboro, however, has written me since this work went to press that Lady Dale "came to America, and, insofar as I have been able to ascertain, died in Virginia in 1640" (Hamor's *True Discourse,* 41, and Scarboro's letter of September 24, 1968). See also Chapter 11, note 18.

3. "Breife Declaration," fo. 81^{v} (see Chapter 7, note 14). The following long quotation is from fo. 82^{r}.
4. Brown, *Genesis,* 751.
5. "Breife Declaration," fo. 82^{v}.
6. Chamberlain, *Letters,* II, 12. The date of the letter is June 22, 1616. By the time Dale sailed, the Virginia Company's affairs in England were ailing, but there is no evidence that his determination to take Pocahontas to London was in any way affected by that. It is, in fact, doubtful if he could have known of the company's troubles. Nevertheless, it was an inspired gesture.
7. Brown, *Genesis,* 783–84.
8. *Letters of George Lord Carew,* 36. See also Arber, *Smith, Works,* 529, and Barbour, *John Smith,* 330–31.
9. Because of its significance, the entire letter has been copied, slightly modernized (Smith, *Generall Historie,* 121–23, Arber, *Smith, Works,* 530–33).
10. Chamberlain, *Letters,* II, 57.
11. The information on the Belle Sauvage Inn is based on Kent's *Encyclopaedia of London,* 394–96; Thomas Archer, *Highway of letters,* 179–80; Bell, *Fleet Street,* 234 and valuable sketch map; and Treloar, *Ludgate Hill,* 12, 46–48, 55, 68, and 128–29, with sketch. See also William Prynne, *Histrio-Mastix,* fo. 556^{r}, and Gosson, *Schoole of Abuse* (in Arber, *English Reprints*), 40. The Sir Thomas Wyatt who is mentioned in Bell, *Fleet Street,* 232–35 (he rested outside the Belle Sauvage yard), was the grandfather of Sir Francis Wyatt who succeeded Sir George Yeardley as Governor of Virginia in 1621.
12. For Ben Jonson and *The Staple of News,* see the complete edition by C. H. Herford and Percy Simpson, 11 vols., Oxford, 1925–1952 (consult Index).
13. *Rolfe Family Records,* II, 14.
14. Samuel Purchas' *Pilgrimage* first appeared in 1613, in a folio volume of 754 pages; the second edition of 900 pages was published the next year. The third edition, of 1617, came to 1096 pages. Eight years later, in 1625, Purchas' huge *Pilgrimes* appeared in four folio volumes. It was reprinted in Glasgow in twenty, 8vo., in 1905–1907. This is the edition usually used for reference purposes, as it is here. One year later, the *Pilgrimage*

was reprinted in uniform size and type with the *Pilgrimes* and issued as a fifth volume. Though it is only a reprint, it is often mistakenly called the fourth edition. See further details in the Publishers' Note to the *Pilgrimes* (Glasgow ed.), I, xxi–xxvii, and Barbour, *Jamestown Voyages,* 1–7.

15. Purchas, *Pilgrimes,* XIX, 118.
16. Stow, *Survey* (1633), 412, at the end of the description of Castle Baynard Ward.
17. Treloar, *Ludgate Hill,* 47.
18. Brett-Jones, *Stuart London,* 497.
19. The move to Brentford (see Arber, *Smith, Works,* 533, and Barbour, *John Smith,* 331–32, with some revision necessary) requires explanation. I here offer one which seems sound.

Chapter 13

1. The only source for John Smith's meetings with Pocahontas and Uttamatómakkin (Tomocomo) is Smith himself. See Arber, *Smith, Works,* 533–34. Lord and Lady De La Warr did, on one occasion at least, accompany Pocahontas, but we have no details.
2. The account of Purchas and his conversations with Uttamatomakkin (Smith's spelling) is based on two complementary sources, both by Purchas: the *Pilgrimage,* 1617 ed. (reprinted in 1626), 954–55; and the *Pilgrimes,* XIX, 117–18. I have accented the name on the basis of "Tomocomo" to facilitate reading.
3. Dr. Theodore Gulston (*DNB,* Goulston), 1572–1632, was a renowned M.D., a parishioner of Purchas' church, a scholar, a free brother of the East India Company, and interested in the Virginia Company (see biographies in *DNB* and Brown, *Genesis*).
4. On Okee/Okeus, see Barbour, *Jamestown Voyages,* 149–50, 333, 364–65, and 368.
5. See Land, "Henrico and Its College," especially 474ff.
6. Brown, *First Republic,* 243. I have "toned down" Brown's categorical statements, perhaps mistakenly.
7. Taylor, *Two Richard Hakluyts,* I, 66.
8. Strickland, Queens of England, VII, 314.
9. All the details regarding this masque are based on the Herford-

Simpson edition, vol. X, 462–71 and 568–73. See also Chapter 12, note 12.

10. "The Vision of Delight" was revived on June 27, 1911, in honor of King George V's coronation festivities (*ibid.,* X, 570).

Chapter 14

1. See Appendix I for a discussion of this matter. Simon van de Passe (1595?–1647) was the son of Crispin, a famous Dutch engraver of Utrecht. He had arrived in England in 1615, and before he left for Copenhagen in 1622, he not only made many engravings of noted persons but also contributed to the development of English engraving.
2. Chamberlain, *Letters,* II, 56–57.
3. John Keats, "Ode on a Grecian Urn."
4. My entire study of Pocahontas' last two or three months is little more than an attempt to reconstruct happenings on which recorded history throws no light.
5. The date March 20 is given in Brown, *First Republic,* 249. Mystery surrounds so many of the details published in this work that I dare go no further than to say that the *recorded burial* of Pocahontas at Gravesend on the very next day militates against Argall's waiting until March 20 to receive his grant.
6. Wenceslaus Hollar (1607–1677), a native of Prague who came to England in 1635, made a drawing of Gravesend in 1662 which is on exhibit (1967) in the London Museum, Kensington. It is faded and cannot be reproduced properly, but it shows the ancient Christopher Inn conspicuously, the church of St. George less so, and the waterfront much as it must have looked when Pocahontas was carried ashore.

   The church was entirely destroyed in the "Great Fire" which broke out the night of August 24, 1727, and wiped out the greater part of the town itself. An edifice, charitably described as "an excellent . . . period piece," has replaced the old church, and no trace of anything relating to Pocahontas remains. On the outside church wall, however, there is a modern commemorative plaque, and in the churchyard there is a replica of William Ordway

Partridge's statue of Pocahontas in Jamestown, Va. It stands pathetically and almost ridiculously in the small enclosure whose original tombstones have been stacked up along the low surrounding wall. On Gravesend, see Cruden, *History,* 286–87 and 398–400.

7. Purchas, *Pilgrimes,* XIX, 118.
8. Chamberlain, *Letters,* II, 66.
9. Book No. 5 of the Parish Registers, St. George's Church.
10. All of this account is based on John Rolfe's letter of June 8, 1617, to Sir Edwin Sandys, supplemented by Argall's letter of March 10, 1617/18 to the Virginia Company (Kingsbury, *Records,* III, 70–2 and 92).
11. Arber, *Smith, Works,* 529.
12. *Ibid.,* 106 and 134 (also in Barbour, *Jamestown Voyages,* 395 and 424).
13. *Ibid.,* 535–36.
14. Kingsbury, *Records,* III, 73–74.
15. Moyomps (May-umps) was distinct from Moyaone (Moyaoncer, Moyowance). The former, a village friendly to Powhatan, may have been near or at Occoquan Creek; the latter, an enemy, on the other side of the Potomac, near modern Accokeek. See Ferguson, *Moyaone,* 10–11, which first called attention to the distinction, I believe. However, her suggestion that the "river Moyumps would probably be the upper Potomac" seems to me unnecessary and perhaps mistaken. The important point, in any case, is that Powhatan had indeed moved as far from the Englishmen as he well could.
16. See note 10.
17. See Chap. 11, and Brown, *Genesis,* 777.
18. See Forman, "Bygone 'Subberbs'," 476–77. Bermuda City was later re-named Charles City, and was on the right bank of the James just below the mouth of the Appomattox. It was nearly 15 miles west of modern Charles City.
19. Kingsbury, *Records,* III, 92.
20. Arber, *Smith, Works,* 539.
21. Kingsbury, *Records,* III, 93.
22. Kingsbury, *Records,* II, 401.
23. In a document ascribed to 1625, it appears that Argall finally got

the upper hand and that Brewster was crying quits (Steer, *Earl Marshal's Papers,* 4–5, a reference for which I am much indebted to Mrs. Alison M. Quinn). As will be seen, "finis" was written to the case only a few months later by Argall's death.

24. See Brock, *Abstract,* II, 29–35, which shows six signatures on the letter to the Captain, and Kingsbury, *Records,* II, 51–55, which shows only five—a matter of little consequence. Otherwise the two versions of the same document are in agreement.
25. Just when or how Lord De La Warr died seems to be uncertain (Brown, *First Republic,* 281–82). For a sound study of Argall's government and the circumstances under which he left, see the "Aspinwall Papers," 4–49 (notes to John Pory's letter).
26. Brock, *Abstract,* II, 37, in which the date is given as May 28. This must be a misreading for Mar[ch], a not uncommon error. As to when Argall left, John Smith quotes John Rolfe (Arber, *Smith, Works,* 540).

Chapter 15

1. From Nelle Richmond Eberhart, "The Moon Drops Low," lyric composed for Charles Wakefield Cadman's song of that name, op. 45, no. 4. The end of the first verse and the beginning of the second read:

   And the deep dark lies like a death-web spun
   'Twixt the setting moon and the rising sun.
   Our glory sets like the sinking moon;
   The Red Man's race shall be perished soon;
   Our feet shall trip where the web is spun . . .
2. "Aspinwall Papers," 15–16. There is an intelligent account of Yeardley in the lengthy notes, beginning on p. 14. As to Yeardley's acreage, see Hatch, "First Seventeen Years," 42 and 71–72.
3. Brown, *First Republic,* 290.
4. *Ibid.,* 294.
5. Chamberlain, *Letters,* II, 188.
6. The "Instructions" are in Kingsbury, III, 98–109, with the "Ordinance and Constitution" on pp. 482–84, and are briefly analyzed in

Brown, *First Republic,* 292–93. For the General Assembly, see John Pory's "Report" (Kingsbury, *Records,* III, 153–77). There are studies of the "Great Charter" in Professor Craven's *Dissolution,* 52–80, and ". . . And So the Form of the Government . . ."

7. Hatch, "First Seventeen Years," 106.
8. See "Aspinwall Papers," 21–34. Robert "Poole" is mentioned but once in Smith (Arber, *Smith, Works,* 528). The details are in Kingsbury, *Records,* III, 174–75, 242, 244–45, and 253. There seems to be no account of what happened to him in the end.
9. The best account of this incident is in Craven, *Dissolution,* 127–31. On the Negroes, see Rolfe's letter in Kingsbury, *Records,* III, 243. On slavery in this connection, see Stanard, *Story,* 158, Hendrick, *Lees,* and "Aspinwall Papers," notes on pp. 4 and 10.
10. Kingsbury, *op. cit.,* III, 244 and 247.
11. *Ibid.,* 251.
12. Published in a "broadside," or handbill, of the company, May 17, 1620 (Kingsbury, *op. cit.,* III, 275–80).
13. John Smith, "Extracted out of the Councels Letters for Virginia" (Arber, *Smith, Works,* 562).
14. His aunt married Argall's uncle. Wyatt's grandfather was involved in a conspiracy to prevent the marriage of Queen Mary I to Philip of Spain which developed into an armed rebellion. He was executed on April 11, 1554. See Chapter 12, note 11.
15. On George Thorpe, see Arber, *Smith, Works* (consult Index) and Kingsbury, *Records,* III, 230, 417–18, 446–47, 462, and 552.
16. Nemattanon is spelled in various ways. For this affair and for the later incident as well, see Arber, *Smith, Works,* 572 and 587, and Kingsbury, *op. cit.,* III, 228. Massituppamohtnock may be a distortion of Monasukapanough (see Smith's map of 1612 and Lederer, *Discoveries,* 116).
17. Letter dated July 25, 1621 (Kingsbury, *Records,* III, 487).
18. Kingsbury, *op. cit.,* III, 547–49.
19. Brown, *First Republic,* 463.
20. Kingsbury, *op. cit.,* III, 550. The rest of the chapter is based on Edward Waterhouse's "Declaration of the State of the Colony and . . . a Relation of the Barbarous Massacre" (Kingsbury, *op. cit.,* III, 541–71).

Chapter 16

1. Governor Wyatt's letter to the Virginia Company, undated but evidently written after April 20, 1622, is in Kingsbury, *Records,* III, 611–15.
2. See Arber, *Smith, Works,* 577. As to the number of inhabitants, a census taken in February, 1622/3, shows 1277 men, women, and children living (though the addition is not quite correct). Several ships arrived between March, 1622, and February, 1623, but the number of emigrants they brought is uncertain. It would seem, however, that barely enough newcomers arrived to replace those killed. At the same time, it must be remembered that no *statistics,* in the modern sense of the word, existed or exist. The true figures may have been wildly different. In any event, John Smith's optimistic estimate must be pretty far from the truth. (See the uncertain details supplied in Brown, *First Republic,* 467–75 and 499–506).
3. Kingsbury, *Records,* II, 96. The matter was aired at a court held on July 17, 1622.
4. The letter of August 1 is in Kingsbury, *Records,* III, 666–73, the last two pages of which are reproduced, modernized, in the text.

Chapter 17

1. See Carson, "Will of John Rolfe," with a transcription, 61–64. Of the witnesses, Lady Yeardley was living in Jamestown with the ex-Governor at the time of the "census" of February 16, 1623/4, as were John Cartwright and a Robert Davis (another Robert Davis was killed at the College site during the massacre). Neither Richard Buck nor his wife appears in this list, although their four children do. Since no colonists seem to have been killed at Jamestown, where Buck was minister, it can only be said that the cause of their death is unknown. John Milward is not mentioned elsewhere, to the best of my knowledge, but a Henry Milward is listed as killed at a plantation adjoining Charles City,

along with his wife, his child, and his sister. See P.R.O., State Papers, Colonial, C.O. 3/2, printed in *Colonial Records* (1874), 37–60. The list of those massacred is in the same work, 61–66, and in Kingsbury, *Records,* III, 565–71.

2. See Brown, *Genesis,* 986–87, and *Colonial Records,* 42.
3. On Thomas Rolfe, see genealogical notes in *VMHB,* XXI (1913), 208–11, and Appendix II, where his "traditional" early marriage in England is explained. I have omitted this aspect of Thomas' career from the main narrative because it apparently is supported only by Norfolk family word-of-mouth transmission. Fort James was approximately at modern Lanexa, New Kent County (see Nugent, *Cavaliers,* 234). The story of the massacre of 1644 is well told in Beverley, *History,* 60–62, and an accurate modern account is in Washburn, *Virginia under Charles I,* 33–37.
4. The details on Thomas Rolfe's posterity are taken from Robertson, *Pocahontas,* 29–32, 70–74, and (the "Resumé"), 84. Wyndham Robertson was the son of Elizabeth Bolling and William Robertson. Elizabeth Bolling was the daughter of Thomas, eldest son of John Bolling the younger. John Bolling was the grandson of Jane Rolfe and Colonel Robert Bolling, respective daughter and son-in-law of Thomas Rolfe.
5. See "Aspinwall Papers," 39–41, and Purchas, *Pilgrimes,* 92–93.
6. *Calendar of State Papers, Colonial, East Indies, 1617–1621,* 288–89, dated August 6, 1619.
7. Kingsbury, *Records,* II, 50–51.
8. See the lists of those present at courts, Kingsbury, *Records,* I, 215–359. Brewster brought the matter up on May 12 when Argall was not present. Argall appeared at the next Quarter Court, held on June 9, and missed only four meetings until Christmas time. After that he seems to have been out of town for ten weeks or so.
9. The examination extended to 104 questions asked, at least in part, of twenty-six witnesses. The record is very long and is to be found in P.R.O., Chancery Papers, C. 24/473, Part 1. I have extracted a few pertinent details regarding Argall from it. Many of its sidelights are interesting but lie outside the scope of this book.
10. Kingsbury, *Records,* III, 231–32.
11. On Sir Richards Hawkins and the Algiers expedition, see Mark-

ham, *Hawkins' Voyages,* xxxvii–xxxix; Williamson, *Observations,* lxxxvi–lxxxviii; Gardiner, *History,* scattered references in vols. III–IV — consult index; and Purchas, *Pilgrimes,* VI, 131–45.

12. Chamberlain, *Letters,* II, 535.
13. Markham, *Hawkins' Voyages,* xxxix.
14. The source for this is a letter from Captain John Mason (founder of New Hampshire) to Secretary Sir John Coke, dated April 2, 1632, P.R.O., State Papers, Colonial, C.O. 1/6, folios 129r–30r.
15. On Argall and Gorges and for general background, see Preston, *Gorges,* 170, 182, 204–10, 245, and 329.
16. Arber, *Smith, Works,* 257.
17. Preston, *op. cit.,* 235.
18. See Gardiner, *History,* Vol. VI, Chapter LV, 1–23, for historical perspective; also the detailed study of Sir Edward Cecil in the *DNB,* ably written by Sir John Knox Laughton, with mention of Glanville's *Voyage to Cadiz,* a valuable source of information.
19. P.R.O., State Papers, Domestic, S.P. 16/6, dated September 8, 1625.
20. P.R.O., State Papers, Domestic, S.P. 16/11, the source of most of what follows. A most useful early map is that of William Borough, in Hakluyt, *Principal Navigations,* VI, 448.
21. P.R.O., State Papers, Domestic, S.P. 16/19, dated January 28, 1625/6.
22. The original will (not the registry copy, P.C.C. 69 Hele) was made available to me by the kindness of Miss Alice Stanley, Literary Department, Somerset House. The handwriting gradually becomes more crowded, until five lines on the last page occupy the space allotted three lines on the first, but it is clear, careful, and legible throughout. So far, I have found no clue to the full identity of Annie Percivall, although it seems obvious that she was a "natural" daughter. What happened to Samuel Percivall as well as when Annie (or Anne) married Bolling are still unknown to me. It is merely a curious coincidence, I believe, that she married a cousin of the young Bolling who married Pocahontas' grandson.
23. The account of Smith's life is very much abridged from Barbour, *John Smith.*

24. I have a study of the debt of John Smith to Sir Henry Mainwaring in preparation.
25. Miss Alice Stanley located Smith's original will for me in 1966. A study of this has appeared in Barbour, "Note on the Discovery."
26. From Thackeray's "Ballads," available in many editions — it is on p. 88 of Vol. XXI (1888) in the edition in twenty-six volumes.

Appendix III

1. The Bodleian copy has no inscription, but the printed copy appended to Hamor's *True Discourse* reads: "Honourable Sir, and most worthy Gouernor: when your leasure shall . . ."
2. Originally written "never," the "n" has been crossed out.
3. "Opened" is the first word on the verso of fo. 118. The letter has been bound so tightly that the last word or words of each line of this and 119 verso are difficult or impossible to read. Recourse has been had to the reasonably accurate transcription in the Günthers' *Rolfe Family Records,* 15–20. Since this agrees in most major points with the Hamor version, it has been thought unnecessary to point out each instance of words supplied in this manner.
4. So in Günther; "hath" in Hamor.
5. The words in square brackets have been added from Hamor, and the punctuation altered. The Bodleian MS seems inaccurate here.
6. The bracketed explanations have also been taken from the Hamor copy.
7. The signature appears to be that of Rolfe himself, and the whole letter may be holographic.

Note: While this book was in press, I discovered a letter among the Ferrar Papers in the Old Library, Magdalene College, Cambridge, which after further study may supply a clue to Samuel Argall's maritime activities in 1606. Meanwhile, my text as it appears on pages 71–73 remains basically sound.

Bibliography

Bibliography

While this work is in no sense a "sequel" to my *Three Worlds of Captain John Smith,* the bulk of the sources and references is the same for both works. It would therefore be wasteful of space to repeat here all the details of the earlier bibliography which are pertinent to the story of Pocahontas and the search for peace between the Indians and the white invaders.

I have therefore, somewhat rashly, decided to make this primarily a bibliography of such sources as have been mentioned in the notes to the present book. For that reason, it is divided into six sections:

A. Dictionaries and the like, with abbreviations used
B. Contemporary manuscripts, by location (The many folios consulted in the Public Record Office are not listed in detail, since the "average reader" will not be in a position to consult them and the specialist will know how to find them.)
C. Primary printed sources (mentioned in the notes)
D. Secondary works (mentioned in the notes)
E. Works dealing with Pocahontas not listed in C and D (This necessarily is incomplete, for a thorough search is unfeasible.)
F. Other works, mostly unbibliographized (Broadly speaking, this includes material not available in 1964 or not precisely pertinent to my book on Smith of that year. A few repetitions appear because they are important.)

It should be noted, generally, that many significant sources and references have been ignored because already mentioned, as stated above. The result may seem arbitrary. If so, space has been the deciding factor.

A

Dictionaries, etc., and periodical publications, with abbreviations

A.H.R. American Historical Review.
B.M. British Museum. *See* Section B.
C.S.P. Calendar of State Papers. See Section C.
DCB/DBC. Dictionary of Canadian Biography—Dictionaire biographique du Canada. Vol. I. Toronto, 1966.
DNB. Dictionary of National Biography. 63 vols. London, 1885–1900.
Encyclopaedia Britannica, 11th ed., 29 vols. Cambridge, 1910–1911.
H.M.C. *See* Historical Manuscripts Commission, Section C.
Names. Journal of the American Name Society.
Notes and Queries. 1850– .
OED. Oxford English Dictionary. 12 vols. and supplement. Oxford, 1933.
P.R.O.. Public Record Office. *See* Section B.
VMHB. Virginia Magazine of History and Biography.
WMQ. William and Mary Quarterly.

B

Contemporary Manuscripts

1. Public Record Office
   Chancery Papers
   State Papers, Colonial. America and West Indies
   State Papers, Colonial. East Indies, China, and Japan
   State Papers, Domestic
   State Papers, Holland

2. British Museum
   Cotton Manuscripts
3. Somerset House
   Registers of the Prerogative Court of Canterbury
   Original wills preserved in the Literary Department
4. Bodleian Library
   Ashmole Manuscripts
5. Library of the Virginia Historical Society
   Randolph Manuscripts

C

Primary Printed Sources (mentioned in the notes)

Arber, *Smith, Works. See* Smith, John. *Works.*

Archer, Gabriel. "A relatyon . . . written . . . by a gent. of y[e] Colony," in Barbour, *Jamestown Voyages.*

"Aspinwall Papers, The." *Collections,* Massachusetts Historical Society, 4th ser., IX (1871), 4–73. A letter of John Pory . . . to Sir Dudley Carleton, followed by John Harvey's "Declaration," published with copious notes.

Barbour, Philip L., ed. "The Jamestown Voyages under the First Charter," *Hakluyt Society,* 2 vols, 2nd ser., CXXXVI–CXXXVII (1969).

Batho, G. R., ed. "The Household Papers of Henry Percy, Ninth Earl of Northumberland (1564–1632)," *Camden Society,* 3rd ser., XCIII (1962).

Beverley, Robert. *The History and Present State of Virginia.* (London, 1705.) ed. Louis B. Wright. Chapel Hill, 1947.

Brock, R. A., ed. "Abstract of the Proceedings of the Virginia Company of London, 1619–1624 . . . ," prepared by Conway Robinson, *Collections,* Virginia Historical Society, new ser., VII–VIII (1888–1889).

Brown, Alexander. *The Genesis of the United States.* 2 vols. Boston, 1890.

Calendar of State Papers, Colonial, East Indies, China, and Japan, II, 1513–1616. London, 1862.

Campeau, Lucien, S.J. *La première mission d'Acadie.* (*Monumenta Missionum Societatis Iesu.* Vol. XXIII. Missiones Occidentales, *Monumenta Novae Franciae,* I.) Rome and Quebec, 1967.

Carew, George. *Letters from George Lord Carew to Sir Thomas Roe . . . 1615–1617.* (Camden Society, old ser., LXXVI.) 1860.

Carson, Jane. "The Will of John Rolfe," *VMHB,* LVIII (1950), 58–65.

Chamberlain, John. *The Letters of John Chamberlain,* ed. Norman Egbert McClure. 2 vols. (The American Philosophical Society, *Memoirs,* XII, parts I and II.) Philadelphia, 1939.

Collins, Arthur, ed. *Letters and memorials of state, written and collected by Sir Henry Sidney.* 2 vols. London, 1746.

Colonial Records of Virginia. Senate Document (Extra). Richmond, 1874. Reprinted, Baltimore, 1964.

Glanville, Sir John. *The voyage to Cadiz in 1625 . . . ,* ed. Alexander B. Grosart. (Camden Society, new ser., XXXII.) 1883.

Gosson, Stephen. *The Schoole of abuse.* London, 1579. (Ed. Edward Arber, *English Reprints,* no. 3. London, 1869.)

Hakluyt, Richard. *The principal navigations, voyages traffiques & discoveries of the English nation.* 3 vols. London, 1598–1600. (Reprinted, 12 vols. [Hakluyt Society, extra ser., I–XII], Glasgow, 1903–1905.)

Hamor, Raphe [Ralph]. *A true discourse of the present estate of Virginia . . . till . . . 1614.* London, 1615. (Reprinted, with introd. by A. L. Rowse, Virginia State Library, Richmond, 1957.)

Harcourt, Robert. *A relation of a voyage to Guiana (1613),* ed. Sir C. Alexander Harris. (Hakluyt Society, 2nd ser., LX.) 1928.

Harleian Society Visitations. *Essex,* Vols. XIII–XIV (1878–1879); *Kent,* Vol. XLII (1898).

Historical Manuscripts Commission. *De L'Isle and Dudley MSS,* II (1934); III (1936). [Ser. 77.]

Jonson, Ben. *Works,* eds. C. H. Herford and Percy Simpson. 11 vols. Oxford, 1925–1952.

Kingsbury, Susan Myra. *The Records of The Virginia Company of London.* 4 vols. Washington, 1906–1935.

Lawson, John. *History of North Carolina.* London, 1714. (Reprinted, ed. Frances Latham Harriss, Richmond, 1937, 1952, 1960, without index.)

Lederer, John. *The Discoveries . . . collected and translated out of Latine . . .* by Sir William Talbot, Baronet. London, 1672. (Reprinted, ed. William P. Cumming, Charlottesville, Va., 1958.)

Morton, Thomas. *New English Canaan . . .* Amsterdam, 1637. (Reprinted, Prince Society, Boston, 1883.)

Percy, George. "Discourse" (a fragment). (See Purchas, *Pilgrimes,* and Barbour, *Jamestown Voyages.*)

——— "A Trewe Relacyon . . ." (Printed, with minor slips, from a transcript, in *Tyler's Quarterly Historical and Genealogical Magazine,* III [1922], 259–82. The original MS is in the Free Library of Philadelphia.)

Prynne, William. *Histrio-Mastix . . .* London, 1633.

Purchas, Samuel. *Purchas his Pilgrimage . . .* London, 1613. Another (enlarged) edition, 1614. Another (further enlarged) edition, 1617. (Reprinted from the 3rd ed. as Vol. V of the *Pilgrimes,* 1626.)

——— *Hakluytus Posthumus, or Purchas his Pilgrimes . . .* 4 vols. London, 1625. (Reprinted, 20 vols. [Hakluyt Society, extra ser., XIV–XXXIII], Glasgow, 1905–1907.)

Quinn, David Beers, ed. *The Roanoke Voyages 1584–1590.* 2 vols. (Hakluyt Society, 2nd ser., CIV–CV.) 1955.

Relation of the Right Honourable the Lord De-La-Warre . . . London, 1611.

Rolfe, John. "Letter to Sir Thomas Dale," appended to Ralph Hamor's *True discourse.* (A contemporary copy is in the Bodleian Library, MS Ashmole, 830.)

——— *True Relation.* New Haven, 1951. (A facsimile of Rolfe's original [the Pembroke-Taylor MS], addressed to the Earl of Pembroke. Other copies exist, addressed to King James [printed in the *Southern Literary Messenger,* V ((1839), p. 401ff; and in the *Virginia Historical Register,* I (1848), 101–13] and to Sir Robert Rich.)

Smith, John. *Capt. John Smith . . . Works. 1608–1631,* ed. Edward Arber. (The English Scholar's Library, No. 16.) Birmingham, 1884. (Reprinted with the same pagination, but with a new introduction by A. G. Bradley. 2 vols. Edinburgh, 1910. Lacks the *Sea Grammar* and two commendatory verses by Captain Smith.)

——— *The Generall Historie of Virginia, New-England, and the Summer Isles* . . . London, 1624. (Reprinted in Arber, *Smith, Works,* and in facsimile with an introduction by A. L. Rowse and bibliographical notes by Robert O. Dougan. Cleveland, 1966.) (For a full bibliography of Smith's writings, see Barbour, *John Smith.*)

Spelman, Henry. "Relation of Virginea." In Arber, *Smith, Works.*

Steer, F. W., ed. *A catalogue of the Earl Marshal's papers at Arundel Castle.* (Harleian Society Visitations, CXV–CXVI.) 1964.

Stow, John. *Annales* . . . Continued by Edmund Howes. London, 1631.

——— *The Survey of London* . . . [*enlarged*] *and now completely finished by the study and labour of A*[*nthony*] *M*[*unday,*] *H. D. and others* . . . London, 1633.

Strachey, William. *The Historie of Travell into Virginia Britania* (*1612*), eds. Louis B. Wright and Virginia Freund. (Hakluyt Society, 2nd ser., CIII.) 1953.

——— "A true reportory of the wracke . . ." In Purchas, *Pilgrimes.*

Taylor, Eva G. R., ed. *The writings and correspondence of the two Richard Hakluyts.* 2 vols. (Hakluyt Society, 2nd ser., LXXVI–LXXVII.) 1935.

A true and sincere declaration of the purpose of the plantation begun in Virginia. London, 1610. (Entered for publication December 14, 1609.)

Williamson, James A., ed. *The 'Observations' of Sir Richard Hawkins.* London, 1933.

Winwood, Sir Ralph. *Memorials of affairs of state* . . . Collected . . . by Edmund Sawyer. 3 vols. London, 1725.

D

Secondary works (mentioned in the notes)

Allan, Mea. *The Tradescants. Their plants, gardens and museum, 1570–1662.* London, 1964.

Archer, Thomas. *The highway of letters and its echoes of famous footsteps.* London, 1893.

Barbour, Philip L. "Chickahominy Place-names in Captain John Smith's *True Relation.*" *Names,* XV (1967), 216–227.

——— "A Note on the Discovery of the Original Will of Captain John Smith; With a Verbatim Transcription." *WMQ.* 3rd ser., XXV (1968), 625–28.

——— *The Three Worlds of Captain John Smith.* Boston, 1964.

Bell, Walter George. *Fleet Street in seven centuries . . .* London, 1912.

Bosworth, George F. "The Manors of Low Hall and Salisbury Hall, Walthamstow." Walthamstow Antiquarian Society, *Official Publication No. 7,* 1920.

Brett-Jones, Norman G. *The Growth of Stuart London.* London, 1935.

Brown, Alexander. *The First Republic in America.* Boston, 1898.

Brown, George W. *See* Rousseau, Jacques.

Brydon, George MacLaren. *Virginia's Mother Church . . .* Richmond, 1947.

Bushnell, David I., Jr. "Virginia—From Early Records," *American Anthropologist,* new ser., IX (1907), 31–44.

Craven, Wesley Frank. *Dissolution of the Virginia Company.* New York, 1932. (Reprinted, Gloucester, Mass., 1964.)

Cruden, Robert Pierce. *History of Gravesend.* London, 1843.

Culliford, S. G. *William Strachey 1572–1621.* Charlottesville, Va., 1965.

Cuvelier, Joseph, and Lefèvre, Joseph. *See* Lonchay, Henri, and Cuvelier, Joseph.

Eberhart, Nelle E. "The Moon Drops Low," lyric for Charles Wakefield Cadman, *Four American Indian Songs,* Op. 45. Boston, New York, Chicago, n.d.

Faujas de Saint-Fond, Bartolomé, ed. *Oeuvres de Bernard Palissy.* Paris, 1777.

Feest, Christian F. "Virginia Indian Miscellany II," *Archiv für Völkerkunde,* XXI (1967), 5–25.

Ferguson, Alice L. L. *Moyaone and The Piscataway Indians.* Washington, D.C., 1937.

Flannery, Regina. *An Analysis of Coastal Algonquian Culture.* (The Catholic University of America, Anthropological Series, No. 7.) Washington, D.C., 1939.

Forman, Harry Chandler. "The bygone 'Subberbs of James Cittie,'" *WMQ,* 2nd ser., XX (1940), 475–86.

Gardiner, Samuel R. *History of England . . . 1603–1642.* New impression, 10 vols. London, 1904–1909.

Gilliam, Charles E. "Pocahontas-Matoaka," *Names,* II (1954), 163–65.

Gunther, Albert Everard. *Rolfe Family Records, I, III.* p.p. [London], 1962.

Günther, Robert William Theodore and Amy. *Rolfe Family Records, II.* London and Aylesbury, 1914.

Halliday, F. E. *A Shakespeare Companion, 1564–1964.* Revised ed., Penguin Books, 1964.

Hasted, Edward. *History and Topographical Survey of Kent.* 4 vols. London, 1778–1799.

Hatch, Charles E., Jr. "The First Seventeen Years. Virginia, 1607–1624." (*Jamestown 350th Anniversary Booklets,* no.6.) Williamsburg, 1957.

Heilbronner, Walter Leo. "The earliest printed account of the death of Pocahontas," *VMHB,* LXVI (1958), 272–77.

Hendrick, Burton J. *The Lees of Virginia. Biography of a Family.* Boston, 1935.

Hodge, Frederick Webb, ed. *Handbook of American Indians north of Mexico.* (Smithsonian Institution, Bureau of American Ethnology, Bulletin no. 30.) Washington, D.C., 1907–1910.

Hoffman, Bernard G. "Ancient Tribes Revisited . . ." *Ethnohistory,* XIV (1967), 1–46.

Jennings, John Melville. "A Biographical Sketch [of John Rolfe]." *See* Rolfe, John, *True Relation.*

Johnson, Robert C. "The Lotteries of the Virginia Company," *VMHB,* LXXIV (1966), 259–92.

Kent, William. *An Encyclopaedia of London.* London, 1937.

Land, Robert Hunt. "Henrico and its college," *WMQ,* 2nd ser., XVIII (1938), 453–98.

León-Portilla, Miguel, and Garibay K., Ángel Ma., *Visión de los Vencidos.* 2nd ed. (Biblioteca del Estudiante Universitario, 81.) Mexico, D.F., 1961.

Lewis, Clifford M., S.J., and Loomie, Albert J., S.J. *The Spanish Jesuit Mission in Virginia 1570–1572.* Chapel Hill, 1953.

Lonchay, Henri, and Cuvelier, Joseph. *Correspondance de la Cour d'Espagne sur les affaires des Pays-Bas au XVIIe siècle.* Vol. I, Brussels, 1923. Vol. VI (*Supplément* by Cuvelier, Joseph, and Lefèvre, Joseph), Brussels, 1937.

McKenney, Thomas Lorraine, and Hall, James. *History of the Indian Tribes of North America.* 3 vols. Philadelphia, 1836–1844.

Markham, Clements R., ed. *The Hawkins' Voyages.* (Hakluyt Society, 1st ser., LVII.) 1877.

Meillet, A., and Cohen, Marcel. *Les langues du monde . . .* New ed., Paris, 1952.

Müller, Werner. *Die Religionen der Waldlandindianer Nordamerikas.* Berlin, 1956.

Neill, Edward Duffield. *History of the Virginia Company of London . . .* Albany, 1869.

Nugent, Nell Marion. *Cavaliers and Pioneers.* Richmond, 1934.

Preston, Richard Arthur. *Gorges of Plymouth Fort.* Toronto, 1953.

Prince, Walter F. "The First Criminal Code of Virginia," American Historical Association, *Annual Report for 1899,* I, 309–63.

Quarles, Marguerite Stuart. *Pocahontas. Bright Stream Between Two Hills.* Richmond, 1939.

Robertson, Wyndham. *Pocahontas, alias Matoaka, and Her Descendants . . .* Richmond, 1887.

Rolfe Family Records. See Günther and Gunther.

Rousseau, Jacques, and Brown, George W. "The Indians of Northeastern North America," *DCB/DBC,* I, 5–16.

Scarboro, David Dewey, Jr. "Sir Thomas Dale: a study of the Marshal and Deputy Governor of Virginia." (Unpublished thesis, Emory University Library, Atlanta, 1963.)

Scott, James Renat. *Memorials of the Family of Scott.* London, 1876.

Shakespeare's England. An Account of the Life & Manners of his Age. 2 vols. Oxford, 1917.

Shirley, John W. "George Percy at Jamestown, 1607–1612," *VMHB,* LVII (1949), 227–43.

Smith, Bradford. *Captain John Smith: His Life and Legend.* Philadelphia, 1953.

Speck, Frank G. "Chapters on the ethnology of the Powhatan tribes of Virginia," *Indian Notes and Monographs,* Vol. I, No. 5, Museum of the American Indian, New York, 1928.

Stanard, Mary Newton. *The Story of Virginia's First Century.* Philadelphia, 1928.

Stokes, Isaac Newton Phelps. *Iconography of Manhattan Island.* 6 vols. New York, 1915–1928.

Strickland, Agnes [and Elizabeth]. *Lives of the Queens of England . . .* New ed., 12 vols. in 6. Philadelphia, 1848.

Swanton, John R. *The Indians of the Southeastern United States.* (Smithsonian Institution, Bureau of American Ethnology, Bulletin 137.) Washington, D.C., 1946.

Tooker, Elisabeth. *An Ethnography of the Huron Indians, 1615–1649.* (Smithsonian Institution, Bureau of American Ethnology, Bulletin 190.) Washington, D.C., 1964.

Treloar, Sir William Purdie, 1st Baron. *Ludgate Hill: past and present.* London, 1892.

Turman, Nora Miller. *George Yeardley, Governor of Virginia . . .* Richmond, 1959.

Tylor, Edward B. "Powhatan's Mantle," *Internationales Archiv für Ethnographie,* I (1888), 215–17.

Washburn, Wilcomb E. "Virginia Under Charles I And Cromwell, 1625–1660." (*Jamestown 350th Anniversary Booklets,* no. 7.) Williamsburg, 1957.

Zubillaga, Félix. *La Florida. La Misión Jesuítica [1566–1572] . . .* (Bibliotheca Instituti Historici Societatis Iesu, Vol. I.) Rome, 1941.

E

Works dealing with Pocahontas not listed above (a selection)

Blathwayt, Mrs. Raymond. "The Story of Two Names," *Wide Awake,* XXIII (1886), 379–92. (Basically factual.)

Brougham, John. . . . *Po-ca-hon-tas: or, the gentle savage.* New York, n.d. (Drama.)

Carpenter, Frances. *Pocahontas and her world.* New York, 1957. (Fiction.)

Crane, Nathalia Clara Ruth. *Pocahontas.* New York, *ca.* 1930. (Dramatic poem.)

Custis, George Washington Parke. *Pocahontas; or, The settlers of Virginia.* Philadelphia, 1830. (Reprinted in Quinn, A. H., ed. *Representative American plays,* 5th ed., New York, 1930.) (Drama.)

Davis, John. *Travels of four years and a half in the United States of America; during 1798, 1799, 1800, 1801, and 1802* . . . London and New York, 1803.

Dixon, Margaret Collins (Denny). *The princess of the Old Dominion* . . . New York, 1953. (Fiction.)

Dorsey, Ella Loraine. *Pocahontas.* Washington, D.C., 1906. (Sympathetic study.)

Edmunds, Pocahontas Wight. *The Pocahontas-John Smith story.* Richmond, 1956.

Eggleston, Edward, and Seelye, Elizabeth Eggleston. *Pocahontas; including an account of the early settlement of Virginia* . . . New York, 1879. (Republished, *ca.* 1890.)

Fletcher, John Gould. *John Smith — Also Pocahontas.* New York, *ca.* 1928.

Fraser, Georgia. *Princess royal.* New York, 1926. (Poetry.)

Garnett, David. *Pocahontas; or, The nonparell of Virginia.* London, 1933. (Fiction.)

Gaston, Edward Page. "Pocahontas's last resting place," *Landmark,* V (1923), 255–58.

Geddes, Virgil. *Pocahontas and the elders.* Chapel Hill, 1933. (Drama.)

Gibbs, Henry Philip. *The poems of John Yaller Cat* (the author's pseudonym). Colony, Okla., 1924.

Guide to Rolfe Portraits. Hunstanton, Norfolk, 1955.

Harnwell, Anna Jane (Wilcox). *Pocahontas and John Smith.* In Sanford, A. P., compiler. *Plays of story and legend.* New York, 1937. (Drama.)

Hendrick, Welland. *Pocahontas.* Chicago, *ca.* 1886. (Burlesque operetta.)

Hillersohn, Estelle. *Grubb's corner; or, The Dutch on the Delaware.* [Wilmington? Del., 193–?] (Operetta.)

Howell, John Edward. *Pocahontas.* New York, 1869. (Poetry.)

Hubbell, Jay B. "The Smith-Pocahontas story in literature," *VMHB,* LXV (1957), 275–300. (Scholarly study, with mention of many other poems, plays, and so on.)

Jacques, Violet Wilbur (MacKenzie). *Pocahontas, Indian princess.* New York, 1957. (Poetry.)

Johnston, Edward F. *Pocahontas.* New York, *ca.* 1916. (Comic operetta.)

Koogle, Effie Louise. . . . *Royalty in old Virginia.* Lebanon, Ohio, *ca.* 1906. (Drama.)

Lossing, Benson John. *Description of the marriage of Pocahontas* . . . London, [1887?] (Description of Henry Brueckner's imaginative painting.)

McDavid, Mittie Owen. *Princess Pocahontas.* New York, 1907.

Mooney, N. . . . *Pocahontas* . . . New York, 1946. (Drama.)

Murray, William Henry. *Murray's essays on Pocahontas and Pushmataha* . . . p.p. Ardmore, Okla., *ca.* 1924.

Musick, John Roy. *Pocahontas: a story of Virginia.* New York, 1893. (Fiction.)

Neill, Edward Duffield. *Pocahontas and her companions* . . . Albany, 1869. (Basically factual.)

Owen, Robert Dale. *Pocahontas.* New York, 1837. (Historical drama.)

P. *The memory of Pocahontas vindicated against the erroneous judgment of Weddy Thompson;* by a Kentuckian. Washington, D.C., 1847.

Philip, Alex. J. "The Princess Pocahontas," *Home Counties Magazine,* XI (1909), 161–66.

Picture, The, of the baptism of Pocahontas, Painted by John Gadsby Chapman, by order of Congress, for the rotunda of the Capitol. Washington, D.C., 1840. (Descriptive.)

Platt, Charles Davis. *Pocahontas and the dawn of our nation.* Dover, N.J., 1921? (Drama in verse.)

Pocahontas, the Indian princess . . . New York, 185–? (A Golden Picture book.)

Pocahontas Memorial Association. (Officers, history of the association, and Ode to Jamestown.) Washington, D.C., 1906.

Robertson, Wyndham. "The marriage of Pocahontas." *Virginia Historical Reporter,* II (1860), 65–87.

Sheets, Catherine Randolph. *Love will find the way; the marriage of John Rolfe and Pocahontas.* Washington, D.C., *ca.* 1907.

Sheppard, William L. *The Princess Pocahontas. Her story.* Richmond, [1907]. (Documents.)

Sigourney, Lydia Howard (Huntley). *Pocahontas, and other poems.* London, 1841. (Poetry.)

Slaughter, P. *A sketch of the life of Randolph Fairfax . . .* 3rd. ed. n.p., 1878.

Southall, James P. C. "Captain John Smith (1580–1631) and Pocahontas (1595?–1617)," *Tyler's Quarterly Historical and Genealogical Magazine,* XXVIII (1946–47), 209–25.

Stanard, William G. "Pocahontas, her son and granddaughter," *VMHB,* XXX (1922), 295–98.

Straubenmüller, Johann. *Pocahontas, oder: Die Gründung von Virginien.* Baltimore, 1858. (Poetic tale.)

Towner, Lawrence W. "*Ars Poetica et Sculptura:* Pocahontas on the Boston Common," *The Journal of Southern History,* XXVIII (1962), 482–85.

United States. Library, Committee on (House, 60:1.). "Memorial monument to Pocahontas." Hearing . . . Washington, D.C., 1908.

Waldron, William Watson. *Pocahontas, princess of Virginia . . .* New York, 1841. (Poetry.)

Wall, Mary Virginia. *The daughter of Virginia Dare.* New York and Washington, 1906. (Fiction.)

Watson, Virginia Cruse. *The Princess Pocahontas.* Philadelphia, 1916. (Fiction.)

Young, Philip. "The Mother of us all," *The Kenyon Review,* XXIV (1962), 391–415. (Essay.)

F

Other works

Adolf, Leonard A. "Squanto's Role in Pilgrim Diplomacy," *Ethnohistory,* XI (1964), 247–61.

Barbour, Philip L. "Pocahontas." (Biography in *Notable American Women.* In press.)

Beatty, John Louis. "The olde rebell Warwick," *Delaware Notes,* Newark, Del., ser. 26 (1953), 51–75.

Bemiss, Samuel M. "The Three Charters Of The Virginia Company." (*Jamestown 350th Anniversary Booklets,* no. 4.) Williamsburg, 1957.

Binford, Lewis R. "An Ethnohistory of the Nottoway, Meherrin and Weanock Indians of Southeastern Virginia," *Ethnohistory,* XIV (1967), 103–218.

Conner, Seymour. "Sir Samuel Argall: A Biographical Sketch," *VMHB,* LIX (1951), 162–75.

Craven, Wesley Frank. ". . . And So the Form of Government Became Perfect," *VMHB,* LXXVII (1969), 131–45.

——— "The life of Robert Rich, second Earl of Warwick, to 1642." (Unpublished thesis, Cornell University, 1928.)

——— "The Virginia Company of London, 1606–1624." (*Jamestown 350th Anniversary Booklets,* no. 5.) Williamsburg, 1957.

Davis, Richard Beale. "America in George Sandys' 'Ovid,' " *WMQ,* 3rd ser. IV (1947), 297–304.

——— "The gentlest art in seventeenth century Virginia," *Tennessee Studies In Literature,* II (1957), 51–63.

——— *George Sandys: Poet-Adventurer.* London and New York, 1955.

Day, Gordon M. "English-Indian Contacts in New England," *Ethnohistory,* IX (1962), 24–40.

Farb, Peter. *Man's Rise to Civilization.* New York, 1968.

Feest, Christian F. "Powhatan: A Study in Political Organization," *Wiener völkerkundlicher Mitteilungen,* VIII (1966), 69–83.

——— "Tomahawk und Keule im östlichen Nordamerika," *Archiv für Völkerkunde,* XIX (1964–1965), 39–84.

——— "Virginia Indian Miscellany I," *Archiv für Völkerkunde,* XX (1966), 1–7.

——— "The Virginia Indian in Pictures," *The Smithsonian Journal of History,* II (1967), 1–30.

——— ed. *Indianer Nordamerikas.* Vienna, 1968.

Goodrich, John Gould. *Lives of Celebrated American Indians.* Boston, 1843.

Gorges, Sir Ferdinando. "A brief relation of the discovery and plantation of New England," Massachusetts Historical Society, *Collections,* 2nd ser., IX (1822), 1–25.

Gunther, A. E. *A guide to Heacham, its history and architecture.* p.p., London, 1963.

Hagan, William T. *American Indians.* (The Chicago History of American Civilization.) Chicago, 1961.

Harvey, John. "Harvey's Declaration [1624]." *See* "The Aspinwall Papers," section C, above.

Hicks, George L. "Cultural Persistence Versus Local Adaptation . . ." *Ethnohistory,* XII (1965), 343–54. [*Caveat studiosus!*]

Hiscock, Robert Heath. *A History of the parish churches of Gravesend and the burial place of Princess Pocahontas.* Gloucester, n.d. [1958 or later].

Historical Manuscripts Commission. *8th report,* part II. (Duke of Manchester's MSS.)

Hitchin-Kemp, Frederick, *et. al. A General History of the Kemp and Kempe Families* . . . London, [1902].

Hoffman, Bernard G. "John Clayton's 1687 Account of the Medicinal Practices of the Virginia Indians," *Ethnohistory,* XI (1964), 1–40.

——— *Observations on certain ancient tribes of the northern Appalachian province.* (Smithsonian Institution, Bureau of American Ethnology, Bulletin 191. Anthropological Papers, no. 70, 191–245.) Washington, D.C., 1964.

Juricek, Bernard T. "The Westo Indians," *Ethnohistory,* XI (1964), 134–73.

Keiser, Albert. *The Indian in American Literature.* New York, 1933.

Küsters, Ludwig. *Die kurkölnische Festung Rheinberg . . .* 2nd ed., Rheinberg, 1967.

Leroi-Gourhan, André, *et al. La préhistoire.* ("Nouvelle Clio," no. 1.) Paris, 1966.

Lysons, Daniel. *Environs of London, IV.* London, 1796.

McCary, Ben C. "Indians in Seventeenth Century Virginia." (*Jamestown 350th Anniversary Booklets,* no. 18.) Williamsburg, 1957.

Miller, Perry. *Errand into the Wilderness.* Cambridge, Mass., 1956. (Reprinted, New York, 1964.)

Neill, Edward Duffield. *The English Colonization of America.* London and Edinburgh, 1871.

Newton, Arthur Percival. *The Colonizing Activities of the English Puritans.* New Haven, 1914.

Nordenskiöld, Nils Erland Herbert, Baron. *The American Indian as Inventor.* London, 1929.

Otterbein, Keith F. "Why the Iroquois Won . . ." *Ethnohistory,* XI (1964), 56–63.

Penington, John. *An examination of Beauchamp Plantagenet's 'Description of the Province of New Albion.'* Philadelphia, 1840.

"Rolfe, John, Letter of [to Sir Edwin Sandys, dated June 8, 1617]," *VMHB,* X (1899–1900), 134–38. (Slightly careless transcription.)

Rolfe, Thomas, "Note" on, *VMHB,* XXI (1913), 208–11.

Rutman, Darrett B. "The Historian and the Marshal; a note on the Background of Sir Thomas Dale," *VMHB,* LXVIII (1960), 284–94.

——— ed. *The Old Dominion . . .* Charlottesville, 1964.

Sanders, Charles Richard. "William Strachey, the Virginia Colony and Shakespeare," *VMHB,* LVII (1949), 115–32.

Serrano y Sanz, Manuel, ed. *Documentos históricos de la Florida.* Madrid, 1912.

Sheehan, Bernard W. "Indian-White Relations in Early America: A Review Essay," *WMQ,* 3rd ser., XXVI (1969), 267–86.

Stith, William. *The History of the First Discovery and Settlement of Virginia.* Williamsburg, 1747. (Often in error.)

Sturtevant, William C. "Spanish-Indian Relations in Southeastern North America," *Ethnohistory,* IX (1962), 41–94. (Emphasis on Florida.)

Swanton, John R. "Sun Worship in the Southeast," *American Anthropologist,* n.s., XXX (1928), 206–13.

Swem, Earl G., and Jennings, John M. (with Servies, James A.). "A Selected Bibliography of Virginia, 1607–1699." (*Jamestown 350th Anniversary Booklets,* no. 1.) Williamsburg, 1957.

Trelease, Allen W. "Indian-White Contacts in Eastern North America: The Dutch in New Netherland," *Ethnohistory,* IX (1962), 137–46.

Trigger, Bruce Graham. "The Jesuits and the Fur Trade," *Ethnohistory,* XII (1965), 30–53.

——— "Trade and Tribal Warfare on the St. Lawrence in the Sixteenth Century," *Ethnohistory,* IX (1962), 240–56.

van der Aa, Pieter. *Naaukeurige Versameling* . . . 29 vols. Leyden, 1706–1707.

Voyages d'un François . . . avec une description de la Virgine & Marilan dans l'Amérique. The Hauge, 1687. (Reprinted and ed. by Gilbert Chinard, Historical Documents, Institut Français de Washington, Cahier V. Baltimore, 1932.)

Washburn, Wilcomb E. "A Moral History of Indian-White Relations . . ." *Ethnohistory,* IV (1957), 47–61.

——— ed. *The Indian and the white man.* (Documents in American Civilization Series.) Garden City, N. Y., 1964.

Wertenbacker, Thomas J. *Pocahontas.* (Biography in the *Dictionary of American Biography.*)

Whitley, W. T., D.D. "The colonizing of America by the owners of Leez Priory," *The Essex Review,* XLV (1936), 160–65.

Wirt, William. *The British Spy* . . . Newburyport, Mass., 1804.

Wright, Irene A. "Documents: Spanish Policy toward Virginia, 1606–1612 . . ." *American Historical Review,* XXV (1920), 448–79.

Wright, James V. "The Application of the Direct Historical Approach to the Iroquois and the Ojibwa," *Ethnohistory,* XV (1968), 96–111.

Index

Index

Note: Pocahontas and Powhatan, John Smith, Samuel Argall, and John Rolfe, along with all the other individuals named in this book, were pawns as well as leaders in the struggle between Indians and Englishmen for survival in North America. Since it is this struggle which is our basic theme, specific references to the two peoples involved have not been listed. Indians and Englishmen appear on almost every page, from the first to the last.

The Appendixes have not been indexed in detail, but a few significant references have been included. The titles seem to be sufficient guide to the contents.

A

Abbot, George, Archbishop of Canterbury, 173
Acadia (Nova Scotia), 120, 123, 146, 149
Acanack-China, 204
Adams, Captain Robert, 89–90, 124
Algiers, 218–20
Algonkian Indians, 1–4, 131, 214
Algonkian languages. *See* Powhatan
America, 1–2, 5, 23, 75, 120, 212
Annapolis, Md., 110
Anne of Denmark, Queen of Great Britain, 155–58, 170, 175–76
Apokant, 18
Appamatuck tribe and village[s], 11, 13, 24, 44, 86
Appomattox River, 151
Aquia Creek, 102
Archer, Captain Gabriel, 74
Argall, family, 67, 69

Argall, John, 67, 70
Argall, Margaret, née Tallakarne, 67
Argall, Mary, née Scott, 68–69
Argall, Mary. *See* Kemp, Mary
Argall, Richard, 68
Argall, Samuel, Captain, Admiral, knighted, 1622, navigator for Virginia, 60, 66–76, 82–85, 87–89, 96–110, 119–24, 128, 134–36, 138, 145–53, 167, 174, 180, 183–193; later career, 194, 198–99, 201, 215–24; proclamations and edicts, 189–90
Argall, Thomas, 67–68, 220
Argall's Gift (Argall's Town, Paspahegh), 187, 197, 208
Argull, Lieutenant ———, 70
Arkil, Danish name, 67
Arrohattoc, tribe and village, 94
Ashmole, Elias, antiquarian, 232
Atlantic Ocean, 183, 218
Atquanachuck, tribe or village, 40
A true and sincere declaration . . . , 74
Azores Islands, 124
Aztec Emperor (Motecuhzoma), 6, 23, 31

B

Banks, ———, a Scottish showman, 159
Bargrave, John, 70–71, 218
Barking Reach, Thames River, 181
Bay of Fundy. *See* Fundy, Bay of
Beacon Hill, Essex, 181
Bedford, Earl of. *See* Russell, Edward
Bedfordshire, 68
Belgium, 222
"Belle Sauvage Inn," London. *See* London
Berg (Bergh). *See* Rheinberg
Berkeley, family and estate, 201, 225
Berkeley, Sir William, Governor of Virginia, 214
Bermuda Islands, 66, 76, 82–83, 104, 115, 117, 150, 198, 218
"Bermudas, the," plantations (including Bermuda City, Hundred, Nether Hundred, etc.), 118, 138, 144, 150–51; Bermuda City incorporated, 187
Beverley, Robert, 162; *History . . . of Virginia,* 162
Biard, Pierre, S.J., 122–24
Biencourt de Saint-Just, Charles de, 123
Blackfriars' Church, London. *See* London
Blackwall, London. *See* London
Blair, Elizabeth. *See* Bolling, Elizabeth, née Blair
Blount, Charles, Earl of Devonshire and 8th Baron Mountjoy, 97
Bolling, Alexander, 2nd husband of Anne Percivall, daughter of Samuel Argall, 224
Bolling, Elizabeth, née Blair, 215
Bolling, Jane, née Rolfe, 214–15, 224

Bolling, John (of Yorkshire), father of Robert, 224
Bolling, John, great-grandson of Pocahontas, husband of Elizabeth Blair, 215
Bolling, John the Younger, his son, 215
Bolling, Colonel Robert, husband of Jane Rolfe, 214–15, 224
Brent River, Herts. and Middlesex, 164
Brentford, Middlesex, 163–64, 166
Brewster, Captain Edward, 76, 84, 95, 190–91, 217
Brewster, William, Virginia colonist, his father (?), 84
Brinton, Edward, Virginia colonist, 52
Bristol, 168, 224
Browne, ———, servant of Ralph Hamor, 206
Browne, Sir William, Lieutenant Governor of Flushing, 70
Buck, Rev. Richard, minister at Jamestown, 118, 133, 213
Buckingham, Earl and Duke of. *See* Villiers, George
Buckinghamshire, 68
Bugsby's Reach, Thames River, 180

C

Cadiz, Spain, 222–23
Calvin, John, 130; *Institutions,* 130
Cambridge (University), 70
Canada, 119–20, 146
Canary Islands, 72
Canterbury, 91
Canterbury, Archbishop of. *See* Abbot, George
Canute (Cnut), the Dane, King of England, 68
Capahowasic, 26, 38
Cape Charles, 83–84, 100, 110, 151
Cape Cod, 82–83, 147, 184, 219, 225
Cape Hatteras, 4, 15, 115
Cape Henry, 34, 76, 110
Carew, George, Baron Carew of Clopton and Earl of Totnes, 150, 155
Carleton, Sir Dudley, Viscount Dorchester, diplomatist, 175–76, 179, 182, 194–95, 232
Carolinas (North and South), 5; *see also* North Carolina
Cartwright, John, Virginia colonist, 213
Cecil, Sir Edward, Viscount Wimbledon, 221–23
Cecil, Sir Robert, Earl of Salisbury, Secretary of State, 94, 152, 155, 221
Chamberlain, John, letter-writer, 154, 176, 179, 182, 194–96, 219, 232
Charles, Prince of Wales, later Charles I of Great Britain, 175–176, 221
Charles City, 197, 202
Charles Emanuel the Great, Duke of Savoy, 198
Chawopo, 44
Chesapeake, tribe and village, 9

Chesapeake Bay, 1, 4–5, 8, 28, 30, 34, 60, 73, 76, 82–83, 94, 102, 110, 115, 117, 204, 214
Chesapeake Bay Bridge, 110
Chester, 30
Chickahominy, tribe, 17–18, 43, 59, 79, 133–37, 202
Chickahominy River, 11–12, 14, 17–18, 20, 25, 40, 43, 57, 135
Chippoke Creek, 44
Chowan River, N.C., 204
Christian IV, King of Denmark, 224
Cinquaoteck, 31–32
"Cleopatra," a sister (cousin?) of Pocahontas, 214
Cleves (Kleve), Germany, 70
Clopton House, Warwickshire, 150
Coles, Edward, Virginia colonist, 144
Company of Adventurers, etc. *See* Virginia Company
Coquonassum, werowance of Appamatuck, 11
Cornelius, John, London merchant, 73
Cornwall, 184
Cortés, Hernán, *conquistador,* 23
Covert, Richard, 67
Cowes, Isle of Wight, 75
Croatoan, tribe and village, N.C., 15

D

Dale, Sir Thomas, Marshal of Virginia, 89–91, 93–96, 99–100, 103, 109–111, 117–20; first meeting with Pocahontas, 122–26, 128, 130–35, 138–45, 147; back to London, 150–55, 162, 169, 171, 184–85, 187–88, 201
Dale, Lady Elizabeth, née Throckmorton, 153
Danbury, Essex, 226
Daniel, Jewish prophet, 130
Davis, Captain ———, 80–81
Davis, Robert, Virginia colonist, 213
Dekker, Thomas, dramatist, 159
Delaware Bay, 83, 149, 219
De La Warr, Lord. *See* West, Thomas
Denmark, 224
Devereux, Penelope. *See* Rich, Penelope
Devereux, Robert, 2nd Earl of Essex, her brother, 97
Devereux, Robert the Younger, 3rd Earl of Essex, his son, 222
Devon, 184
Digges, Sir Dudley, diplomatist, 187
Dorset, 68
Dorset, Earl of. *See* Sackville, Richard
Dover Road, Dover, Kent, 96
Downs, the, Kent, 148
Dowse (Dawse), Thomas, Virginia colonist, 86
Dunkirk, France (held by Spain, a pirate rendezvous), 221–22
"Dutchmen" (Germans?) in Virginia, 37, 45, 47, 52–53, 58–59
Dutch Wars of Independence, 70

E

Eason, Bermudas, son of Edward, 116
Eason, Edward, Virginia colonist, 116
East India Company, 70–71, 73, 147–48, 216
East Sutton, Kent, 67, 69–70
Egypt, 214
Elfrith, Captain Daniel, 198–99
Elizabeth I, Queen of England, 78, 148, 218
Elizabeth (Stuart), Queen of Bohemia, 180, 221
Elizabeth City, incorporated, 187
England, 32, 34, 37, 39, 41, 44, 62, 64, 67, 71, 74, 78, 88–89, 100, 113, 117, 119, 124, 145–50, 153; Pocahontas' arrival, 157, 168, 175, 178, 180–81; after her death, 184–85, 188–89, 191, 193, 201, 204, 212, 216, 218, 221, 223
English Channel, 183
Erith, Kent, 181
Essex, 68, 181
Essex, Earl of. *See* Devereux, Robert, and his son
Europe, 26, 37, 53, 93, 221
Ezra, Book of, 128

F

Falmouth, Cornwall, 222–23
Farrar's Island, James River, 95
Fettiplace (Phettiplace), William, Virginia colonist, 54
Fiddler's Reach, Thames River, 181
Fleet Street and Valley, London. *See* London
Florida, 4, 75, 144
Flowerdieu, Temperance. *See* Yeardley, Temperance
Flowerdieu Hundred, James River, 188, 208
Flushing (Vlissingen), Netherlands, 70
Forest, Mistress Thomas, Virginia colonist, 45
Fort Henry, James River, 142
Fort James, in Chickahominy territory, 214
France and the French, 4–5, 36, 97, 119–24, 138, 146–47, 149, 216, 221–22
Frederick V, Elector Palatine, King of Bohemia, 180, 221
Fredericksburg, Va., 102
Frenchman Bay, Me., 120
Frethorne, Richard, Virginia colonist, 197
Frobisher, Sir Martin, navigator, 116
Frobisher, Richard, Gravesend shipwright, 116
Fundy, Bay of, 119, 123

G

Gallions Reach, Thames River, 181
Gates, Sir Thomas, patentee and Governor of Virginia, 66, 71, 75–79, 95–96, 100, 104, 109, 113–16,

Gates, Sir Thomas (*cont'd.*) 118–20, 124, 144, 150, 154, 188, 218
Georgia, 5
Germans (?) in Virginia, 37
Gibraltar, 219
Gilbert, Captain Bartholomew, navigator-explorer, 6
Giustinian, Zorzi, Venetian Ambassador in London, 39
Gorges, Sir Ferdinando, member of Virginia Council, 219–20
Gosnold, Anthony, Virginia colonist, brother of Bartholomew, 56
Gosnold, Captain Bartholomew, explorer, Virginia colonist, 56
Gouge, Rev. William, Blackfriars' Church, London, 132
Gravesend, Kent, 181–83, 206; St. George's Church, 183, 206
Great Britain, 36, 76
Great Dismal Swamp, Va.–N.C., 5
Great Lakes, U.S.A.–Canada, 2, 7
Great Mogul. *See* Jahāngīr
Guercheville, Marquise de. *See* Pons, Antoinette de
Gulstone (Goulston), Dr. Theodore, physician, 169
Guyana, 117

H

Hakluyt, Rev. Richard, Virginia patentee, 119, 174–75, 194
Hamor, Ralph, Secretary of the Virginia colony, 104, 131, 136–44, 146, 149, 152, 174, 205–6
Hampshire, 68
Harcourt, Robert, Guyana patentee, 117
Hariot, Thomas, mathematician, 93
Hawes, Nicholas, Virginia adventurer, 101
Hawkins, Sir John, navigator, 219
Hawkins, Sir Richard, naval commander, 219, 223
Heacham, Norfolk, 112–13, 161–162
Heidelberg, Germany, 180
Henrico, settlement, 94–96, 118, 145, 151, 153, 174; incorporated, 187; 197, 214
Henry VIII, King of England, 67–68, 180
Henry Frederick, Prince of Wales, 76, 94, 170
Henry's Town, Cape Henry, 110
Herbert, Philip, Earl of Montgomery, 176
Hog Island, James River, 58
Hole, William, engraver, 238–39
Holland and Hollanders. *See* Netherlands
Horton, Mistress Alexander, 116
Howard, Frances, Countess of Somerset, 179
Howard, Frances, Duchess of Richmond and Lennox. *See* Stuart, Frances, née Howard
Hudson, Henry, navigator, 83
Hudson River, 219
Huguenots, 119
Hulsius, Levinus, German publisher, 238

I

Iapassus, werowance of Pastancie, 88, 101, 104–8
India, 150, 155
Ireland, 36, 79
Iroquoian Indians, 35
Isle of Wight, 75
Itopatin. *See* Opitchapan

J

"Jack of the Feathers." *See* Nemattanon
Jackson, Andrew, President, 215
Jahāngīr, the Great Mogul, 150, 155
James I, King of Great Britain, 26, 36, 40, 71, 85, 97, 113, 119, 121, 123; Chickahominies, his subjects, 133–36, 145–46, 148, 153, 155–56, 158, 161–62, 168–71; Pocahontas, and the masque, 173, 175–77; later Virginia problems, 192, 195, 200, 207–9, 211, 217, 220–21, 232
James Fort, Jamestown, 76, 87, 90
James River, 1–2, 9–10, 13–14, 19, 25, 42, 44, 59, 62, 75, 77, 86, 94–95, 99–100, 133, 148, 150–52, 154, 164, 187, 189, 197, 206, 214
Jamestown (James City), beginnings, 6, 13, 23, 27–28, 32, 35, 37, 39–40, 42, 44–45; Powhatan's hostility, 49–50, 52, 55–62, 64–66, 68, 73–74; after rebirth in 1610, 75–76, 78, 83–84, 87–88, 90–91, 93, 95–96, 98, 100, 109, 115, 117–18, 122–24, 126, 128, 133; after Pocahontas' wedding, 138, 144, 146–48, 152–53, 156–157, 164, 185 (James City incorporated, 187), 189, 193, 196, 198, 200, 206–8, 213–14
Jamestown Council. *See* Virginia, Council in
Jesuits (members of the Society of Jesus), 5, 120, 122–24
John Baliol, King of Scots, 68
Johnson, Robert, alderman, deputy treasurer of the Virginia Company, 173, 192; *New Life of Virginia,* 173
Jonson, Ben, dramatist, 159–60, 175; "The Staple of News," 160; "The Vision of Delight," 176
Jordan, Samuel, Virginia colonist, 208

K

Kecoughtan, 9–10, 17, 59, 65, 77, 94, 99, 197, 208
Kekataugh, half-brother of Powhatan, 32
Kemp, family, 69
Kemp, Emmeline. *See* Scott, Emmeline
Kemp, Mary, née Argall, 69
Kemp, Reginald, 69
Kemps, an Indian, 79
Kenchill, Kent, 67
Kennebec River, Me., 83
Kent, 67–69
Kent Island, Md., 110

King, John, Bishop of London, 162–163, 173
"King Philip," Metacom, son of Massasoit, 75
Kiskiack (Chiskiac), tribe and village, 13–14, 28, 94, 151, 154, 197
Kitchin, ———, Virginia colonist, 144
Kocoum, an Indian "private Captain," 99, 131

L

La Mothe, Nicolas de, called La Motte-le-Vilin, lieutenant to René Le Coq de la Saussaye, 124
Lane, Sir Ralph, Governor of the first Roanoke colony, 204
La Saussaye. *See* Le Coq de la Saussaye, René
La Warr's Fort. *See* Powhatan village
Laydon, John, Virginia colonist, 45
Le Coq de la Saussaye, René, French colonial agent, 120–23
Lennox, Duke of. *See* Stuart, Ludovic
Lescarbot, Marc, French colonial propagandist, 119; *Relation dernière,* 119
Levant Company, 71
Leyden, Netherlands, 220
Liancourt, Duc de. *See* Plessis, Charles du
Limehouse. *See* London
Lincolnshire, 226
London, 27, 34, 36, 39, 42, 55, 67–69, 73–74, 77, 87, 90, 94, 96, 100, 145, 147, 152, 154; Pocahontas in, 161–66, 169–70, 174, 178–79, 181–84; after her death, 190–91, 200, 203, 207–8, 216–17, 220, 224, 226.
Belle Sauvage Inn, 159, 163; Blackfriars' Church, 132; Blackwall, 221; Fleet Street, 159; Fleet Valley, 163; Limehouse parish, 6; Ludgate, 159, 163; St. Martin's, Ludgate, 163; St. Paul's, 159; Tower of London, 90, 162
London Council. *See* Virginia Council in London
Long Reach, Thames River, 181
Louis XIII, King of France, 121, 146
Ludgate and Ludgate Hill. *See* London

M

Machumps, brother-in-law of Powhatan, 92
Maidstone, Kent, 67, 69
Maine, 83, 119–20, 147
Mainwaring, Sir Henry, naval commander, 225
Manahata River. *See* Hudson River
Manhattan Island, 124, 220
Mansell, Sir Robert, Admiral, 218–219
Marlowe, Christopher, dramatist, 159
Martin, Captain John, Virginia colonist, 62, 65, 90, 174

Martin Brandon, plantation, 188
Martins Hundred, plantation, 188, 197
Maryland, 83
Maskunt, village, 139
Mason, Dorothy. *See* Rolfe, Dorothy, née Mason
Massachusetts, 220, 225
Massasoit, chief of the Wampanoag Indians of Rhode Island, 75
Massawomecks, an Iroquoian people of northern Appalachia, 105
Massituppamohtnock, 202
Matachanna, daughter of Powhatan, 168
Matchcot, village, 139
Matoaka. *See* Pocahontas
Mattaponi River, 2
Matthew, Tobias, Archbishop of York, 173
Maycock Hundred, plantation, 188
Mediterranean Sea, 218
Menapacant, village, 21, 31–32
Mexico, 2–4, 6
Mildmay, Sir Humphrey, country gentleman, 226; Mildmay Manor, Danbury, 226
Milward, John, Virginia colonist, 213
Molina, Don Diego de, an obscure Spanish magistrate, 92–95, 109–110, 144, 154
Monacans, upper James River tribe, probably Siouans, 25, 40, 42–43, 47, 61
Montgomery, Earl of. *See* Herbert, Philip
Morgan, (Edward?), Virginia colonist, 205
Mount Desert Island, Me., 120
Mountjoy, Lord. *See* Blount, Charles
Moyaone and Moyomps, villages and tribes on the upper Potomac, one subject to Powhatan, the other inimical; confused in the accounts, they are listed here together, 25, 185
Mulberry Island, James River, 133, 214
Munetute. *See* Nemattanon
Muscovy (or "Russia") Company, 71

N

Namontack, Powhatan's servant, 28, 30–31, 37, 39, 41–42, 44, 139, 169
Nansemond, river, tribe and village, 9, 44, 48, 62, 90, 92
Nantaquaus (Nantaquond), son of Powhatan, 26, 28, 30, 156
"Narrow Seas." *See* English Channel
National Portrait Gallery, Smithsonian Institution, Washington, D.C., 233–34
Negroes in Jamestown, 199, 214
Nemattanon ("Jack of the Feathers"), 95, 202, 205
Netherlands (Holland) and the Dutch, 70–71, 79, 124, 150, 153, 175, 219–20, 222
Netherlands, Spanish. *See* Belgium

Nettlestead, Kent, 68
Nevis, West Indies, 88
New England ("North Virginia"), 119, 122, 146–47, 149, 158, 166, 168, 219–21, 224–25
New England Council. *See* Virginia Council for New England
Newfoundland, 121
Newmarket, Suffolk, 195
Newport, Captain Christopher, navigator, 6, 10, 15, 26–28, 30–33, 36–37, 40–44, 49, 75, 77–79, 86, 89–90, 101, 113, 116, 141, 147
Newport News, Va., 208
New York Bay, 124, 149
Norfolk, England, 67, 112–13, 161
North Carolina, 204
North (or German) Sea, 179
Northumberland, Earl of. *See* Percy, Henry
Northumbria, Earl of. *See* Waltheof
North Virginia Company, etc. *See* Virginia
Norwich, 161
Nova Scotia, 120

O

Okee (Okeus), Indian god, 171–73
Old Point Comfort, Va., 9, 44, 62–66, 77, 89–90, 92, 95, 98–102, 109–10, 153, 184, 197
Opachisco, Pocahontas' uncle, 131
Opechancanough, half-brother of Powhatan, 15, 18–21, 25, 31–32, 52–56, 125–26, 169, 185, 188–189, 196, 198, 202–3, 205–6, 211, 214
Opitchapan (Itopatin, Taughaiten), half-brother of Powhatan, 32, 185, 189, 203
Opossunoquonuske, werowansqua of an Appamatuck village, 24, 29
Orapaks, 57, 60, 99
Oxford (University), 70; Ashmolean Museum, 231; Bodleian Library, 232

P

Pacific Ocean, 204
Pamunkey (modern York) River, 2, 8, 13, 15, 20–21, 28, 52, 63, 94, 99, 124, 134, 139, 151, 164, 197
Pamunkey tribe, 15, 18, 21, 52, 203, 214
Parahunt, son of Powhatan, 13–14, 16, 22, 43, 60, 86, 88, 99
Paris, 146
Paspahegh "Queen," 80–81
Paspahegh tribe, 10–11, 15, 17, 30, 59, 78–80, 84, 87, 134
Paspahegh village (near Dancing Point, James River), 17, 59, 87, 99
Paspahegh werowance. *See* Wowinchopunk
Passe, Simon van de, 178
Pastancie, village, 101, 103
Patawomeck, tribe and werowance, 25, 63–64, 87–88, 99–100, 103–106, 110, 197, 216

Patawomeck (Potomac) River, 35, 87, 99, 101–2, 185, 204
Patrixbourne, Kent, 70
Pennington, John, navigator, 223
Penobscot Bay, Me., 83
Percivall, Anne (Annie), (natural?) daughter of Samuel Argall, 224
Percivall, Samuel, her husband, 224
Percy, George, brother of Henry, 42–43, 54, 61–66, 76, 79–80, 84, 86–91, 93–96, 164
Percy, Henry, 9th Earl of Northumberland, 42, 54, 61, 76, 93, 164–65
Philip II, King of Spain, 5
Philip III, King of Spain, 39, 222
Pierce, Jane. *See* Smith, Jane, née Pierce
Pierce, Joan, her mother, 213
Pierce, Captain William, her father, Virginia colonist, 213
Pilgrims, the, of *Mayflower* fame, 220, 225
Pippsco (Pepiscunimah), werowance of a Quiyoughcohanock village, 16
Plessis, Charles du, Duc de Liancourt, 120
Plymouth, Devon, 113, 155, 166, 168–69, 171, 184, 193, 219, 222–225
Plymouth, Mass., 220, 225
"Plymouth Group." *See* under Virginia, Council for New England
Pocahontas (Matoaka), baptized Rebecca, Indian "princess," 1–2, 5–8, 22; rôle with the English, 23–28, 32, 34–35; John Smith, President, 38–39, 51–52, 56–57, 61, 63–64; new Englishmen, 75, 81, 98–99, 103–11; John Rolfe, 118–19, 122, 125–33, 137–40, 151–52, 154; in London, 155–64; last meeting with John Smith, 165–68; at court, 173–77; the end, 178–83; later references, 188, 206, 212–16, 223–27, 231–238, 241–45
Pochins, son of Powhatan, 9–10, 77, 99
Pocoughtaonacks, Iroquoian (?) tribe to the northwest, 25
Poles in Virginia, 37; *see also* Poole, Robert
Pons, Antoinette de, Marquise de Guercheville, 120–21, 146
Poole, Robert (Robert the Pole), interpreter, intrigant, 197–99
Port Royal (Annapolis), Nova Scotia, 120, 123
Pory, John, Secretary of the Jamestown colony, 194–95, 204
Potomac. *See* Patawomeck
Potomac Heights, D.C., 102
Powell, Captain Nathaniel, Virginia colonist, 184, 193
Powhatan, overlord of Tidewater Virginia, 2–18, 20, 22; confrontation with John Smith, 23–35, 227; coronation, and resultant problems for the English, 36–53,

Powhatan (*cont'd.*)
55–61, 63, 75, 77–79, 81, 87–88, 91, 94–95, 99, 103–9, 185, 216; peace with the English, 118, 125–26, 131–36, 138–44, 154–156, 166, 168–71, 173, 180, 182–183, 185, 188–89, 211; his "mantle," 231–32
Powhatan language (Algonkian), 19, 23, 26, 60, 88
Powhatan tribe, 30, 43, 46, 105, 203
Powhatan village and fort, 2, 13, 16, 37, 42–43, 59–60, 62, 86, 88, 94, 99
Poythress, Captain Francis, Virginia colonist, 214
Poythress, Jane, his daughter. *See* Rolfe, Jane, née Poythress
Privy Council, the, 146, 149, 208, 219–20
Prynne, William, pamphleteer, 159
Puerto Real, Bay of Cadiz, 222
Puerto Santa María, Bay of Cadiz, 222
Purchas, Rev. Samuel, 162–63, 165, 169–74, 181–82; *Pilgrimage,* 162; *Pilgrimes,* 162, 174
Purtan Bay, York River, 8

Q

Quantico, Prince William Co., 88
Quentin, Jacques, S.J., 122
Quiyoughcohanock, tribe and village, 13

R

Ralegh, Sir Walter, 5, 171
Ralegh, Elizabeth, née Throckmorton, his wife, 201
Randolph, John, descendant of Pocahontas, 215
Randolph, Ryland, a cousin, 235
Rappahannock River, 6, 8, 21, 35
Rassawek, hunting lodge, 20–21
Ratcliffe, Captain John. *See* Sicklemore, Captain John
Ravens, Henry, master's mate, 115–116
Rawhunt, Powhatan's servant, 27
Rebecca. *See* Pocahontas
Redmayne, Dorothy, née Mason, widow of Rolfe, John Rolfe's mother, 112, 161
Redmayne, Dr. Robert, her 2nd husband, 161
Rheinberg ("Berg"), Rheinland, Germany, 70
Rich, Penelope, née Devereux, 97
Rich, Robert, 1st Earl of Warwick and 3rd Baron Rich, her husband, 97
Rich, Sir Robert, 2nd Earl of Warwick, their son, 97, 198, 217
Richmond, Va., 2, 91, 94, 99, 202
Richmond and Lennox, Duchess of. *See* Stuart, Frances, née Howard
Richmond and Lennox, Duke of. *See* Stuart, Ludovic
Roanoke Island, N.C., and colony, 5–6, 75, 171
Roanoke tribe, N.C., 203

Rochester, Kent, 220
Rolfe, family, 113, 161–62, 241–45
Rolfe, Bermuda, daughter of John, Jr., 116, 118
Rolfe, Dorothy, née Mason. *See* Redmayne, Dorothy, née Mason
Rolfe, Edward, brother of John, Jr., 112
Rolfe, Elizabeth, daughter of John, Jr., 213–14
Rolfe, Eustace, grandfather of John, Jr., 112
Rolfe, Eustace the Younger, twin-brother of John, Jr., 112
Rolfe, Henry, brother of John, Jr., 161–62, 184
Rolfe, Jane, daughter of Thomas. *See* Bolling, Jane
Rolfe, Jane, née Pierce, third wife of John, Jr. *See* Smith, Jane
Rolfe, Jane, née Poythress, wife of Thomas, 214
Rolfe, John, son of Eustace, 112, 161
Rolfe, John the Younger, his son (throughout, it is assumed that this John Rolfe is the same person as the John Rolfe who married Pocahontas), 111–13, 116–18, 127–33, 137, 146, 148, 152, 154–155, 157, 159–68, 174–76, 178–180; after Pocahontas' death, 183–86, 188–89, 199, 213–15; further comments, 232, 234, 237, 241–45; letter to Dale, 247–52
Rolfe, Thomas, son of John, Jr., and Pocahontas, 154, 157, 161, 180, 183–84, 186, 188, 214, 224
Rolfe, unnamed, first wife of John, Jr., 113, 116–17
Rome, 170
Russell, Edward, 3rd Earl of Bedford, 54
Russell, John, Virginia colonist, 50, 54–55
Rye, Sussex, 68

S

Sackville, Sir Edward, 4th Earl of Dorset, 208–9
Sackville, Richard, 3rd Earl of Dorset, his older brother, 208
Sagadahoc (Kennebec) River, Me., 83
St. Augustine, Fla., 4
Sainte-Croix, Bay of Fundy, Canada, 123
St. George's Church, Gravesend. *See* Gravesend
St. John's River, Fla., 4
St. Lawrence, Gulf of, 2
St. Martin's Ludgate. *See* London
St. Paul's (Cathedral). *See* London
St. Peter and St. Paul, church. *See* Swanscombe, Kent
Salisbury, Lord. *See* Cecil, Robert
Saltonstall, Sir Samuel, collector of the customs, 226
Sandys, Sir Edwin, statesman, 183, 185–87, 199, 202–3, 217
Savage, family, 30, 159

Savage, Thomas, Virginia colonist, 30, 88, 138–40, 142–44, 204
Savage's Inn. *See* London, Belle Sauvage Inn
Scotland, 68, 175
Scot's Hall, Kent, 68
Scott, family, 69
Scott, Anthony, standard-bearer, 75
Scott, Emmeline, née Kemp, 68–69
Scott, Mary. *See* Argall, Mary
Scott, Mary, née Tuke, 68
Scott, Sir Reginald, father of Mary (Scott) Argall, 68
Scrivener, Matthew, Virginia colonist, 28, 43, 45, 56
Shakespeare, William, 150, 175
Sherburne, Edward, financial agent, 175
Ships: unnamed, 5–6, 8–9, 14, 27, 34, 60, 70, 88, 94–95, 121–22, 124, 147, 198, 221–22; *Blessing,* 213; *Bona Nova,* 207; *De La Warr,* 75, 84; *Deliverance,* 116; *Discovery,* 207; *Expedition,* 147; *George,* 180–81, 183–84, 186–187, 191–92; *Mary and Margaret,* 42; *Patience,* 116; *Sea Adventure,* 113–15, 213; *Swiftsure,* 222–23; *Tiger,* 204; *Treasurer,* 97, 102, 109, 120–24, 149, 153, 198; *Trial,* 96; *William and Thomas,* 193
Shirley Hundred, plantation, 208
Shortridge, Jeffrey, Virginia colonist, 63
Sicklemore, Captain John, *alias* Ratcliffe, 63–64, 103
Sidney, Sir Philip, soldier-poet, 97
Sistine Chapel, Vatican City, 170
Smith, Jane, née Pierce, widow of John Rolfe, Jr., 213–14
Smith, Captain John, colonist, 1, 6–7, 17–35; President of the Council, 36–62, 69–71, 73, 76, 86–90, 94, 98–101, 103, 106–7, 110, 125, 133, 139, 177, 184–85; in England and New England, 146–47, 155–60 (sees Pocahontas and Tomocomo, 165–68, 170–71, 174), 179, 182, 190, 200, 208, 219–20, 224–27, 232; *Advertisements for the unexperienced Planters of New England,* 226; *Description of New England,* 155; Letter to Queen Anne about Pocahontas, 156–58; *Generall Historie,* 156, 225; *Sea Grammar,* 225; *True Travels,* 226
Smith, Captain Roger, commandant, 214
Smith's Fort, opposite Jamestown, 133, 214
Smith's Hundred, plantation (no connection with Captain John), 188, 208
Smith's Isles, off Cape Charles, 100, 151
Smyth, John, of Nibley, Berkeley family steward, 225
Smythe, Sara, née Blount, wife of Sir Thomas, 114
Smythe, Sir Thomas, Treasurer of the Virginia Company, 64, 70–

74, 100, 110, 114, 145, 147, 192, 217–18
Smythe's Island. *See* Smith's Isles
Somers, Sir George, Admiral of Virginia, 66, 75–77, 82–83, 113, 115
Somerset, Countess of. *See* Howard, Frances
Southampton, Earl of. *See* Wriothesley, Henry
Southampton Hundred. *See* Smith's Hundred
South Virginia Company. *See* Virginia Company
Spain and the Spaniards, 4–6, 15, 31, 70, 72, 75, 92–93, 95, 109, 117, 122, 135, 138, 144, 199, 219, 221–22; the Invincible Armada, 5, 69
Spanish ambassadors in London. *See* Velasco, Alonso de, and Zúñiga, Pedro de
Spelman, Henry, Virginia colonist, nephew of Sir Henry Spelman, historian, 62–64, 88, 169, 198; "Relation of Virginia," 64
Strachey, William, Secretary of the Jamestown colony, 2–4, 6, 75–76, 90, 94, 113–14, 116; *Historie*, 6; *Lawes divine, morall and martiall*, 188; "True reportory" (not named in text), 114–17
Stuart, Frances, née Howard, Duchess of Richmond and Lennox, 179, 225
Stuart, Ludovic, Duke of Richmond and Lennox, her husband, second cousin and closest surviving relative of James I, 220–21, 225
Stukely, Sir Lewis, vice-admiral of Devon, 184
Suffolk, 6
Susquehanna River, 35
Swanscombe, Kent, 181
Swift, Ensign James, Virginia colonist, 104, 110
Syon House, Middlesex, 164

T

Tackonekintaco, werowance of Warraskoyack, 84
Tallakarne, Margaret. *See* Argall, Margaret
Thames River, 164, 180, 183, 212
Thanet, Isle of, Kent, 183
Thirty Years War, 221
Thorpe, Captain George, friend of the Indians, 200–203, 205
Thorpe, Margaret, née Throckmorton, grandmother of George, 200
Throckmorton, Elizabeth. *See* Dale, Elizabeth
Tindall, Robert, Prince Henry's gunner, 76
Tomocomo. *See* Uttamatómakkin
Tossantessas. Indian name for the Englishmen, meaning not definitely established, 133, 135
Tradescant, John, 232
Tradescant, John, the Younger, 231
Trinidad, West Indies, 117
Tucker, Captain Daniel, navigator, 62, 65, 218

Tuke, Sir Bryan, secretary of Henry VIII and Cardinal Wolsey, 68
Tuke, Mary, his daughter. *See* Scott, Mary
Turkish pirates, 204
Turner, Lieutenant William, shipmaster under Samuel Argall, 124, 146

U

Uttamatómakkin, son-in-law of Powhatan, 168–73, 176, 178–79, 185

V

Van de Passe. *See* Passe, van de
Velasco, Don Alonso de, Spanish Ambassador in London, 110, 144–45
Velasco, Don Luis de, viceroy of Mexico, 4
Velasco, Don Luis, an Indian, 4–5
Venetian Ambassador. *See* Giustinian, Zorzi
Villiers, George, Duke of Buckingham, 176, 221–23
Virginia (random mention), 1–2, 8, 25, 36, 39, 45, 71–72, 75, 90–91, 94, 100, 102, 115–17, 119, 121, 131, 141, 147, 149–50, 153, 155–57, 160, 165, 167, 169, 172–174, 176, 180–81, 184, 187–91, 193, 195–96, 198–201, 203–9, 213, 217–18, 225
NORTH VIRGINIA COMPANY (New England), 97, 219–20
[SOUTH] VIRGINIA COMPANY (Company of adventurers and planters in Virginia), 39, 41–44, 70, 72–73, 96–97, 100, 104, 113, 145, 147–48, 151, 158–62, 173–175, 179–80, 188, 194–96, 199–200, 202, 216–18, 225
VIRGINIA COUNCIL IN LONDON (for Virginia), 36–37, 72, 74, 87, 90, 97, 113–14, 119, 151, 183, 187, 189–93, 195, 200, 203, 208–9, 211, 217–18, 220
[VIRGINIA] COUNCIL FOR NEW ENGLAND, 219–21, 225
VIRGINIA COUNCIL IN VIRGINIA, 28, 33, 35, 44, 55, 75–76, 165, 203–4, 207–9
VIRGINIA COUNCIL OF ESTATE AND GENERAL ASSEMBLY, 195–197, 204, 209

W

Wahunsonacock. *See* Powhatan
Wainman (Wenman), Sir Ferdinand, first cousin of Lord De La Warr, 76, 84
Waldo, Captain Richard, Virginia colonist, 44, 56
Waller, John, Virginia colonist, 87
Walthamstow, Essex, 68; Walthamstow Bedyk, manor, 68, 220
Waltheof, Earl of Northumbria,

married Judith, niece of William the Conqueror, 68
Warraskoyack, tribe and village(s), 77, 84, 154, 206
Washington, General George, President, 69, 215
Washington, Lawrence, a collateral ancestor, 69
Washington, D.C., 102
Weanoc, tribe and village, 13, 44, 189
Werowocomoco, Powhatan's "seat," 8, 22–23, 26, 28, 37, 39–41, 44–45, 49, 51, 53, 56–57, 81, 105, 108, 125, 167, 182
West, Cicely, née Sherley, wife of Sir Thomas, 191
West, Captain Francis, younger brother of Sir Thomas, 42, 54, 62, 64, 90, 218
West, Sir Thomas, 3rd Baron De La Warr, 42, 54, 71, 73–80, 83–89, 99, 118, 150, 165, 174, 188, 190, 192–95; "Short Relation," 87
West, Captain William, a relative, 79
"West Country" (the southwestern English counties), 166, 179, 224
West Indies, 72, 88, 117, 135, 148, 198
Westminster, city, 164
Westminster Abbey, 174
West Point, King William Co., Va., 15, 21, 53
Weyanoke and Weyanoke Point. *See* Weanoc
Weyanoke Hundred, plantation, 188
Whitaker, Rev. Alexander, 91–92, 110, 117–18, 132, 150, 173, 187
White, William, Virginia colonist, 16
Whitehall Palace, Westminster, 175
Wickham, Master William, curate, 187
Wiffin, Richard, Virginia colonist, 56
Wimbledon, Viscount. *See* Cecil, Sir Edward
Winganuske, "dearest wife" of Powhatan, sister of Machumps, 6, 39
Wingfield, Edward Maria, Virginia patentee and colonist, first President of the Council, 15, 96, 165
Winne (Wynne), Captain Peter, Virginia colonist, 53, 57
Winwood, Sir Ralph, Secretary of State, 155
Wolsey, Thomas, Cardinal, 68
Woolwich Reach, Thames River, 180
Wowinchopunk, werowance of Paspahegh, 10–17, 87, 89, 99
Wriothesley, Henry, 3rd Earl of Southampton, 209, 218
Wrothe, Rebecca. *See* Pocahontas
Wyatt, Sir Francis, Governor of Virginia, 200, 203–5, 207–11

Y

Yeardley, Sir George, Governor of Virginia, 76, 150–51, 153–54, 184–85, 189, 193–200, 204, 218

Yeardley, Temperance, née Flowerdieu, his wife, 189, 213
York, Yorks., 173
York, Archbishop of. *See* Matthew, Tobias
York River, Va. *See* Pamunkey
Youghtanund, tribe and perhaps village, 18, 63, 88
Youghtanund (modern Pamunkey) River, 57

Z

Zúñiga, Pedro de, Spanish Ambassador in London, 39